SUPER FOOTBALL CHALLENGE

SUPER FOOTBALL CHALLENGE

600 TRIVIA QUIZZES TO TEST YOUR FOOTBALL KNOWLEDGE

Dennis Purdy

STERLING

New York / London
www.sterlingpublishing.com

STERLING and the distinctive Sterling logo are registered trademarks of
Sterling Publishing Co., Inc.

Library of Congress Cataloging-in-Publication Data
Purdy, Dennis.
    Super Football Challenge : 600 trivia quizzes to test your football knowledge
/ Dennis Purdy.
       p. cm.
    ISBN 978-1-4027-5627-6
    1. Football—United States—Miscellanea. I. Title.
    GV950.5.P87 2008
    796.33—dc22
2007049938

10 9 8 7 6 5 4 3 2 1

Published by Sterling Publishing Co., Inc.
387 Park Avenue South, New York, NY 10016
© 2008 by Dennis Purdy
Distributed in Canada by Sterling Publishing
C/o Canadian Manda Group, 165 Dufferin Street
Toronto, Ontario, Canada M6K 3H6
Distributed in the United Kingdom by GMC Distribution Services
Castle Place, 166 High Street, Lewes, East Sussex, England BN7 1XU
Distributed in Australia by Capricorn Link (Australia) Pty. Ltd.
P.O. Box 704, Windsor, NSW 2756, Australia

Sterling ISBN 978-1-4027-5627-6

For information about custom editions, special sales, premium and corporate
purchases, please contact Sterling Special Sales Department at 800-805-5489 or
specialsales@sterlingpublishing.com.

CONTENTS

A NOTE ABOUT THE ANSWERS

The answers to each quiz can be found in a separate section, beginning on *page 367*. The answers are arranged by tens, starting with numbers ending in ones and ending with numbers ending in zero. This is to ensure that you, dear reader, are not tempted to peek at them.

Also, please note that the quizzes refer to records, feats, etc., for games played through the 2006 season (which includes January 2007 bowl games).

From **1990 to 2006,** I promoted the largest sports card shows in the Pacific Northwest. As part of my promotion, I would bring in former and current sports stars to sign autographs for the fans, and many of these guests were some of the greatest football players of all time.

One of my perks as promoter was that I got to pick the player up from the airport, take him to and from the show, sit with him on stage during his signing session, and then take him back to the hotel and/or airport. It was during these many one-on-one times that I got to know the players behind the legends on a personal basis, and this has given me many wonderful memories (and a few bad ones!) over the years, all of them unforgettable.

One funny moment came when I picked up Gale Sayers, the legendary running back, at the Sea-Tac Airport. The airport parking garages were undergoing massive construction at the time and concrete barriers and fencing were everywhere. As we were driving through the garage and its maze of obstacles, Sayers kept darting his head left, then right, seeking an opening just as he had for years against defensive lines on the football field. "Go right!" he'd shout. "Quick, go left around that next barricade!" And then another, "Go right! Right, I said!" With his help, we made it out of the garage that day.

And there were revealing moments, like the time I picked up Paul Hornung at the airport. Our topic of conversation eventually got around to Pete Rose and his legal difficulties. Hornung readily admitted to me his problems with gambling on sports when he was younger and how he had been appropriately suspended by NFL commissioner Pete Rozelle. He said he was able to come back into public favor in time because he openly admitted what he had done and had sought the forgiveness of fans. He also said that (baseball all-time hits leader) Pete Rose's problem with the public was his own stubbornness, refusing to admit his involvement in gambling when all the signs pointed to his guilt.

Another funny incident occurred with Otis Sistrunk, the fearsome former Oakland Raider lineman. I'd had Otis as a guest four or five times previously at other shows and after he relocated locally we had become friends, so it was business as usual for him to come to my Tacoma Dome show in early 1996. Now, if you don't know who Otis Sistrunk is, let me fill you in. He's about nine feet tall and weighs almost a ton. At least it seems like it. Anyway, I was sitting behind a table on my raised stage (it was six feet above ground level) with my hands laced behind my head and my feet extended to the edge of the stage.

Suddenly, someone grabbed my foot and started shaking it … and shaking it, and shaking it and shaking it. I couldn't see who it was because my table was draped with a table cover and whoever was shaking my foot had such a tight grip on me that I couldn't sit up in my chair. Finally, irritated beyond measure, I said, "I don't know who's on the other end of my foot, but if you don't stop it I'm going to come down there and kick your ass!" The shaking stopped and Otis backed up so that I could see him. This giant black man, dressed all in black, said, "Well, I guess I better stop then." He then let loose with the biggest, pearliest white smile I've ever seen in my life, we all had a good laugh, and I proved that Otis Sistrunk is, for the record, a pussycat.

I was also able to learn what real gentlemen most of these former NFL players were. Truly first class. Guys like Bob Lilly, Roman Gabriel, Harold Carmichael, Gale Sayers, Jim Taylor, Jack Ham, and Dick Butkus, among many others. As for Butkus, I saw firsthand what years of playing in the NFL had done to his knees, and I wondered if the difficult, painful way in which he walked was an equitable trade for his remarkable (but short) NFL career. I suspect he thinks it was.

One truly amazing incident occurred in June 1991 when I had the recently retired and local fan favorite Steve Largent to one of my shopping mall shows. Huh, fan favorite? The guy walked on water as far as Seattle-area fans were concerned. And they proved it that day.

Largent was scheduled for a 2:00 pm signing that would last for two hours. At most we were going to get 500–600 autographs signed. At 6:30 that morning, as soon as the mall doors opened, fans rushed inside and began to line up for the signing session. By 10:00 we had 4,000 people in line. By noon the line had grown to 9,000 people, and it wound like a snake all around the massive parking lot ... and it was raining outside! The mall manager was forced to call in an additional two dozen police and security officers just to manage the traffic jam.

The mall manager told me later that the average automobile traffic count at the mall was 22,000 cars on a Saturday. (They have underground sensors that count every car that enters the mall lots.) That day the count was 46,000. Anyway, we repeatedly announced that Largent was only going to sign for two hours and that the vast majority of people who still waited in line were never going to get to meet their hero. But they didn't believe us and remained in line until the bitter end.

And what an end it was. The mall's marketing director had ordered hundreds of photos for the signing session, and when she announced that the signing was over, much to the dismay of about 8,000 people still standing in line, she decided that the best thing to do was ... (gulp!) ... throw the remaining unsigned photos out into the crowd. Well, crowd became mob, and we had, to say the least, the most interesting conclusion to a signing session ever: a riot!

But those days are behind me. Thank goodness. Now all I do is write books (this is my seventh), one of which you hold in your hands. It's quieter and—hopefully you'll agree—more enjoyable.

Dennis Purdy

CHAPTER 1

COLLEGE FOOTBALL BY THE DECADE

Long before the NFL came into being, college football was the game of the land. Some of the perennial powerhouses of the 19th century had fan followings that would make today's NFL teams jealous, and the genesis of many of today's rules and traditions began with the college game. In this chapter, match the year to its bit of college football history.

1. 1870   A. Year Columbia first fielded a football team, joining Rutgers and Princeton

2. 1872   B. Year Yale became the first team ever to go a perfect 8–0–0

3. 1882   C. Year Princeton and Rutgers were the only two football teams in the country

4. 1885   D. Only year since football's invention that there were no games played

5. 1869   E. Year Yale fielded the country's fourth football team

6. 1874   F. Year Princeton became the first team ever to go a perfect 9–0–0

7. 1871   G. Year Harvard fielded the country's fifth football team

1. 1883   A. Year Yale became the first team ever to go a perfect 13–0–0

2. 1889   B. Year football expanded to the West Coast with the addition of California to the college ranks

3. 1876   C. Year Yale became the first team ever to go a perfect 16–0–0

4. 1876   D. First year consensus All-Americans were elected

5. 1894   E. Year Harvard became the first team ever to win 12 games in one season (12–2)

6. 1886   F. Year football expanded from New England to the Midwest with the addition of Northwestern to the college ranks

7. 1896   G. Year the Big Ten became college football's first conference, though it only had seven teams, not 10

1. 1890   A. Year Navy first fielded a team, going 0–0–1, tying the Baltimore Athletic Club, 0–0, in the only game they played

2. 1897   B. Year the Rocky Mountain Conference became college football's second conference

3. 1900   C. Only year from 1869–1903 that neither Yale nor Princeton laid claim to the national title (Harvard was the unanimous selection)

4. 1889   D. Year Chicago won the Big Ten with a 4–0–0 conference record, and went 12–0–2 overall

5. 1879   E. Year Edgar Allan Poe was a consensus All-American (okay, so he wasn't *that* Edgar Allan Poe)

6. 1890   F. Year Pennsylvania went a perfect 15–0–0

7. 1899   G. Year Army joined the ranks of college football, playing only one game, a 24–0 loss to (ugh!) ... Navy

(Note: One year is the answer to two clues)

1. 1907   A. Year the Missouri Valley Conference became college football's third conference

2. 1901   B. Year Michigan repeated as Big Ten champs, going a perfect 11–0–0 for the second straight season

3. 1906   C. Year that three teams (Colorado, North Carolina State, and Washington) incredibly all played four tie games each

4. 1905   D. First 20th century year to feature a unanimous choice as the national champion (Yale)

5. 1902   E. Year Minnesota had the best record in the country at 13–0–0

6. 1904   F. Year Chicago won the Big Ten by going 7–0–0, a record they would match in 1913, but which would not be equaled again until Ohio State accomplished it in 1954

        G. Season the Rose Bowl became college football's first bowl game (played on Jan. 1 of the following calendar year)

(Note: One year is the answer to two clues)

1. 1915   A. First season in which the Big Ten Conference actually-fielded 10 teams

2. 1918   B. Season the Rose Bowl was resumed with its second game

3. 1917   C. Season in which the Great Lakes Naval Air Station team defeated the Mare Island Marines, 17–0, in a Rose Bowl featuring two military schools

4. 1912   D. Year Kansas State went 10–1–0, surprisingly the only team in the country that year to win 10 games

5. 1910   E. Year the Southwest Conference began play as a football conference, making it the country's fourth college conference

6. 1916   F. Year touchdowns were first counted as worth six points (had previously been worth 2, 4, and 5 points at various times in history)

G. Season the Pacific Coast Conference started play, making it the country's fifth college conference

1. 1927   A. Two more bowl games make their debut this season, the Dixie Classic and the San Diego East-West Christmas Classic

2. 1920   B. Notre Dame has the first 10–0–0 season in its 38-year history

3. 1922   C. Season in which a second bowl game made its debut, the Fort Worth Classic, in which Centre routed TCU, 63–7

4. 1928   D. Georgia Tech wins the 22-team Southern Conference championship with a 7–0–0 record, then defeats California 8–7 in the Rose Bowl to cap a perfect 10–0–0 season

5. 1921   E. The Rose Bowl once again was the only bowl game played, with Alabama defeating Washington, 20–19, giving the Crimson Tide the country's best record at 10–0–0

6. 1925   F. The goal posts are moved back ten yards to the end lines

7. 1924   G. The Southern Conference makes its debut as the country's sixth athletic conference and North Carolina takes the title

1. 1939   A. The Heisman Trophy is awarded for the first time, and Jay Berwanger of Chicago is the recipient

2. 1933   B. The SEC makes its debut, and Alabama wins the title with a 5–0–1 conference record

3. 1934   C. Clinton Frank is the first recipient of the Maxwell Award, given annually to the player judged to be college's best

4. 1936   D. The Associated Press weekly college football polls debut

5. 1932   E. The Sugar and Orange Bowls both make their debuts following the completion of this season

6. 1935   F. The last year in college football history that only one bowl game was played at the completion of the season

7. 1937   G. All players are now required to wear helmets

1. 1941   A. Referees are given discretion to put a white ball in play for night games

2. 1948   B. The best record in the country this year (12–0–0) belongs to ... (gulp!) *Randolph Field?!*; they outscored their opponents 508–19, defeating, among others, Rice 59–0, Texas 42–6, and Air Force 13–6 in the Treasury Bond Bowl

3. 1940   C. The use of a one-inch kicking tee is now permitted

4. 1944   D. Blockers are now required to keep their hands against their chests

5. 1945   E. USC, undefeated and ranked #3 with two games to go, gets crushed first by #1 Notre Dame, 38–7, then 49–0 by #2 Michigan in one of the sourest ends to a season ever

6. 1947   F. Doc Blanchard wins the Heisman Trophy in a close vote over his teammate Glenn Davis

7. 1949   G. Tom Harmon wins the Heisman Trophy and the Maxwell Award

1. 1958   A. Navy's Ron Beagle wins the Maxwell Award as college football's best player, but doesn't finish in the top 10 of the Heisman voting

2. 1951   B. Institution of the two-point conversion

3. 1950   C. Notre Dame, ranked #1 in the preseason poll, finishes 4–4–1 and out of the rankings well before season's end

4. 1953   D. Syracuse wins the national title, finishing 11–0–0, including a 23–14 win over #4 Texas in the Cotton Bowl

5. 1956   E. Notre Dame's Paul Hornung wins a close Heisman vote over Tennessee's John Majors and Oklahoma's Tommy McDonald even though McDonald gets more 1st place votes

6. 1959   F. Face masks added to helmets

7. 1954   G. Notre Dame's Johnny Lattner wins his second consecutive Maxwell Award, the only player to win it more than once

1. 1967   A. Southern California wins the national title, finishing 11–0–0, including a dramatic 42–37 win over #2 Wisconsin in the Rose Bowl

2. 1960   B. #2 Navy's Roger Staubach wins both the Heisman Trophy and Maxwell Award by wide margins, but is stymied by #1 Texas in the Cotton Bowl, 28–6

3. 1964   C. Coaching from the sideline is now permitted

4. 1962   D. Mississippi begins the season ranked #1, but finishes a dismal 2–4–1 in SEC play, which illustrates—as the old saying goes—why they play the games

5. 1965   E. O.J. Simpson runs away with the Heisman Trophy collecting 855 first-place votes to runner-up Leroy Keyes' 49

6. 1968   F. In one of the most incredible turnabouts in college football history, three teams finish the season 10–0–0, and all three lose their bowl games; Alabama, 8–1–1, wins its bowl game and vaults to the national title with a lesser record

7. 1963   G. Mississippi wins the national title, finishing 10–0–1, including a 14–6 win over Rice in the Sugar Bowl

1. 1970   A. Teams are now allowed to schedule an 11-game season

2. 1973   B. The top five teams in the country all finish 11–1–0, creating a mad scramble for the national title, won by Notre Dame, which had entered the New Year's Day bowl games as #5

3. 1979   C. Nebraska wins the national title, finishing 13–0–0, including a 38–6 romp over #2 Alabama in the Orange Bowl

4. 1977   D. Freshmen are now allowed to play

5. 1971   E. Notre Dame wins the national title in exciting fashion: they enter the Sugar Bowl ranked #3, but knock off #1 Alabama, 24–23, to vault to the top over idle #2 Oklahoma

6. 1974   F. Rule passed requiring at least one team, starting in 1981, to wear white jerseys

7. 1972   G. All players are required to wear shoulder pads

1. 1983   A. Clemson had the only perfect record among ranked teams, finishing 12–0–0 to win the national title, including a 22–15 win over #4 Nebraska in the Orange Bowl

2. 1985   B. White jerseys are made mandatory for visiting teams

3. 1988   C. Auburn's Bo Jackson wins the Heisman Trophy in a very close vote over Iowa's Chuck Long, 1,509–1,464

4. 1986   D. Three teams (Oklahoma, Miami of Florida, and Syracuse) head into bowl week with identical 11–0–0 records, but only Miami wins, and it captures the national title

5. 1987   E. An incredible nine teams enter bowl week with records of 11–0–0 or 10–1–0, setting the stage for a wild finish; Notre Dame emerges as the national champs, finishing 12–0–0, including a 34–21 Fiesta Bowl win over #3 West Virginia

6. 1984   F. Kickoff is moved to the 35-yard line

7. 1981   G. Brigham Young had the only perfect record among ranked teams, finishing 13-0–0 to win the national title, including a 24–17 win over Michigan in the Holiday Bowl

(Note: One year is the answer to two clues)

1. 1996   A. The NCAA institutes a tiebreaker system to be used in all games tied after four periods

2. 1994 B. Michigan's Desmond Howard romps to the Heisman Trophy with 640 first-place votes to runner-up Casey Weldon's 19

3. 1991 C. Visible bandannas are ruled an illegal uniform attachment

4. 1999 D. The Big 12 Conference debuts, a reformation of the Big 8 and Southwest Conferences

5. 1995 E. Tennessee wins the national title, finishing a perfect 13–0–0, including an exciting 23–16 win over #2 Florida State in the Fiesta Bowl

6. 1998 F. #2 Florida was ripped by #1 Nebraska in the Fiesta Bowl, 62–24, but somehow managed to stay #2 in the final AP poll that came out afterwards

    G. Jerseys that extend to the top of the pants must be tucked in

1. 2002 A. Three quarterbacks (Philip Rivers, Ben Roethlisberger, and Ryan Dinwiddie) all throw for more than 4,350 yards during the season, but are dwarfed by B.J. Symons who sets a new NCAA record with 5,833 yards

2. 2005 B. Oklahoma is the only ranked school to go through the season with a perfect record, finishing 13–0–0, including a 13–2 win over #3 Florida State in the Orange Bowl

3. 2000 C. Miami of Florida is the only ranked school to go through the season with a perfect record, finishing 12–0–0, including a 37–14 win over #4 Nebraska in the Rose Bowl

4. 2006 D. After two seasons of experimental use, the NCAA approves the use of instant replay for reviewing a game official's call

5. 2001   E. Navy defeated Colorado State, 51–30, in this year's bowl game with the longest name: *The San Diego County Credit Union Poinsettia Bowl*

6. 2004   F. Ohio State is the only ranked school to go through the season with a perfect record, finishing 14–0–0, including a 31–24 win over then #1 Miami of Florida in the Fiesta Bowl

7. 2003   G. Southern California and Auburn both finish the season at 13–0–0, but SC wins the national title on the strength of its 55–19 pounding of #2 Oklahoma in the Orange Bowl

CHAPTER 2

THE NFL BY THE DECADE

The success of the college game naturally led to the formation of a professional league. This first pro league was called the American Professional Football Association. Two years later it became the National Football League (NFL), although many of the rules in place at the league's beginning have continued to evolve over the years, as you'll see in this chapter. In the games that follow, match the year to its bit of NFL history.

1. 1925   A. Year the Chicago Staleys changed their name to the Bears

2. 1920   B. The New York Giants win their first NFL title in dominating fashion, shutting out 10 of their 13 opponents

3. 1922   C. First year an NFL team won 11 games (the Canton Bulldogs finished 11–0–1)

4. 1927   D. Year the NFL began play

5. 1929   E. The Cardinals win their first NFL Championship

6. 1921   F. The Green Bay Packers win their first NFL Championship

7. 1923   G. First season to see an African-American head coach (Fritz Pollard of the Akron Pros)

1. 1920   A. The Decatur Staleys relocate to Chicago and become known as the Chicago Staleys

2. 1925   B. The sixth and final year the Rock Island Independents were members of the NFL

3. 1923   C. Year the Akron Pros won the first professional title

4. 1921   D. Year the NFL contracted from 22 teams the year before to 12

5. 1926   E. First year an NFL team won 14 games (the Frankford Yellow Jackets finished 14–1–2)

6. 1929   F. Only year in the NFL's first decade of existence to feature a team with at least 10 losses (the Oorang Indians finished 1–10)

7. 1927   G. Ernie Nevers of the Cardinals scores a still NFL-record 40 points in one game against the Bears

1. 1923   A. The NFL plays its first night game as Providence hosts the Chicago Cardinals

2. 1925   B. First year pro football issued standings

3. 1929   C. The American Professional Football Conference was formed

4. 1922   D. In a game this year, George Halas picked up a Jim Thorpe fumble and returned it 98 yards for a TD, a record that stood until 1972

5. 1920   E. The NFL passes a rule that prohibits the drafting of players whose college classes hadn't yet graduated

6. 1926   F. The NFL establishes its first limit on the number of players per team—16

7. 1921   G. The American Professional Football Association officially changed its name to the National Football League

18

1. 1932   A. First year the NFL went to divisional play (Eastern and Western Divisions)

2. 1935   B. The Lions win their first-ever NFL title

3. 1934   C. The only year from 1920–1943 that the NFL had two teams which lost 10 or more games (the Newark Tornadoes were 1–10–1 and the Frankford Yellow Jackets were 4–13–1)

4. 1930   D. NBC telecasts the first football game, a 23–14 victory by the Brooklyn Dodgers over the Philadelphia Eagles, watched on about 1,000 television sets then in New York

5. 1936   E. First year the NFL race ended in a tie and a playoff game was used as a tiebreaker

6. 1939   F. The NFL agrees to hold its first-ever college player draft, starting the next year

7. 1933   G. First NFL season to feature a team that went through the regular season without suffering a loss or tie (13–0)

19

1. 1932   A. Andrew Farkas of the Redskins becomes the first player to score 10 touchdowns in a season when he finishes with 11

2. 1933   B. Year the Boston Braves relocated to Washington and became the Redskins

3. 1937   C. Beattie Feathers of the Bears becomes the first 1,000-yard runner in NFL history

4. 1936   D. Year the Chicago Bears finished with six ties (7–1–6), most in NFL history

5. 1934   E. Last season in which the leader in touchdown passes had fewer than 10 (Bob Monnett of Green Bay had 9)

6. 1939   F. Year the NFL title game with Green Bay was moved from its scheduled site of Boston to New York because Boston's owner was upset with his team's poor attendance that year

7. 1938   G. The Pittsburgh Pirates begin play in the NFL, but later change their name to the Steelers

1. 1933   A. First year the NFL played a championship game that had been planned and scheduled before the season began

2. 1936   B. Year the NFL only had eight teams, the lowest number ever

3. 1939   C. The rival AFL folded after a two-year stint

4. 1934   D. In the NFL's first-ever Pro Bowl, the New York Giants defeat the Pro All-Stars, 13–10

5. 1932   E. The first Chicago College All-Star Game was held, and the collegians and pros played to a 0–0 tie in front of 79,432 fans

6. 1937   F. Dayton, one of the league's original teams, relocates to Brooklyn and becomes the Dodgers, taking the same name as that city's popular baseball team

7. 1930   G. First year in NFL history that all league teams played the same number of games

1. 1942   A. Only year in NFL history since divisional play began in 1933 to feature two teams that went through the entire regular season without a win or tie (both teams were 0–10–0)

2. 1944   B. The Philadelphia Eagles win their first NFL title, a 7–0 affair played against the Cardinals in a snowstorm

3. 1949   C. The Cardinals win their second and, to date, final NFL title

4. 1947   D. The Philadelphia Eagles and Pittsburgh Steelers merge and become the Phil-Pitt Steagles

5. 1940   E. The Pittsburgh Pirates change their name to the Steelers

6. 1943   F. Second of only three years in NFL history to feature a team that went through the regular season without suffering a loss or tie (11–0)

7. 1948   G. The Cleveland Browns win the last AAFC title before the league folds up shop, losing its battle with the NFL

1. 1940   A. The Rams disband temporarily and sit out this season

2. 1949   B. Steve Van Buren rushes for 1,008 yards to set a new NFL record, eclipsing the old record by only 4 yards

3. 1946   C. The Cleveland Rams relocate to Los Angeles and begin play as the Los Angeles Rams

4. 1945   D. The Chicago Bears maul the Washington Redskins, 73–0, to win the NFL title

5. 1943   E. Green Bay's Cecil Isbell becomes the first quarterback to crack the 2,000-yard passing mark in a season

6. 1947 F. The Philadelphia Eagles defeat the Los Angeles Rams, 14–0, to win the NFL Championship

7. 1942 G. The Rams reach the postseason for the first time and defeat the Redskins, 15–14, for the NFL title

1. 1941 A. The NFL adopts a new rule which requires all players to wear helmets

2. 1946 B. For the first time, the NFL had two 1,000-yard rushers in the same season (Steve Van Buren and Tony Canadeo)

3. 1947 C. The third rival league to call itself the American Football League begins play with six teams

4. 1940 D. The Rams become the first team to sport helmet emblems when one of their players paints horns on his helmet

5. 1948 E. Elmer Layden becomes the first Commissioner of the NFL

6. 1943 F. Bert Bell becomes the second Commissioner of the NFL

7. 1949 G. The NFL adds a new "bonus" choice in the draft in which one team wins a lottery for the right to take the first pick

1. 1957 A. The Cleveland Browns win the NFL title the first year they join league play

2. 1955 B. The Baltimore Colts begin play in the NFL

3. 1950 C. Vince Lombardi becomes the head coach of the Packers

4. 1953 D. The Lions win their fourth and, to date, final NFL title

5. 1958   E. The Rams win their second NFL title, this time playing in Los Angeles, defeating the Cleveland Browns, 24–17

6. 1959   F. The Steelers draft Louisville quarterback Johnny Unitas in the ninth round, but later release him without letting him appear in a preseason game. The rest, as they say, is history.

7. 1951   G. The Baltimore Colts win their first NFL title, beating the New York Giants, 23–17, in overtime

1. 1957   A. After losing hard-fought NFL title games three years in a row, frustrated Cleveland crushes Detroit, 56–10, to capture their second NFL title

2. 1953   B. First season to see an African-American assistant coach (Lowell Perry of the Pittsburgh Steelers)

3. 1955   C. Jim Brown rushes for 1,527 yards, smashing the old record by nearly 400 yards (1,146 by Steve Van Buren in 1949)

4. 1956   D. Marion Motley becomes the first African-American to lead the NFL in an individual statistical category (rushing)

5. 1954   E. The Giants romp over the Bears, 46–7, in the first NFL title game in seven years that doesn't include Cleveland

6. 1958   F. The Browns win their sixth straight Conference title, the only NFL team in history to do so

7. 1950   G. Willie Thrower (no kidding!) becomes the first African-American quarterback in the NFL

1. 1952   A. The Rams become the first team in NFL history to have all of their games—home and away—televised

2. 1955   B. A brown ball with white end stripes replaces the white ball with black end stripes for all night games

3. 1956   C. The Dallas Texans fold, the last NFL team ever to fail

4. 1950   D. Lamar Hunt announces the formation of a new professional league—the American Football League

5. 1953   E. The NFL title game was televised nationally for the first time

6. 1959   F. The Browns and Colts make a trade involving 15 players, the largest in NFL history

7. 1951   G. The sudden death overtime rule was used for the first time, and the Rams defeated the Giants, 23–17, three minutes into the extra period of a preseason game

1. 1967   A. First year the NFL has four Divisions

2. 1968   B. The Miami Dolphins begin play in the AFL

3. 1963   C. The New York Jets become the first AFL team to win the Super Bowl, defeating the Colts 16–7

4. 1960   D. The Cincinnati Bengals begin play in the AFL

5. 1966   E. The American Football League (AFL) begins play

6. 1969   F. Last year the Cleveland Browns won the NFL title

7. 1964   G. Don Shula becomes head coach of the Colts, replacing Weeb Ewbank

1. 1969   A. First year the Cowboys, Eagles, Redskins, and Saints comprised the Capitol Division

2. 1964   B. Last year the Rams, Colts, Falcons, and 49ers comprised the Coastal Division

3. 1963   C. The Houston Oilers become the first pro football team to play indoors and on artificial turf

4. 1966   D. Season Kansas City won the AFL title and appeared in the Super Bowl

5. 1968   E. The NFL Hall of Fame announces its first inductees

6. 1961   F. The Los Angeles Chargers relocate to San Diego

7. 1967   G. The Buffalo Bills win their first AFL title, defeating the San Diego Chargers, 20–7

1. 1963   A. Green Bay halfback Paul Hornung is suspended for the season for betting on league games

2. 1967   B. Burl Toler becomes the first African-American to officiate an NFL game

3. 1963   C. The Atlanta Falcons begin play in the NFL

4. 1961   D. The Minnesota Vikings begin play in the NFL

5. 1966   E. The Dallas Texans relocate to Kansas City and become the Chiefs

6. 1960   F. The Eagles defeat the Packers, 17–13, to win the NFL title

7. 1965   G. The Oakland Raiders win their first AFL title

1. 1961   A. The Pro Football Hall of Fame opens in Canton, Ohio

2. 1963   B. NFL officials' penalty flags changed in color from white to bright gold

3. 1968   C. Pete Gogolak becomes the NFL's first soccer-style kicker

4. 1965   D. Both the NFL and AFL adopt a rule that prohibits the grabbing of any player's facemask

5. 1960   E. The Raiders defeat the Jets, 43–32, in the famous "Heidi" game, scoring two TDs in the last 42 seconds after NBC preempted the game's last 50 seconds for the movie

6. 1964   F. The Houston Oilers defeat the Los Angeles Chargers, 24–16, in the first AFL title game

7. 1962   G. Pete Rozelle becomes the NFL Commissioner as a compromise candidate on the 23rd ballot and moves the league offices to New York

1. 1978   A. Tony Dorsett wins the NFL Rookie of the Year Award

2. 1973   B. O.J. Simpson wins the NFL's MVP Award as he becomes the first player in history to rush for 2,000 yards in a season

3. 1977   C. Earl Campbell selected as the NFL's #1 draft choice

4. 1972   D. The year of Tom Dempsey's 63-yard field goal

5. 1971   E. First year the NFL topped the 10-million mark in regular-season paid attendance (10,076,035)

6. 1974   F. The only year in the 43-year history of the Chicago College All-Star Game that the game wasn't held

7. 1970   G. Mean Joe Greene wins the NFL's Defensive Player of the Year Award

1. 1970   A. Last year the NFL featured a team that lost every regular season game it played (Tampa Bay finished 0–14–0)

2. 1972   B. The Boston Patriots move to Foxborough and change their name to the New England Patriots

3. 1976   C. First year the NFL has six Divisions

4. 1974   D. The Seattle Seahawks switch from the NFC to the AFC

5. 1971   E. The only season in NFL history to feature a team that finished with a perfect record (no losses or ties) in both the regular season and the playoffs

6. 1977   F. Now playing for the Chargers, Johnny Unitas becomes the first quarterback in NFL history to pass for more than 40,000 yards in his career

7. 1973   G. The Steelers have one of the greatest drafts in NFL history, selecting four future Hall of Famers in the first five rounds (Lynn Swann, John Stallworth, Jack Lambert, and Mike Webster)

1. 1972   A. The Steelers win a coin flip with the Bears for the right to choose Terry Bradshaw in the NFL draft

2. 1976   B. Quarterback Joe Montana of Notre Dame is selected by San Francisco in the (gulp!) third round of the draft

3. 1975   C. The Tampa Bay Buccaneers end their NFL record string of 26 straight losses, defeating the Saints, 33–14

4. 1970   D. The Seattle Seahawks begin play in the NFL

5. 1977   E. Season that Dallas won their first Super Bowl

6. 1971   F. Franco Harris'"Immaculate Reception" gives the Steelers their first postseason victory in franchise history after forty years of drought

7. 1979   G. The New Orleans Saints begin play in the Superdome

1. 1970   A. The World Football League, the newest rival to the NFL, begins play

2. 1976   B. The first AFC-NFC Pro Bowl takes place

3. 1972   C. The NFL institutes the 30-second clock

4. 1973   D. The NFL adopts a jersey numbering system in which all players are given numbers within a certain group based on a player's position

5. 1971   E. The owners of the Rams and Colts exchange teams

6. 1978   F. The NFL begins playing a 16-game schedule

7. 1974   G. Vince Lombardi dies; seven days later the Super Bowl Trophy is renamed the Vince Lombardi Trophy

1. 1984   A. The only year from 1967 to current day that the NFL did *not* use a divisional format

2. 1982   B. The Saints appear in their first-ever postseason game, but lose to the Vikings, 44–10

3. 1983   C. The Patriots choose quarterback Tony Eason with their first pick in the draft, passing over quarterback Dan Marino

4. 1980   D. The St. Louis Cardinals relocate to Phoenix and begin play as the Phoenix Cardinals

5. 1987   E. First NFL season in which a wild card team won the Super Bowl

6. 1988   F. Season that culminated in the AFC Championship Game known as "The Deep Freeze," a 27–7 victory by Cincinnati over San Diego, a game played in –9 degree temperature with a wind chill factor of –60 degrees

7. 1981   G. The year the Super Bowl first became a venue for high-concept advertising (Apple Computer began the trend)

1. 1984   A. Steve Largent of the Seahawks becomes the NFL's all-time leader in pass receptions

2. 1989   B. The Colts move from Baltimore to Indianapolis

3. 1982   C. Johnny Grier becomes the first African-American referee

4. 1980   D. Year the Vikings began playing indoors at the Metrodome

5. 1987   E. Season that culminated in the NFC Championship Game that featured "The Catch" by Dwight Clark

6. 1988   F. Art Shell becomes the first African-American head coach in the NFL since Fritz Pollard of the Akron Pros in 1921

7. 1981   G. Season the Eagles played in their first Super Bowl

1. 1984   A. The Los Angeles Rams begin playing their games in Anaheim Stadium

2. 1980   B. The NFL begins using instant replay to assist officials

3. 1987   C. Eric Dickerson rushes for an NFL single-season record of 2,105 yards

4. 1988   D. First season to see an African-American as a starting quarterback in the Super Bowl

5. 1982   E. Year the Chicago Bears went 18–1, their only loss coming at the hands of the Miami Dolphins, the only team ever to go 17–0 for a season

6. 1985   F. Steve Largent of the Seahawks becomes the NFL's all-time leader in receiving yards

7. 1986   G. Year the NFL season was cut from a 16-game season to a 9-game season because of a players' strike

1. 1982   A. After deliberating five days, a jury awarded the USFL one dollar in damages in their $1.7 billion suit against the NFL

2. 1986   B. The Oakland Raiders sue the NFL over their refusal to allow the team to move to Los Angeles

3. 1988   C. Dan Marino set a new record for yards passing in a season (5,084), Eric Dickerson set a new record for yards rushing in a season (2,105), and Art Monk set a new record for passes caught in a season (106)

4. 1980   D. The 30-second clock is replaced by the 45-second clock

5. 1989   E. ESPN begins telecasting NFL games

6. 1987   F. Paul Tagliabue becomes the NFL's seventh Commissioner

7. 1984   G. The Raiders win their lawsuit against the NFL and move to Los Angeles and become the Los Angeles Raiders

1. 1998

2. 1996

3. 1995

4. 1991

5. 1997

6. 1993

7. 1994

A. The Jacksonville Jaguars begin play in the NFL

B. The season Buffalo earned the right to play in its first of four consecutive Super Bowls

C. The Baltimore Ravens begin play in the NFL

D. The Phoenix Cardinals are renamed the Arizona Cardinals

E. First year that FOX telecast the Super Bowl

F. Last year that NBC telecast the Super Bowl

G. Don Shula wins his 325th career game, breaking the long-held record of George Halas for coaching wins

1. 1997

2. 1998

3. 1995

4. 1994

5. 1990

6. 1991

7. 1999

A. Season that the 49ers became the first team to win five Super Bowls

B. Year Jim Kelly passed for five touchdowns in a Monday night game against the Cincinnati Bengals

C. The Houston Oilers relocate to Nashville and become the Tennessee Oilers

D. Year Kurt Warner became the second quarterback in history to have 40 TD passes in a season (he had 41)

E. The Carolina Panthers begin play in the NFL

F. Season in which the Broncos repeated as Super Bowl champs

G. Year Thurman Thomas rushed for 214 yards in a Monday night game against the New York Jets

1. 1994

   A. The Seahawks are forced to play five of their home games outdoors at nearby Washington Husky Stadium when tiles fall off the Kingdome ceiling necessitating repairs that will ultimately kill several repair workers

2. 1999

   B. Only year Bill Cowher of the Steelers won the NFL Coach of the Year Award

3. 1997

   C. The Los Angeles Rams relocate to St. Louis and begin play as the St. Louis Rams

4. 1992

   D. The year Red Grange died

5. 1995

   E. Last season in which the player who was the league's MVP also led his team to a win in the Super Bowl

6. 1991

   F. Season the Atlanta Falcons made it to the Super Bowl

7. 1998

   G. Season that Brett Favre and Barry Sanders were co-MVPs

1. 1993

   A. The Raiders relocate back to Oakland from Los Angeles

2. 1990

   B. Carolina and Jacksonville are awarded NFL franchises

3. 1995

   C. Former NFL Commissioner Pete Rozelle dies

4. 1992

   D. To give all teams a week off during the season, the NFL institutes its staggered bye-week schedule, thereby letting teams play a 16-game schedule over 17 weeks

5. 1997

   E. The use of instant replay is discontinued when only 17 owners of the necessary 21 vote to continue using it

6. 1996

   F. Seattle defeats Tennessee, 16–13, in the 10,000th game in NFL history

7. 1994

   G. The optional two-point conversion attempt is instituted

1. 2002

A. First season to see an African-American head coach take a team to the Super Bowl

2. 2000

B. The Seattle Seahawks switch from the AFC to the NFC

3. 2001

C. Only year from 1985–2006 that a safety (Ed Reed) won the NFL Defensive Player of the Year Award

4. 2007

D. Kansas City quarterback Elvis Grbac passes for 504 yards in one game

5. 2005

E. Year the NFL played its first regular season game outside the United States

6. 2006

F. Year the NFL played its first regular season game outside of North America

7. 2004

G. Emmitt Smith becomes the NFL's all-time rushing leader, passing Walter Payton

1. 2003

A. The Houston Texans become the first expansion team in 41 years to win their first game, a 19–10 win over Dallas

2. 2005

B. Beginning this year, the NFL changed its season-opening date to the weekend after Labor Day

3. 2004

C. Year the Indianapolis Colts started the season with nine straight wins

4. 2000

D. Year the 49ers and Cardinals set the NFL regular season record for single-game attendance (103,467)

5. 2002

E. The first season in 34 years to feature a quarterback as the winner of the NFL Offensive Rookie of the Year Award

6. 2001   F. On January 26 of this year, the Tampa Bay Buccaneers defeat the Raiders in the Super Bowl, 48–21

7. 2006   G. Year the Indianapolis Colts beat the Steelers in an exciting game in Mexico City, 24–23 in a preseason game

CHAPTER 3

WHO AM I?

E **ach of the games** in this chapter has four clues that all refer to one major football personality. The clues start off tough, revealing only a little information. Each subsequent question reveals a bit more. Your objective is to guess the name of the person in question in as few clues as possible.

1 I finished my collegiate career as the third highest rated passer in NCAA history.

2 An All-American at UCLA, I was the first overall pick in the NFL Draft in 1989.

3 I took over the starting quarterback job as a rookie, and even though I showed a lot of promise, as in my 379-yard game (a record for rookies), my team finished a dismal 1–15.

4 With 90 victories for the Dallas Cowboys to my credit in the 1990s, I was the winningest quarterback during any decade in NFL history.

1 After graduating from college, I was drafted 82nd overall in the NFL Draft.

2 Though I was apparently not too highly thought of out of college, by the time I retired as a member of the Kansas City Chiefs, I had accumulated more than 40,000 yards passing in my career.

3 Three times I was named to the All-NFL team, the same number of times I won the Super Bowl MVP Award.

4 My main claim to fame, however, was my 14 seasons spent with the San Francisco 49ers where I led my team to four Super Bowl victories.

1 I was the first president of the NFL, though in that year the league was known as the American Professional Football Association.

2 I played 52 games in my NFL career, rushing for six touchdowns and passing for four more.

3 An All-American halfback at Carlisle College, I was also an Olympic decathlon champion.

4 I was voted as the top American athlete of the first half of the 20th century, quite an honor considering the prejudice that existed against Native Americans at the time.

1 I was a three-time All-American at the University of Illinois.

2 I was such a huge star in college that the fledgling NFL recruited me as a gate attraction, and it worked—big time!

3 In fact, I was such a popular gate attraction, that it went to my head. Since the Chicago Bears didn't meet my exorbitant salary demands the next season (not to mention my request for one-third ownership of the team!), my agent and I formed a rival league to compete against the NFL.

4 I returned to the NFL the following year, but I suffered a leg injury that prevented me from ever again running with the ghostlike elusiveness that gave me my nickname, "the Galloping Ghost."

1 During my career, I played in four Pro Bowls and was named the Offensive Player of the Game in three of them.

2 Even though I returned kickoffs for just five years, by the time I retired, I was the NFL's all-time leader in kickoff returns.

3 I scored 22 touchdowns in my rookie season, including six in one game against San Francisco on a muddy field.

4 Though I was one of the NFL's greatest running backs of all time, my short career with the Chicago Bears ended prematurely due to injury after the 1971 season.

1 I had a legendary career at the University of Minnesota before turning pro.

2 Some consider me the poster boy of power football in the NFL's early days. For sheer brutal line-smashing, I had no peer.

3 A two-way player, I was All-NFL five times, retiring with more than 4,000 yards of offense as a fullback and a bone-crushing legacy as a linebacker.

4 I retired in 1937 after eight seasons with the Bears, but six years later came out of retirement and helped Chicago win another NFL title in 1943.

1 In 1938, I startled the sports world by signing "Whizzer" White to a $15,000 contract, unheard of at the time.

2 But even Whizzer didn't change my sad fortunes. My team didn't have a winning record until my ninth year of ownership (1942), and we'd lost money every year.

3 In 1947 we tied Philadelphia for the Eastern Division title, but lost to them in a playoff game, 21–0. That was the closest thing to a championship for us until ...

4 The 1974 season, when my beloved Pittsburgh Steelers won the Super Bowl, 16–6, over the Minnesota Vikings, the first of four Super Bowl wins in six years as we made up for lost time.

1 Expectations of me were high, especially after I became a Heisman-trophy winning quarterback from Notre Dame.

2 In 1961, I was home on Christmas leave from the Army, so I joined my teammates and led them to the NFL Championship over the New York Giants by scoring a record 19 points.

3 After initially floundering between different positions for two different coaches, I eventually settled in as the team's halfback and placekicker, scoring an NFL-record 176 points in 1960.

4 Nicknamed "The Golden Boy," I spent nine seasons with Vince Lombardi and the Packers, though I did miss one full season when I was suspended for gambling.

1 At Syracuse University, I was an All-American in lacrosse as well as football, and I was a letterman in basketball, too.

2 The NFL's unanimous Rookie of the Year in 1957, I never missed a game in my nine-year NFL career.

3 I played in the Pro Bowl all nine years of my career, and won the NFL's MVP Award four times (1957, 1958, 1963, 1965).

4 When I retired from the Cleveland Browns at the age of 29 to become a movie actor, I had rushed for 12,312 yards and set many NFL records, leaving fans to wonder what kind of numbers I could have put up if I hadn't retired at the peak of my career.

1 In 1949, I came out of the University of Kentucky and became the back-up quarterback and backup placekicker for the Chicago Bears.

2 I became the starting quarterback for the Bears in 1953, but after two years I lost my job and became the backup again through the 1958 season, although I was doing more kicking.

3 In 1959, the Bears tried to make me a kicker only, so I retired. After sitting out the year, I came back in 1960—as a member of the new AFL's Houston Oilers, leading them to the AFL title in both 1960 and 1961 as the team's fulltime quarterback and fulltime kicker.

4 In 1967, I went to the Raiders, continuing to be both a quarterback and kicker. I played nine more seasons—until I was 48!—before retiring as pro football's all-time leading scorer with 2,002 points.

1 I was the first player to win All-Southwest Conference honors for four years.

2 In 1977 I became the first University of Texas player to win the Heisman Trophy.

3 By the time I retired from the New Orleans Saints after the 1985 season, I had rushed for over 9,400 yards, even though I was only 30 years old.

4 Perhaps the highlight of my career was 1978, when I was the #1 pick in the NFL Draft, was named the NFL's Rookie of the Year, and won the league's MVP Award as well, all after rushing for 1,450 yards and 13 touchdowns for the Houston Oilers, the team I played most of my career for.

1 I was a coach's player: steady, a quiet leader, and punctual. In fact, I showed up on time for all 15 of the Pro Bowls I was selected to.

2 After winning the Outland Trophy while playing for Utah State, I was voted the NFL's Rookie of the Year in 1962.

3 And I was as durable as I was good. During my career I played in 208 games, including 198 in a row.

4 I was considered the leader of the Los Angeles Rams'"Fearsome Foursome," joining forces with Lamar Lundy, Deacon Jones, and Roosevelt Grier.

1 In 1955, the Pittsburgh Steelers drafted me in the 9th round, but later cut me before I ever threw a pass for them. Because I loved playing football, I played the rest of the year on the Pittsburgh sandlots for $6 a game.

2 Weeb Ewbank heard about me and, after watching me play, offered me a contract in 1956 for $17,000—provided I made the team.

3 I made the team as a back-up, and when I got my chance to play in the season's fourth game, on my first pass I threw an interception that was returned for a TD.

4 But after that, I never looked back. In 18 pro seasons, 17 with the Baltimore Colts, I threw for over 40,000 yards and 290 TDs, earned the nickname "Mr. Clutch" for my many stirring comeback drives, and led the Colts to three NFL titles, including a win in Super Bowl V.

1 I started coaching late in my career, at age 40, as an assistant coach of the New York Giants, a position I held for five years.

2 In 1969, I took over the reigns of the dismal Washington Redskins, a team that hadn't had a winning record for 13 straight seasons, and turned them around, finishing 7–5–2.

3 I wasn't able to build on that winning record with the Redskins, however, because I developed cancer which spread very quickly, and I died in September of 1970 at the age of 57.

4 In between my time with the Giants and Redskins, however, I was head coach of the Green Bay Packers for nine seasons, leading them to an 89–29–4 record and five NFL titles, including wins in the first two Super Bowls, which is why the Super Bowl trophy is named in my honor.

1 In 1975, I was the star receiver for the Memphis Southmen of the World Football League.

2 I was a dangerous receiver. In 1973, I caught only 29 passes, but 11 of them were for touchdowns.

3 During my 13-year NFL career, I caught 427 passes for 8,565 yards, giving me an amazing per catch average of 20.1 yards, among the best in NFL history.

4 The reason I only averaged about 32 catches per season during my career (besides always being double covered) was that I always played on ball control teams. I spent eight seasons with Cleveland, mostly during the Jim Brown era, and five seasons with the Dolphins when they had Kiick and Csonka.

1 Even though I was an All-America at Oklahoma State, I wasn't drafted until the 40th pick of the 1988 NFL Draft, primarily because teams were concerned about a knee injury I had suffered during my senior year of college.

2 But the pros needn't have worried. In my first 11 years in the NFL, I missed only eight games, not bad considering the beating that running backs who carry the ball around 300 times a year take.

3 In 1991, I led my team to its second straight Super Bowl berth, winning the league's MVP Award in the process.

4 In the eight seasons from 1989–1996, I rushed for more than 1,000 yards each year as the main ground weapon of the Buffalo Bills.

1 As a rookie in 1974, I led the NFL in punt returns with 577 yards on 41 returns, fourth best in the history of the league up to that point.

2 But I didn't stay a punt returner for long. With my great speed and tremendous leaping ability, I became a full-time wide receiver in my second year.

3 That second year was perhaps the best of my career. I did, after all, win the Super Bowl MVP Award after making four catches for a then-record 161 yards, including a 64-yard game-winning touchdown.

4 During my nine-year career with the Pittsburgh Steelers, I caught 336 passes for 5,462 yards, and helped them to four Super Bowl wins.

1 I was a third-round pick out of the University of Oregon in 1973.

2 I was constantly battling injuries during my NFL career, but in 1982 I managed to hold it together enough to win the league's MVP Award.

3 Surprisingly, though, I had better years (statistically) from 1979–1981 when I became the first quarterback ever to throw for 4,000 yards in three straight seasons.

4 By the time I retired after spending my entire 15-year career with the San Diego Chargers, I was only the third quarterback ever to break the 40,000-yard mark, finishing with 43,040.

1 By the time I retired in 1979 as a member of the San Francisco 49ers, I had rushed for 11,236 yards in 11 NFL seasons.

2 But my career didn't get off to a fast start. Even though I was a two-time All-American, a Heisman Trophy winner, and a #1 pick in the NFL Draft, I was used sparingly the first three years, averaging just 642 yards and 4 TDs a season.

3 When Lou Saban took over the team in 1972, he turned me loose, giving me the ball as much as possible, and I rushed for 1,251 yards.

4 The next year, though, I was "juiced." After rushing for 219 and 200 yards in the last two games of the season, I became the first running back in history to rush for more than 2,000 yards in a season, leading my Buffalo Bills teammates to their first winning record in eight seasons.

1 I may have played at a small college (Jackson State), but it didn't stop me from being a first-round pick in the NFL Draft.

2 And I was durable, too. After missing only one game during my rookie season of 1975, I played in 186 straight games.

3 Only the players' strike in 1982 prevented me from having 11 straight seasons with at least 300 rushing attempts.

4 One of the game's true superstars, I retired after 13 seasons with the Chicago Bears with 16,726 yards rushing, 4,538 yards in pass receiving, and 125 TDs.

1 I was a two-time All-American out of the University of Illinois.

2 Named All-NFL six times, I was selected to eight Pro Bowls and was selected the NFL's Defensive Player of the Year in both 1969 and 1970.

3 A punishing tackler, as a rookie in 1965 I led my team in tackles, interceptions, forced fumbles, and fumble recoveries, no small task for a linebacker.

4 My brilliant nine-year career with the Chicago Bears came to an end because of a severe knee injury I suffered in 1973.

1 While in high school, I threw the javelin 245 feet, a national record.

2 I originally signed to play football at Louisiana State, but later enrolled elsewhere after failing to get a high enough score on the ACT college-entrance exam.

3 But I did just fine as Louisiana Tech's quarterback. I even became the NFL's #1 draft choice in 1970.

4 Although I was somewhat erratic and struggled a bit the first few years, and was often perceived by the media as having less than adequate intelligence, once I did get going, I was impressive. I led the Pittsburgh Steelers to four Super Bowl titles in six years, setting many Super Bowl and postseason records in the process.

1 School wasn't for me. That's why I left Oklahoma State after my junior year.

2 Just three days after signing an NFL contract, I saw my first action. The first time I carried the ball, I gained 18 yards.

3 In my rookie season, I rushed for 1,470 yards, finishing just 10 yards behind league leader Christian Okoye who had 90 more rushing attempts than me.

4 By the time I retired from the Detroit Lions after the 1998 season, I had rushed for more than 1,000 yards in all ten of my seasons, the first player in history to accomplish that feat in his first 10 years.

1 I was a late third-round pick out of Georgia by an expansion team.

2 In my first game (and the team's first-ever game), I came off the bench to throw four TD passes to help defeat the Chicago Bears, 37–13.

3 A nine-time Pro Bowl selection, I was the NFL's MVP in 1975.

4 Known for my scrambling ability, I played 18 years in the NFL, 13 for the Vikings and five for the Giants, retiring as the NFL's all-time leader in yards (47,003), completions (3,686), and touchdowns (342).

1 My first two pro seasons were very successful as I threw for over 9,800 yards and 83 touchdowns.

2 Oh, I forgot to mention that those two seasons were with the Houston Gamblers of the USFL.

3 When the USFL folded after the 1985 season, I was forced to take my "no huddle" offense to the NFL.

4 In my 11-year career with the Buffalo Bills, I passed for over 3,000 yards eight times, finishing my NFL career with 35,467 yards, 237 TDs, and an unprecedented (and never matched) four straight trips to the Super Bowl.

CHAPTER 4

FOOTBALL'S NOTABLE QUOTABLES

Many memorable and colorful characters have graced the game of football over its long history. Some have spun pearls of wisdom. Some have given truly inspirational speeches. And some stuck their foot in their mouths. From the inspiring to the hilarious, in this chapter it is your job to match the quote to the person it is attributed to.

1. George Blanda

A. "I'll stay out of bars when women cease to go in."

2. D.D. Lewis

B. "I'm the greatest ever [at my position]. I'd hate to have to play against me."

3. Walter Payton

C. "Franco Harris faked me out so bad one time that I got a 15-yard penalty for grabbing my own facemask."

4. Cecil Johnson

D. "I had a brain transplant. I got a sportswriter's brain so I would be sure I had one that hadn't been used."

5. Norm Van Brocklin

E. "By the time I was finished playing, I was too old to begin coaching."

6. Deacon Jones

F. "Do I watch Monday night football? It would make as much sense as a secretary going home and typing."

7. John Matuszak

G. "Playing middle linebacker is like walking through a lion's cage in a three-piece pork-chop suit."

1. Lou Holtz

A. [In response to his team's poor season] "I feel like the guy in the javelin competition who won the toss and elected to receive."

2. Jerry Glanville

B. "With me, what you see is what you get. Some people just don't like what they see."

3. Bum Phillips

C. "When I get depressed, I just go home and read my five-year contract."

4. Wayne Fontes

D. "If you're a pro coach, NFL stands for 'Not For Long.'"

5. Nick Coso

E. "My job's not in jeopardy. When I drive, the fans still wave to me, and all of their fingers show."

6. Mack Brown

F. "Earl Campbell may not be in a class by himself, but whatever class he's in, it doesn't take long to call the roll."

7. Buddy Ryan

G. [In response to his team's winless season] "It was a building year, but the building caved in on me."

1. Bruce Collie

A. "My mom said it was a good thing I was the third child and not the first, otherwise I would have been an only child."

2. Art Donovan

B. "Football players are like prostitutes—your body is only worth something for so long. When it's no good anymore, nobody wants it."

3. Larry Grantham

C. "My favorite beer? Cold."

4. Alex Karras

D. "I left because of illness and fatigue. The fans were sick and tired of me."

5. Brian Bosworth

E. "The most profitable form of writing? Ransom notes."

6. John Ralston

F. "We didn't have anything like steroids. If I wanted to get pumped up, I drank a case of beer."

7. Art Modell

G. [After a poor season] "There's no truth to the rumor that our highlight film will be a Polaroid shot."

1. John McKay

A. [When asked what his major in college was] "I got a B.S in B.S."

2. Bill Dooley

B. "I've been fined by the league so much I have no salary."

3. Dick Butkus

C. "I never set out to hurt anybody deliberately unless it was important, like a league game or something."

4. Pete Wysocki

D. [When asked about his team's execution that day] "I think it's a good idea."

5. Ron Meyer

E. "Football is a game designed to keep coal miners off the streets."

6. Jimmy Breslin

F. "Whenever you tackle Earl Campbell, it reduces your IQ."

7. Bubba Baker

G. "My golf game reminds me of Woody Hayes' football game—three yards and a cloud of dust."

1. Alex Karras

A. [On what it's like playing at BYU] "They let you chase girls, they just don't let you catch them."

2. Dan Henning

B. [When asked the definition of an Alabama pervert] "Somebody who loves his wife more than football."

3. Glen Kozlowski

C. "All coaches are in the last year of their contracts, only some of them don't know it."

4. Jim McMahon

D. "Our coach was so tough he'd make us run ten laps if we lost the coin toss."

5. Frank Howard

E. "I never graduated from [college]. I was only there for two terms—Truman's and Eisenhower's."

6. Sonny Smith

F. "My fondest memory of BYU? Leaving."

7. Lou Holtz

G. "We're totally committed to defense. I'm not sure our defense is committed to defense, but the rest of the team is."

1. Dan Fouts

A. [On not being drafted until the fourth round] "The scouts said I looked like Tarzan and played like Jane."

2. Russ Francis

B. [On being picked 265th in the draft] "I think they drafted in alphabetical order."

3. Art Donovan

C. [On defensive linemen] "If their IQ s were five points lower, they would be geraniums."

4. Wilbur Young

D. "The toughest part of losing 85 pounds wasn't watching what I ate, it was watching what my friends ate."

5. Dennis Harrison

E. [When asked where he might be drafted] "People say somewhere in the first round. Maybe higher."

6. Craig Heyward

F. "Now that I'm retired, I want to say that all defensive linemen are sissies."

7. Brent Ziegler

G. "I'm a light eater. As soon as it's light, I start to eat."

1. Thomas Henderson

A. "The football season is like pain. You forget how terrible it is until it seizes you again."

2. Ron Meyer

B. [When talking about how overrated emotion is on a football field] "There was a lot of emotion at the Alamo, and nobody survived."

3. Ray Perkins

C. "Football is a wonderful way to get rid of aggressiveness without going to jail for it."

4. Erma Bombeck

D. [When asked what his wife thinks of his 18-hour work days] "I really don't know. I don't see her that much."

5. Sally Quinn

E. "Football players do one-armed pushups so they can count with their other hand."

6. Heywood Broun

F. "If a man watches three football games in a row, he should be declared legally dead."

7. Al McGuire

G. [On being waived by his team] "I'm surprised there wasn't a boycott or march on downtown to protest it."

1. Lou Holtz

A. [On one of his players] "Physically, he's a world-beater. Mentally, he's an eggbeater."

2. Alex Karras

B. [On Redskins fans wearing pig snouts at home games] "The really scary thing is that some of these people work for the government."

3. Lawrence Taylor

C. [On his golf game] "All my life I've been trying to make a hole in one. The closest I ever came was a bogey."

4. Joe Jacoby

D. [On being late to practice] "Don't blame me. Blame the foursome ahead of me."

5. Bobby Bowden

E. [On one of his players] "Sometimes God gives you physical talents and takes away your brain."

6. Mike Ditka

F. [On his golf game] "My best score ever was 103, but I've only been playing 15 years."

7. Matt Elliott

G. [On one of his players] "He doesn't know the meaning of the word fear. In fact, I just saw his grades, and he doesn't know the meaning of a lot of words."

1. Conrad Dobler

A. "The University of Texas has only two major sports—football and spring football."

2. Gary Darnell

B. [On another player] "He has a lot of class. And all of it is third."

3. Walt Garrison

C. [On whether or not his coach ever smiled] "I don't know. I only played there nine years."

4. Don Meredith

D. [On why his team had better linebackers than their opponents] "We're more aggressive, more mobile, and more smarter."

5. Greg Lloyd

E. "I can't wait until tomorrow, because I get better looking every day."

6. Jones Ramsey

F. [On his college team's winless season] "Our kicker only had one bad day last year— Saturday."

7. Joe Namath

G. [On his coach] "He's such a perfectionist that if he were married to Dolly Parton, he'd expect her to cook."

1. Red Grange

A. "We'll definitely be improved this year. Last year we lost 10 games. This year we only scheduled nine."

2. Hayden Fry

B. "If lessons are learned in defeat, our team is getting a good education."

3. Dennis Green

C. [On how he got #77] "The guy in front of me got #76 and the guy in back of me got #78."

4. Ray Jenkins

D. [After losing a game 64–0] "It's hard to believe, but the score started at 0–0."

5. Blaine Nye

E. "It's not whether you win or lose, but who gets the blame."

6. Murray Warmath

F. "They say losing builds character. I have all the character I need."

7. Ray Malavasi

G. [After suffering an upset loss] "The sun doesn't shine on the same hound dog's rump every day."

1. Chuck Knox

A. "Most of my clichés aren't original."

2. Bill Parcells

B. "I want to gain fifteen hundred or two thousand yards, whichever comes first."

3. George Rogers

C. "If Howard Cosell had breakfast and dinner with everybody he bragged about on *Monday Night Football*, he'd weigh 723 pounds."

4. Mike Ditka

D. "If me and King Kong went into an alley, only one of us would come out, and it wouldn't be the monkey."

5. Joe Garagiola

E. "Concentration-wise, we're having trouble crossing the line mentally from a toughness standpoint."

6. Bob Costas

F. "What's the difference between a three-week-old puppy and a sportswriter? In six weeks, the puppy stops whining."

7. Lyle Alzado

G. "Dan Dierdorf and I once didn't speak for two weeks. I didn't think it was right to interrupt him."

1. Fran Tarkenton

A. [On his fear of small planes] "The good Lord might not want to take me, but He might be after the pilot."

2. Steve Largent

B. [Commenting on Green Bay's 1–10–1 season of 1958] "They overwhelmed one opponent, underwhelmed 10, and whelmed one."

3. Red Smith

C. [On why he never pulled a muscle in his career] "Because I don't have one."

4. Mosi Tatupu

    D. [On growing up poor] "When my uncle used to slice the ham at dinner, it only had one side."

5. Bobby Bowden

    E. [On his four pet pit bulls] "Needless to say, people don't stop by very often."

6. Walt Garrison

    F. [On which record he'd broken that he cherishes the most] "Probably the Beatles' *White Album*."

7. Darrell Royal

    G. [On growing up poor] "I had a tumbleweed as a pet."

1. Mack Brown

    A. "When Vince Lombardi said sit down, I didn't even bother to look for a chair."

2. Knute Rockne

    B. [On one of his receivers] "He has the Midas touch—everything he touches turns to mufflers."

3. John Riggins

    C. "I don't know if I'm ahead or behind, but I know I'm not even."

4. Steve Martin

    D. [After losing seven straight games] "I called up dial-a-prayer and they hung up on me."

5. Jim Walden

    E. [On team rules he imposed] "There will be no fighting in barrooms, unless the head coach is pinned down, in which case he should be rescued."

6. Jerry Glanville

    F. [On his team's rivalry with another school] "We'll dominate them physically, mentally, and then we'll steal their girlfriends."

7. Max McGee

    G. "I find that prayers work best when you have big players."

1. Lou Holtz

A. My hometown was so small, the biggest industry was taking the bottles back to the store."

2. Tim Cohane

B. [On why he got married at 11 a.m.] "Because if it didn't work out, I didn't want to waste the whole day."

3. Monte Clark

C. [On his team's third consecutive scoreless tie] "It's much ado about nothing to nothing."

4. Barry Wilborn

D. [On spring practice] "It doesn't tell you anything. It's like having your daughter coming in at four o'clock in the morning with a Gideon Bible."

5. Duffy Daugherty

E. "It didn't bother me that I ranked 234th in my high school graduating class of 273—until I heard the principal say it was a stupid class."

6. Dave Widell

F. [On Roy Green] "He has two speeds—here he comes and there he goes."

7. Paul Hornung

G. "Turnovers are like ex-wives. The more you have, the more they cost you."

And the best for last. There is one coach who rivals baseball's Bob Uecker as his sport's top funnyman, and he made all of the following statements. Do you know who he is?

1 "They gave me a standing observation."

2 "Three things are bad for you. I can't remember the first two, but doughnuts are the third."

3 "I'm the football coach around here, and don't you remember it."

4 "It was a cliff dweller to end all cliff dwellers."

5 "Don't you think for a minute that I'm going to take this loss standing down."

6 "Just remember the words of Henry Patrick—'kill me or let me live.'"

CHAPTER 5

FOOTBALL IN THE MOVIES

Almost from the time silent films were being made, football was a popular topic of filmmakers. Not surprising, since many of the game's early stars were idolized across the country. And some football movies, such as *Brian's Song*, pack a surprisingly emotional punch. In the following 16 games, match the football movies with their plots.

1. *The Freshman (1925)*

2. *Salute (1929)*

3. *The New Halfback (1929)*

4. *Maybe It's Love (1930)*

5. *Touchdown (1931)*

6. *Maker of Men (1931)*

7. *Hold 'em Jail (1932)*

A. Two brothers square off against each other in the annual Army-Navy game

B. A coach will do anything to win, but has a change of heart when a player is injured

C. Two convicts start up a prison football team

D. A college dean is forced to put an old friend on the football team

E. A player joins a rival college for revenge when he is rejected by his coach/father, school, and girlfriend

F. A college loser is out to prove himself worthy

G. A woman tempts eleven All-Americans to play for her football team

1. *Horse Feathers (1932)*   A. A demanding coach deals with problems on the field and in his marriage

2. *Huddle (1932)*   B. Musical with a singing professor

3. *College Coach (1933)*   C. The story of player Tony Amatto's four years at Yale University

4. *College Humor (1933)*   D. A college president tries to build a winning football team to compete with his rival

5. *Saturday's Millions (1933)*   E. Star quarterback tangles with his college's leading radical female

6. *The Band Plays On (1934)*   F. Four delinquent boys grow up to become football heroes known as the "Four Bombers"

7. *Fighting Youth (1935)*   G. Star player discovers that college football is only a business and that others are interested in him only because of his football talent

1. *Pigskin Parade (1936)*   A. Star player speaks out against collegiate political corruption

2. *Rose Bowl (1936)*   B. A husband/wife coaching team recruits a hillbilly star under false pretenses

3. *The Big Game (1936)*   C. Injured player promises his girlfriend he'll never play again, but when she gives in, he is kidnapped by criminals hoping to profit on the upcoming big game

4. *Saturday's Heroes (1937)*   D. Three buddies play football at Annapolis and chase girls

5. *Hold 'em Navy (1937)*

E. Two buddies play football and chase girls at college

6. *Navy Blue and Gold (1937)*

F. Two high school stars enroll in different schools and compete on the field and in a love triangle

7. *Over the Goal (1937)*

G. The team's star quarterback is kidnapped by gamblers

1. *Life Begins in College (1937)*

A. Star player is kidnapped by criminals

2. *Touchdown Army (1938)*

B. Biography of the great Notre Dame coach

3. *The Gladiator (1938)*

C. A wealthy Indian player faces expulsion from his college team because he once played as a pro

4. *$1,000 a Touchdown (1939)*

D. A star player needs tutoring to pass French class so he can play in the big game

5. *Cowboy Quarterback (1939)*

E. A show-biz couple inherits a college on the verge of bankruptcy and tries to recruit players for the football team with promises of money for each touchdown they score

6. *Knute Rockne, All-American (1940)*

F. A scout signs a star player but has difficulty getting him to leave town without his girlfriend

7. *Rise and Shine (1941)*

G. A timid nerd drinks a special serum and becomes a star athlete

1. *Harmon of Michigan (1941)*

2. *The Iron Major (1943)*

3. *The Spirit of West Point (1947)*

4. *Easy Living (1949)*

5. *Father Was a Fullback (1949)*

6. *Jim Thorpe— All-American (1951)*

7. *Saturday's Hero (1951)*

A. Biography of one of the world's all-around best athletes

B. Biography of the great college player who later became a famous broadcaster

C. An ex-high school football coach struggles in his first season as a college coach

D. A naïve prep star wins a scholarship but becomes corrupted by the system in college

E. Biography of football coach Frank Cavanaugh

F. Army's football legends play themselves

G. Story of injured football star Pete Wilson

1. *That's My Boy (1951)*

2. *The Guy Who Came Back (1951)*

3. *Bonzo Goes To College (1952)*

4. *The Rose Bowl Story (1952)*

5. *Hold That Line (1952)*

A. A story about the lives of football players on and off the field

B. Another football star is kidnapped by still another group of gangsters (Eesch!)

C. An ex-football star, searching for himself, plays in a charity game and discovers greater meaning

D. A tutor is hired to help the weakling son of the college's ex-football star

E. Biography of Hall of Famer Elroy Hirsch

6. *All American (1953)*   F. A star player transfers schools after his parents are killed in an auto accident

7. *Crazylegs (1953)*   G. A chimpanzee leads the team to victory

1. *Trouble Along The Way (1953)*   A. A gang robs the Los Angeles Coliseum during a Rams game

2. *Moochie of Pop Warner Football (1960)*   B. An aging quarterback attempts a comeback with the New Orleans Saints

3. *This Sporting Life (1963)*   C. A coach struggles with a recruiting scandal and his attempt to retain custody of his daughter following a divorce

4. *John Goldfarb, Please Come Home (1965)*   D. An 11-year old boy runs afoul of City Hall during a football tryout

5. *Paper Lion (1968)*   E. A sportswriter tries out for the Detroit Lions

6. *The Split (1968)*   F. Story of a frustrated English rugby star

7. *Number One (1969)*   G. Two Americans help organize a game between Notre Dame and an Arabian team

1. *Brian's Song (1971)*   A. A coach is hired by a victory-starved college

2. *A Fan's Notes (1972)*   B. A domineering father pushes his son to become a pro football player

3. *Footsteps (1972)*   C. An ex-pro quarterback, now convict, leads a team of prisoners against a sadistic warden's team of guards

4. *Legend in Granite (1973)* D. Biography of coaching legend Vince Lombardi

5. *Blood Sport (1973)* E. Tragic story of the friendship between two members of the Chicago Bears

6. *The Longest Yard (1974)* F. An aging widower returns to college many years later and, with the help of a spring-loaded shoe, becomes a star kicker for the football team

7. *Return to Campus (1975)* G. A disillusioned football fan becomes dangerously obsessed

1. *Two-Minute Warning (1976)* A. A sniper threatens a sold-out football stadium

2. *Gus (1976)* B. A football-kicking mule is brought in from Yugoslavia to save the team

3. *Black Sunday (1977)* C. A killer stalks the Super Bowl in New Orleans

4. *Something For Joey (1977)* D. True story about star player John Cappelletti and his leukemia-stricken younger brother

5. *Semi-Tough (1977)* E. Nine-Oscars nominated movie about a pro quarterback who returns to Earth in another man's body after mistakenly being pronounced dead

6. *Heaven Can Wait (1978)* F. Terrorists threaten to blow up the stadium during the Super Bowl

7. *Superdome (1979)* G. Two pro players seek the attention of the same woman—the team owner's daughter

1. *North Dallas Forty (1979)*

2. *Coach of the Year (1980)*

3. *Fighting Back (1980)*

4. *The Club (1980)*

5. *Grambling's White Tiger (1981)*

6. *All The Right Moves (1983)*

7. *Quarterback Princess (1983)*

A. True story of a high school girl who tries out for the varsity football team

B. Story of the dehumanizing and painful side of professional football

C. A coach is forced into off-field politics

D. Star high school player is at odds with his demanding coach

E. A former pro football player, wounded in Vietnam, coaches a team of boys from his wheelchair

F. Biography of Jim Gregory, a white quarterback on an all-black football team

G. Biography of the Pittsburgh Steelers' Rocky Bleier

1. *The Bear (1984)*

2. *Off Sides (1984)*

3. *Against All Odds (1984)*

4. *The Best of Times (1986)*

5. *Wildcats (1986)*

A. A female track coach takes over the reigns of the junior varsity football team

B. Former high school rivals engage in a rematch of the big game—13 years later

C. A town's hippies and police square off in a football game

D. Twenty-five years in the lives of the college football hero and his homecoming queen wife

E. Biography of Alabama Coach Paul Bryant

6. *Lucas (1986)*

    F. An ex-football player is hired by a gangster to find his girlfriend, but when he finds her they end up falling in love

7. *Everybody's All-American (1988)*

    G. A nerd tries to gain acceptance by trying out for the high school football team and standing up to the school bully

1. *Quiet Victory: The Charlie Wedemeyer Story (1988)*

    A. A 53-year-old man returns to the college gridiron when he makes use of an old football scholarship

2. *Glory Days (1988)*

    B. An ex-pro quarterback and a fired Secret Service agent investigate corruption in football

3. *Triumph of the Heart (1991)*

    C. A 1950s Jewish boy attempts to play football and attend Harvard despite religious and social pressures

4. *The Last Boy Scout (1991)*

    D. A dying football coach receives help from his wife in running the team

5. *Necessary Roughness (1991)*

    E. True story of the relationship between NFL star Ricky Bell and a disabled boy he befriended

6. *School Ties (1992)*

    F. Due to a recruiting scandal, a 34-year old man gets a second chance to play football as a college freshman

7. *The Program (1993)*

    G. An inside look at big-college football

1. *Rudy (1993)*

2. *Windrunner (1995)*

3. *Midnight Heat (1996)*

4. *Halfback of Notre Dame (1996)*

5. *Jerry Maguire (1996)*

6. *Weapons of Mass Distraction (1997)*

7. *The Waterboy (1998)*

A. The team's waterboy becomes their best defensive player

B. True story of one small player's attempt to play football for Notre Dame

C. Two billionaires vie for ownership of a pro football team, alienating everyone around them in the process

D. An Indian, possessed by the spirit of Jim Thorpe, helps a high school football player

E. Story of a down-on-his-luck sports agent who sticks to his principles

F. A football player who is having an affair with the wife of the team's owner becomes implicated in his murder

G. A classical pianist inadvertently turns away a star athlete from football and a possible scholarship

1. *Garbage Picking Field Goal Kicking Philadelphia Phenomenon (1998)*

2. *Possums* (1998)

3. *Air Bud: Golden Receiver (1998)*

A. When the local high school team disbands after failing to win a game, the team's radio announcer keeps announcing fantasy broadcasts of team games until they get back together

B. The team's head coach battles quarterback troubles and the deceased owner's daughter who has taken over the pro team

C. Story about the players who took over after the regular players went on strike

4. *Any Given Sunday (1999)*

D. A team's fans become upset when the owner moves the team out of town, so they first try and kidnap him, and when that fails they kidnap the quarterback

5. *Varsity Blues (1999)*

E. A garbage man becomes the field goal kicker for his hometown pro team

6. *Fumbleheads (1999)*

F. Problems result when a high school coach obsessed with winning pushes his players too hard

7. *The Replacements (2000)*

G. A dog plays football

1. *Remember the Titans (2000)*

A. Joining an Alabama high school football team with a tough coach helps a teenage drifter discover new meaning in life

2. *Go Tigers (2001)*

B. A young man finds peace with his mother, girlfriend, and coach of his six-man football team

3. *Full Ride (2002)*

C. True story of the integration of a Virginia high school football team

4. *Second String (2002)*

D. Documentary of the Massillon (Ohio) High School football team

5. *The Slaughter Rule (2002)*

E. Coach Paul "Bear" Bryant puts his Texas A & M team through a summer workout in 1954

6. *Hometown Legend (2002)*

F. When food poisoning knocks out the starters on the eve of the Super Bowl, the backups take over

7. *The Junction Boys (2002)*

G. An undisciplined delinquent is inspired by the love of a woman to pursue a college scholarship in order to play football

1. *The Season: Behind Bars (2003)*

   A. Documentary of a Texas high school team in which all the players are in a maximum security juvenile detention center

2. *Year of the Bull (2003)*

   B. Documentary of a high school player from the Northwest who plays for a team in Miami's impoverished Liberty City neighborhood

3. *Radio (2003)*

   C. True story of a probation officer who forms a high school football team from the teenagers in a juvenile detention camp

4. *Friday Night Lights (2004)*

   D. True story about a college that rebuilds its football program after most of the team is killed in a plane crash

5. *Invincible (2006)*

   E. True story of a 30-year old bartender who never played college football who walks on during a Philadelphia Eagles tryout, makes the team, and rises to become team captain

6. *We Are Marshall (2006)*

   F. The decades-long relationship between a high school football coach and a mentally challenged man whom he mentors

7. *Gridiron Gang (2006)*

   G. A small Texas town rallies behind its high school football team

In the next 17 games, see how well you know the actors who starred in each of these football-themed movies.

1. *The Freshman*

   A. Douglas Fairbanks, Jr., Loretta Young

2. *The Quarterback (1926)*

   B. Richard Dix, Esther Ralston

3. *Salute*   C. Joe E. Brown, Joan Bennett

4. *The New Halfback*   D. George O'Brien, Helen Chandler

5. *The Forward Pass*   E. Richard Arlen

6. *Maybe It's Love*   F. Andy Clyde, Harry Gribbon

7. *Touchdown*   G. Harold Lloyd

1. *Maker of Men*   A. Jack Holt, Richard Cromwell

2. *Hold 'em Jail*   B. Ramon Novarro

3. *Horse Feathers*   C. Robert Young, Andy Devine

4. *Huddle*   D. The Marx Brothers

5. *College Coach*   E. Bing Crosby, Mary Carlisle, Richard Arlen

6. *College Humor*   F. Bert Wheeler, Robert Woolsey, Betty Grable

7. *Saturday's Millions*   G. Dick Powell, John Wayne

1. *The Band Plays On*   A. James Gleason, June Travis, Andy Devine

2. *Fighting Youth*   B. Robert Young

3. *Hold 'em Yale*   C. Cesar Romero, Patricia Ellis

4. *Pigskin Parade*   D. Buster Crabbe

5. *Rose Bowl*   E. Van Heflin

6. *The Big Game*   F. Charles Farrell, Ann Sheridan, Andy Devine

7. *Saturday's Heroes*   G. Stuart Erwin, Judy Garland, Jack Haley

1. *Hold 'em Navy*   A. William Hopper, June Travis

2. *Navy Blue and Gold*   B. Chester Clute, Mary Carlisle

3. *Over the Goal*   C. Lew Ayres, Mary Carlisle

4. *Life Begins in College*   D. Fred Stone, Joan Davis

5. *Touchdown Army*   E. Joe E. Brown, June Travis

6. *The Gladiator*   F. Joe E. Brown, Martha Raye, Susan Hayward

7. *$1,000 a Touchdown*   G. Robert Young, James Stewart, Lionel Barrymore

1. *Cowboy Quarterback*   A. Bert Wheeler, Marie Wilson

2. *Knute Rockne, All-American*   B. Tom Harmon, Anita Louise, Lloyd Bridges

3. *The Quarterback (1940)*   C. Pat O'Brien, Ronald Reagan

4. *Rise and Shine*   D. Pat O'Brien, Ruth Warrick

5. *Harmon of Michigan*   E. Frank Burke, Rod Cameron

6. *The Iron Major*   F. Doc Blanchard, Glenn Davis, Alan Hale, Jr.

7. *The Spirit of West Point*   G. Jack Oakie, Linda Darnell, Walter Brennan

1. *Good News*   A. Fred MacMurray, Maureen O'Hara

2. *Triple Threat*   B. Peter Lawford, June Allyson, Mel Torme

3. *Easy Living*   C. Burt Lancaster, Charles Bickford

4. *Father Was a Fullback*   D. Richard Crane, Mary Stuart, Gloria Henry

5. *Jim Thorpe— All-American*   E. John Derek, Donna Reed

6. *Saturday's Hero*   F. Victor Mature, Lucille Ball, Jack Paar

7. *That's My Boy*   G. Dean Martin, Jerry Lewis, Polly Bergen

1. *The Guy Who Came Back*   A. Tony Curtis, Mamie Van Doren, Lori Nelson

2. *Bonzo Goes To College*   B. Marshall Thompson, Vera Miles, Natalie Wood

3. *The Rose Bowl Story*   C. Paul Douglas, Linda Darnell, Zero Mostell

4. *Hold That Line*   D. Elroy Hirsch, Lloyd Nolan

5. *All American*   E. The Bowery Boys

6. *Crazylegs*   F. Maureen O'Sullivan, Charles Drake

7. *Trouble Along the Way*   G. John Wayne, Donna Reed, Chuck Connors

1. *Moochie of Pop Warner Football*   A. Charleton Heston, Bruce Dern, Jessica Walter

2. *This Sporting Life*   B. Jim Brown, Ernest Borgnine, Diahann Carroll

3. *John Goldfarb, Please Come Home*   C. Peter Ustinov, Shirley MacLaine

4. *Paper Lion*   D. Richard Harris, Rachel Roberts

5. *The Split*   E. James Caan, Billy Dee Williams, Jack Warden

6. *Number One*   F. Alan Alda, Lauren Hutton, Alex Karras

7. *Brian's Song (1971)*   G. Kevin Corcoran, Alan Hale, Jr.

1. *A Fan's Notes*   A. Ernest Borgnine

2. *Footsteps*   B. John Barner, Robert Gutin

3. *Legend in Granite*   C. Richard Crenna, Joanna Pettet, Ned Beatty

4. *Blood Sport*   D. Charleton Heston, John Cassavetes

5. *The Longest Yard (1974)*   E. Jerry Orbach, Burgess Meredith

6. *Return to Campus*   F. Ben Johnson, Larry Hagman, Gary Busey

7. *Two Minute Warning*   G. Burt Reynolds, Eddie Albert, Bernadette Peters

1. *Gus*   A. Nick Nolte, Mac Davis, Charles Durning

2. *Black Sunday*   B. Warren Beattie, Julie Christie, Jack Warden

3. *Something For Joey*   C. Robert Shaw, Bruce Dern

4. *Semi-Tough*   D. Burt Reynolds, Kris Kristofferson

5. *Heaven Can Wait*   E. David Janssen, Edie Adams, Tom Selleck

6. *Superdome*   F. Ed Asner, Don Knotts, Tim Conway

7. *North Dallas Forty*   G. Gerald S. O'Loughlin, Geraldine Page

1. *Coach of the Year*

2. *Fighting Back*

3. *The Club*

4. *Grambling's White Tiger*

5. *All the Right Moves*

6. *Quarterback Princess*

7. *The Bear*

A. Gary Busey, Harry Dean Stanton

B. Robert Urich, Bonnie Bedelia, Art Carney

C. Don Murray, Helen Hunt, Barbara Babcock

D. Jack Thompson, Graham Kennedy

E. Tom Cruise, Lea Thompson, Craig T. Nelson

F. Bruce Jenner, Harry Belafonte

G. Robert Conrad, Erin Gray

1. *Off Sides*

2. *Against All Odds*

3. *The Best of Times*

4. *Wildcats*

5. *Lucas*

6. *Everybody's All-American*

7. *Quiet Victory: The Charlie Wedemeyer Story*

A. Tony Randall, Brian Dennehy, Eugene Roche

B. Robin Williams, Kurt Russell

C. Pam Dawber, Michael Nouri, Bess Meyer

D. Dennis Quaid, Jessica Lange, Timothy Hutton

E. Goldie Hawn, Wesley Snipes, Woody Harrelson

F. Jeff Bridges, Rachel Ward, James Woods

G. Corey Haim, Kerri Green, Charlie Sheen

1. *Glory Days*   A. Bruce Willis, Damon Wayans, Halle Berry

2. *Johnny Be Good*   B. Robert Conrad, Jennifer O'Neill

3. *Triumph of the Heart:*   C. Scott Bakula, Robert Loggia, Sinbad
   The Ricky Bell Story

4. *The Last Boy Scout*   D. Roseanne, Tom Arnold

5. *Necessary Roughness*   E. Anthony Michael Hall, Robert Downey, Jr.

6. *Backfield in Motion*   F. Mario Van Peebles, Susan Ruttan

7. *School Ties*   G. Brendan Fraser, Matt Damon, Chris O'Donnell

1. *The Program*   A. Rick Moranis, Ed O'Neill

2. *Rudy*   B. Tim Matheson, Stephen Mendell

3. *Windrunner*   C. James Caan, Halle Berry

4. *Little Giants*   D. Reggie White, Pat Morita

5. *Midnight Heat*   E. Sean Astin, Ned Beatty, Robert Prosky

6. *Halfback of Notre*   F. Gabriel Hogan, Emmanuelle Vaugier
   Dame

7. *Reggie's Prayer*   G. Jason Wiles, Russell Means, Margot Kidder

1. *Jerry Maguire*

  A. Tom Cruise, Renee Zellweger, Cuba Gooding Jr.

2. *Angels in the Endzone*

  B. Tim Conway, Dick Martin, Kevin Zegers

3. *Weapons of Mass Distraction*

  C. Mathew Lawrence, Christopher Lloyd

4. *The Waterboy*

  D. Ben Kingsley, Gabriel Byrne, Mimi Rogers

5. *Possums*

  E. Adam Sandler, Henry Winkler, Kathy Bates

6. *Air Bud: Golden Receiver*

  F. Mac Davis, Cynthia Sikes, Greg Coolidge

7. *Any Given Sunday*

  G. Al Pacino, Cameron Diaz, Dennis Quaid

1. *Varsity Blues*

  A. Mekhi Phifer, Sean Maher, Ben Gazzara

2. *Fumbleheads*

  B. James Van Der Beek, Jon Voight

3. *The Replacements*

  C. Keanu Reeves, Gene Hackman

4. *Remember the Titans*

  D. Mark Curry, Ed Asner, Barry Corbin

5. *Brian's Song (2001)*

  E. Ryan Gosling, David Morse

6. *Second String*

  F. Denzel Washington, Will Patton

7. *The Slaughter Rule*

  G. Gil Bellows, Jon Voight, Teri Polo

1. *Hometown Legend*

2. *The Junction Boys*

3. *Radio*

4. *Friday Night Lights*

5. *The Longest Yard (2005)*

6. *Invincible*

7. *We Are Marshall*

A. Terry O'Quinn, Lacey Chabert

B. Matthew McConaughey, Matthew Fox

C. Mark Wahlberg, Greg Kinnear

D. Adam Sandler, Chris Rock, Burt Reynolds

E. Cuba Gooding, Jr., Ed Harris, Riley Smith

F. Tom Berenger, Fletcher Humphrys

G. Billy Bob Thornton, Lucas Black

CHAPTER 6

FOOTBALL NUMEROLOGY

The first **19 games** in this chapter concern retired jersey numbers. In the first 13 games, test your memory as you try to match the jersey number to the retired player and the *franchise* he played for. (*Note*: Many of the players are listed with current teams they never played for because the franchise has been relocated. For example, in Game #1, Johnny Unitas is listed as having his number retired by Indianapolis. He never played for Indianapolis, but did play for the Baltimore Colts, the location of the *franchise* before it moved to Indianapolis, and Unitas' number has been retired by Indianapolis.)

1. 12   A. Jim Kelly, Buffalo

2. 13   B. Frank Gifford, New York Giants

3. 14   C. Dan Marino, Miami

4. 15   D. Frank Tripucka, Denver

5. 16   E. Otto Graham, Cleveland

6. 18   F. Johnny Unitas, Indianapolis

7. 19   G. Bart Starr, Green Bay

1. 92

2. 78

3. 89

4. 76

5. 77

6. 85

7. 99

A. Bobby Bell, Kansas City

B. Lou Groza, Cleveland

C. Jack Youngblood, St. Louis

D. Reggie White, Philadelphia

E. Gino Marchetti, Indianapolis

F. Red Grange, Chicago

G. Marshall Goldberg, Arizona

1. 22

2. 20

3. 28

4. 29

5. 31

6. 34

7. 32

A. Willie Galimore, Chicago

B. Buddy Young, Indianapolis

C. Walter Payton, Chicago

D. Eric Dickerson, St. Louis

E. Gino Cappelletti, New England

F. Jim Brown, Cleveland

G. William Andrews, Atlanta

1. 1

2. 3

3. 4

4. 5

A. Bronko Nagurski, Chicago

B. John Elway, Denver

C. Ray Flaherty, New York Giants

D. George McAfee, Chicago

5. 7   E. Phil Simms, New York Giants

6. 8   F. Tuffy Leemans, New York Giants

7. 11   G. Larry Wilson, Arizona

1. 60   A. Ernie Stautner, Pittsburgh

2. 61   B. Lee Roy Selmon, Tampa Bay

3. 63   C. John Hannah, New England

4. 65   D. Elvin Bethea, Tennessee

5. 66   E. Chuck Bednarik, Philadelphia

6. 70   F. Bulldog Turner, Chicago

7. 73   G. Bill George, Chicago

1. 40   A. Floyd Little, Denver

2. 41   B. Don Fleming, Cleveland

3. 42   C. Brian Piccolo, Chicago

4. 43   D. Jim Norton, Tennessee

5. 44   E. Ernie Davis, Cleveland

6. 45   F. Gale Sayers, Chicago

7. 46   G. Sid Luckman, Chicago

1. 12

A. Dan Fouts, San Diego

2. 13

B. Len Dawson, Kansas City

3. 14

C. Steve Bartkowski, Atlanta

4. 15

D. Don Maynard, New York Jets

5. 16

E. Steve Van Buren, Philadelphia

6. 19

F. Lance Alworth, San Diego

7. 10

G. Joe Namath, New York Jets

1. 7

A. Joe Montana, San Francisco

2. 3

B. Don Hutson, Green Bay

3. 12

C. Bob Griese, Miami

4. 22

D. George Halas, Chicago

5. 14

E. Fran Tarkenton, Minnesota

6. 10

F. Bobby Layne, Detroit

7. 16

G. Jan Stenerud, Kansas City

1. 80

A. Steve Largent, Seattle

2. 87

B. Buck Buchanan, Kansas City

3. 88

C. Doug Atkins, New Orleans

4. 86

D. Alan Page, Minnesota

5. 82   E. Chuck Hughes, Detroit

6. 81   F. Dwight Clark, San Francisco

7. 85   G. Raymond Berry, Indianapolis

1. 51   A. Jim Marshall, Minnesota

2. 63   B. Dick Butkus, Chicago

3. 42   C. Ronnie Lott, San Francisco

4. 56   D. Ray Nitschke, Green Bay

5. 66   E. Bob Johnson, Cincinnati

6. 70   F. Willie Lanier, Kansas City

7. 54   G. Lawrence Taylor, New York Giants

1. 39   A. Mack Lee Hill, Kansas City

2. 34   B. Jim Taylor, New Orleans

3. 33   C. Larry Csonka, Miami

4. 31   D. Pat Tillman, Arizona

5. 40   E. Earl Campbell, Tennessee

6. 36   F. Lenny Moore, Indianapolis

7. 24   G. Sammy Baugh, Washington

1. 74   A. Reggie White, Green Bay

2. 92   B. Bob St. Clair, San Francisco

3. 88   C. J.V. Cain, Arizona

4. 99   D. Jackie Slater, St. Louis

5. 73   E. Jerome Brown, Philadelphia

6. 79   F. Merlin Olsen, St. Louis

7. 78   G. Leo Nomellini, San Francisco

1. 39   A. Mike Haynes, New England

2. 40   B. John Brodie, San Francisco

3. 7   C. Joe Klecko, New York Jets

4. 12   D. Hugh McElhenny, San Francisco

5. 14   E. Dutch Clark, Detroit

6. 3   F. Y.A. Tittle, New York Giants

7. 73   G. Tony Canadeo, Green Bay

The next six games contain famous jersey numbers of Hall of Famers, but the teams they played for have surprisingly NOT retired these jersey numbers.

1. 8   A. Sonny Jurgensen, Washington

2. 12   B. Charlie Joiner, San Diego

3. 9   C. Troy Aikman, Dallas

4. 1   D. Norm Van Brocklin, St. Louis

5. 11   E. Paul Hornung, Green Bay

6. 5   F. Warren Moon, Tennessee

7. 18   G. Terry Bradshaw, Pittsburgh

1. 82   A. John Stallworth, Pittsburgh

2. 42   B. Tom Fears, St. Louis

3. 25   C. Fred Biletnikoff, Oakland

4. 80   D. Lynn Swann, Pittsburgh

5. 40   E. Paul Warfield, Cleveland

6. 88   F. Dave Casper, Oakland

7. 87   G. Elroy "Crazylegs" Hirsch

1. 44   A. Charley Trippi, Arizona

2. 32   B. Barry Sanders, Detroit

3. 33   C. John Henry Johnson, Pittsburgh

4. 35   D. Tony Dorsett, Dallas

5. 31   E. O.J. Simpson, Buffalo

6. 20   F. Jim Taylor, Green Bay

7. 2   G. John Riggins, Washington

1. 52   A. Jim Otto, Oakland

2. 00   B. Mike Webster, Pittsburgh

3. 65   C. Ron Yary, Minnesota

4. 66   D. Anthony Munoz, Cincinnati

5. 73   E. Forrest Gregg, Green Bay

6. 75   F. Larry Little, Miami

7. 78   G. Tom Mack, St. Louis

1. 75   A. Mean Joe Greene, Pittsburgh

2. 81   B. Carl Eller, Minnesota

3. 85   C. Nick Buoniconti, Miami

4. 59   D. Jack Ham, Pittsburgh

5. 58   E. Jack Lambert, Pittsburgh

6. 50   F. Mike Singletary, Chicago

7. 87   G. Willie Davis, Green Bay

1. 26   A. Willie Brown, Oakland

2. 20   B. Ken Houston, Washington

3. 83   C. Harry Carson, New York Giants

4. 47   D. Herb Adderley, Green Bay

5. 53   E. Lem Barney, Detroit

6. 27   F. Mel Blount, Pittsburgh

7. 24   G. Ted Hendricks, Oakland

The next four games concern each *franchise's* all-time record for points scored in a game. Match the team with their record-setting final score. (Regular season only.)

1. Baltimore Ravens

2. Buffalo Bills

3. Cincinnati Bengals

4. Cleveland Browns

5. Denver Broncos

6. Houston Texans

7. Indianapolis Colts

8. Jacksonville Jaguars

A. Beat the Miami Dolphins, 58–24, in 1966

B. Beat the Tennessee Titans, 31–21, in 2004

C. Beat the San Diego Chargers, 50–34, in 1963

D. Beat the Houston Oilers, 61–7, in 1989

E. Beat the Green Bay Packers, 48–3, in 2005

F. Beat the Cleveland Browns, 48–0, in 2000

G. Beat the Washington Redskins, 62–3, in 1954

H. Beat the Buffalo Bills, 58–20, in 1976

1. Kansas City Chiefs

2. Miami Dolphins

3. New England Patriots

4. New York Jets

5. Oakland Raiders

6. Pittsburgh Steelers

7. San Diego Chargers

8. Tennessee Titans

A. Beat the New York Jets, 56–3, in 1979

B. Beat the Denver Broncos, 58–20, in 1963

C. Beat the Cleveland Browns, 58–14, in 1990

D. Beat the New York Giants, 63–7, in 1952

E. Beat the Tennessee Titans, 52–25, in 2002

F. Beat the St. Louis Cardinals, 55–14, in 1977

G. Beat the Tampa Bay Buccaneers, 62–28, in 1985

H. Beat the Denver Broncos, 59–7, in 1963

1. Arizona Cardinals
2. Atlanta Falcons
3. Carolina Panthers
4. Chicago Bears
5. Dallas Cowboys
6. Detroit Lions
7. Green Bay Packers
8. Minnesota Vikings

A. Beat the Green Bay Packers, 61–7, in 1980
B. Beat the San Francisco 49ers, 59–14, in 1980
C. Beat the Cincinnati Bengals, 52–31, in 2002
D. Beat the Chicago Bears, 55–20, in 1997
E. Beat the New Orleans Saints, 62–7, in 1973
F. Beat the Detroit Lions, 57–21, in 1945
G. Beat the New York Bulldogs, 65–20, in 1949
H. Beat the Dallas Cowboys, 54–13, in 1970

1. New Orleans Saints
2. New York Giants
3. Philadelphia Eagles
4. St. Louis Rams
5. San Francisco 49ers
6. Seattle Seahawks
7. Tampa Bay Buccaneers
8. Washington Redskins

A. Beat the New York Giants, 72–41, in 1966
B. Beat the Seattle Seahawks, 51–27, in 1976
C. Beat the New Orleans Saints, 48–21, in 2001
D. Beat the Philadelphia Eagles, 62–10, in 1972
E. Beat the Buffalo Bills, 56–17, in 1977
F. Beat the Cincinnati Reds, 64–0, in 1934
G. Beat the Atlanta Falcons, 56–17, in 1992
H. Beat the Baltimore Colts, 70–27, in 1950

CHAPTER 7

THERE'S NO PLACE LIKE HOME

What's in a name? Well, for one thing, the correct answers to all of the trivia games in this chapter. For another, potential marketing ideas (as in, *"Am I the only one who thinks Papa John's Stadium should host The Pizza Bowl?"*). Beginning with the college ranks (the first seven games) and finishing with the NFL, see if you can match these stadium names to the teams that call them home.

141

1. Air Force	A. Rubber Bowl
2. Akron	B. Jordan-Hare Stadium
3. Arkansas State	C. Bronco Stadium
4. Army	D. Falcon Stadium
5. Auburn	E. Floyd Casey Stadium
6. Baylor	F. Michie Stadium
7. Boise State	G. Indian Stadium

1. Boston College
2. Cincinnati
3. Colorado
4. Fresno State
5. Georgia
6. Idaho
7. Iowa

A. Alumni Stadium
B. Bulldog Stadium
C. Nippert Stadium
D. Kinnick Stadium
E. Folsom Stadium
F. Kibbie Dome
G. Sanford Stadium

1. Kent State
2. Kentucky
3. Louisville
4. Maryland
5. Memphis
6. Mississippi
7. Mississippi State

A. Davis Wade at Scott Field
B. Vaught-Hemingway Stadium
C. Liberty Bowl
D. Commonwealth Stadium
E. Byrd Stadium
F. Papa John's Cardinal Stadium
G. Dix Stadium

1. Missouri
2. Nevada
3. UNLV
4. North Carolina

A. Peden Stadium
B. Ryan Field
C. Faurot Field
D. Memorial Stadium

5. Northwestern   E. Sam Boyd Stadium

6. Ohio   F. Kenan Memorial Stadium

7. Oklahoma   G. Mackay Stadium

1. Oklahoma State   A. Beaver Stadium

2. Oregon   B. Ross-Ade Stadium

3. Oregon State   C. Autzen Stadium

4. Penn State   D. Boone Pickens Stadium

5. Pittsburgh   E. Spartan Stadium

6. Purdue   F. Heinz Field

7. San Jose State   G. Reser Stadium

1. South Carolina   A. Williams-Brice Stadium

2. Southern California B. Memorial Coliseum

3. SMU   C. Royal-Memorial Stadium

4. Syracuse   D. Neyland Stadium

5. Temple   E. Carrier Dome

6. Tennessee   F. Gerald J. Ford Stadium

7. Texas   G. Lincoln Financial Field

1. Texas Tech	A. Camp Randall Stadium
2. Toledo	B. Skelly Stadium
3. Troy	C. Glass Bowl
4. Tulsa	D. War Memorial Stadium
5. Utah	E. Jones Stadium
6. Wisconsin	F. Rice-Eccles Stadium
7. Wyoming	G. Movie Gallery Veterans Stadium

Now let's try your hand at some NFL stadium names. (Not all teams are included because some of the answers are obvious, such as Cleveland Browns Stadium for the Cleveland Browns. Duh.)

1. Baltimore Ravens	A. M & T Bank Stadium
2. Buffalo Bills	B. Paul Brown Stadium
3. Cincinnati Bengals	C. Alltel Stadium
4. Denver Broncos	D. RCA Dome
5. Houston Texans	E. Ralph Wilson Stadium
6. Indianapolis Colts	F. INVESCO Field
7. Jacksonville Jaguars	G. Reliant Stadium

1. Kansas City Chiefs	A. Qualcomm Stadium
2. New England Patriots	B. Arrowhead Stadium

3. New York Jets   C. McAfee Coliseum

4. Oakland Raiders   D. Gillette Stadium

5. Pittsburgh Steelers   E. LP Field

6. San Diego Chargers   F. Meadowlands

7. Tennessee Titans   G. Heinz Field

1. Atlanta Falcons   A. Soldier Field

2. Carolina Panthers   B. Hubert H. Humphrey Metrodome

3. Chicago Bears   C. Lambeau Field

4. Dallas Cowboys   D. Texas Stadium

5. Detroit Lions   E. Ford Field

6. Green Bay Packers   F. Georgia Dome

7. Minnesota Vikings   G. Bank of America Stadium

1. New Orleans Saints   A. Qwest Field

2. Philadelphia Eagles   B. Superdome

3. St. Louis Rams   C. Monster Park

4. San Francisco 49ers   D. FedExField

5. Seattle Seahawks   E. Lincoln Financial Field

6. Tampa Bay Buccaneers   F. Edward Jones Dome

7. Washington Redskins   G. Raymond James Stadium

CHAPTER 8

COLLEGE TROPHIES AND TRADITIONS

College football rivalries are among the most intense in all of sports, and many of them award a prized trophy to the winner of their annual meeting. (Although personally I'm not quite sure I'd want to bring home The Old Brass Spittoon as much as The Bourbon Barrel!) In these first seven games, see if you can match up the rivalries with the trophy played for annually.

1. Iowa-Minnesota

2. Akron-Kent State

3. Duke-North Carolina

4. Florida International-
   Florida Atlantic

5. Brigham Young-Utah State

6. Indiana-Michigan State

7. Indiana-Purdue

A. The Wagon Wheel

B. The Old Wagon Wheel

C. The Old Oaken Bucket

D. The Victory Bell

E. Floyd of Rosedale

F. Don Shula Award

G. The Old Brass Spittoon

1. Arizona-Arizona State

2. Bowling Green-Toledo

A. The Illibuck

B. The Territorial Cup (the oldest
   rivalry trophy played for in the
   U.S.—since 1899)

3. Bowling Green-Kent State   C. The Tomahawk

4. Illinois-Northwestern   D. The Peace Pipe

5. Ohio State-Illinois   E. The Cannon

6. Purdue-Illinois   F. The Bourbon Barrel (ended in 1999)

7. Indiana-Kentucky   G. The Anniversary Award

1. Iowa-Iowa State   A. The Governor's Cup

2. Iowa State-Missouri   B. The Telephone

3. Louisville-Kentucky   C. Paul Bunyan

4. Cincinnati-Louisville   D. Victory Bell

5. Miami (Ohio)-Cincinnati   E. The Little Brown Jug

6. Michigan-Michigan State   F. Keg of Nails

7. Minnesota-Michigan   G. The Cy-Hawk

1. Michigan State-Notre Dame   A. The Megaphone

2. Minnesota-Wisconsin   B. Land Grant Trophy

3. Minnesota-Penn State   C. Governor's Victory Bell

4. Kansas-Missouri   D. The Bass Drum

5. Missouri-Nebraska   E. The Fremont Cannon

6. Penn State-Michigan State   F. The Bell

7. Nevada-UNLV   G. Slab of Bacon

(Note: one rivalry is the answer for two awards)

1. Purdue-Notre Dame	A. The Bell
2. USC-UCLA	B. The Shillelagh
3. New Mexico State-UTEP	C. The Mayor's Cup
4. Washington-Washington State	D. The Sawhorse Dollar
5. Princeton-Dartmouth	E. The Silver Spade
6. Ohio-Marshall	F. Victory Bell
	G. The Apple Cup

1. LSU-Arkansas	A. The Bayou Bucket
2. Mississippi-Mississippi State	B. The Bronze Boot
3. Oklahoma-Texas	C. The Golden Egg
4. Wyoming-Colorado State	D. The Steel Tire
5. Oklahoma-Oklahoma State	E. The Bell Clapper
6. Houston-Rice	F. The Golden Hat
7. Akron-Youngstown State	G. The Golden Boot

One final round of trophy games.

1. California-Stanford	A. Paniolo Trophy
2. Ball State-Indiana State	B. Williams Trophy

3. Hawaii-Wyoming	C. The Axe
4. Rice-Tulsa	D. Jefferson-Eppes Trophy
5. Virginia-Virginia Tech	E. The Commonwealth Cup
6. Florida State-Virginia	F. Victory Bell

Almost every college has some sort of long, unusual football tradition. See if you can connect these schools to their enthusiastic endeavors.

1. Air Force	A. After every win, Toomer's Corner, a popular local intersection, is covered in a blizzard of toilet paper
2. Arizona	B. For 24 hours before each homecoming game, freshmen players continuously bang an enormous war drum
3. Arizona State	C. Freshmen annually whitewash a 160-foot high "A" on a nearby mountain peak
4. Arkansas State	D. In honor of one of their team colors, they play on blue artificial turf, the only team with a non-green field
5. Army	E. The student body stands for the entire game
6. Auburn	F. Holds its annual preseason practices at a recreation area 100 miles away from campus
7. Boise State	G. A parachutist delivers the game ball

1. California

   A. Students ring the chapel bell until midnight following any victory

2. Clemson

   B. Ten minutes before kickoff, the team boards two buses and drives around the stadium to the east end zone, then debarks

3. Florida Atlantic

   C. Fans line the 200-yard walkway from the visitor's locker room to the field, hurling insults at the visiting players

4. Florida State

   D. Noted for its student body card stunts during games

5. Fresno State

   E. A student riding a horse charges onto the field just before game time and plants a flaming spear at midfield

6. Georgia

   F. Before each home game, players run onto the field behind Rambling Wreck, a 1930 Model A Ford Sport Coupe

7. Georgia Tech

   G. The coach holds a potluck dinner for all new signees

1. Hawaii

   A. The school that invented Homecoming (1910)

2. Illinois

   B. This team plays all its October home games at night so fans can enjoy a day at the racetracks before the game

3. Kansas

   C. All senior players walk one final time around the stadium, signing autographs as they receive flowers and gifts

4. Kansas State   D. This team's fans mimic the official's motion every time they make a first down

5. Kentucky   E. Each player touches a statue of a bulldog as he comes down a ramp on his way to the field

6. Louisiana State   F. After touchdowns, this team's fans wave their arms in the air

7. Louisiana Tech   G. Proud of their tradition of being among the loudest fans in college football, they once set off their geology department's seismograph after a touchdown

1. Louisiana-Lafayette   A. Began the college tradition of using cheerleaders at its games in 1898

2. Marshall   B. This school's tailgate parties are so good, many fans never make it to the game

3. Maryland   C. This team's players enter their stadium for pregame introductions through plumes of smoke

4. Miami (Florida)   D. Fans ring cowbells at non-conference games (they're banned from conference games)

5. Minnesota   E. Before each home game, this team's players touch a bronze turtle named Testudo on their way to the locker room

6. Mississippi   F. Their tailgate party takes place in the center of campus with men wearing ties, women wearing hats, and much of the food is served on china with linen napkins

7. Mississippi State   G. On their way to the field, this team's players touch a real stuffed buffalo head

1. Navy

2. Nebraska

3. New Mexico State

4. North Carolina State

5. North Texas

6. Northern Illinois

7. Northwestern

A. The team's mascot, Bill the Goat, always faces the direction the offense is going

B. Each team score is celebrated with a blast from a Civil War replica cannon

C. At a ceremony at the beginning of each season, starting defensive players are given black practice jerseys

D. Fans shake their car keys during kickoffs

E. Fans hike up a local mountain to paint and polish a large "A" made out of rocks

F. Players slap a 2x4 with the word "TRUST" on it every time they enter or leave the field

G. Players sing the school fight song in the locker room after each game

1. Notre Dame

2. Ohio State

3. Oklahoma

A. For nearly 80 years this team's fans have gathered every Wednesday during the season to rehash the previous week's game and talk about the upcoming game

B. Home games can't begin until "I Am an American" is read over the public-address system

C. As players leave the locker room for the field, they touch an overhanging sign which reads *"Play like a champion today."*

4. Penn State

D. This team's 36-member spirit group, the Rufneks, fires modified 12-gauge shotguns and carries red-and-white paddles to intimidate their fans into cheering louder

5. Pittsburgh

E. This team's coaches, All-America selections, and opposing coaches engrave their names in a table at a stadium club

6. Purdue

F. After each team victory, the campus' second tallest building, the Cathedral of Learning, is flooded in gold light

7. Rice

G. The school band performs a ceremony each game called "Dotting the 'i'"

165

1. Rutgers

A. Before each game, players touch a statue that memorializes the school as the *"Birthplace of College Football"*

2. SMU

B. The team pours onto the field while the school band plays *"Thus Spake Zarathustra"* (the theme song to *2001: A Space Odyssey*)

3. South Carolina

C. This school's band has long made use of Big Bertha, at 500 pounds and 54 inches in diameter, the largest bass drum in the world

4. Stanford

D. This school has a long tradition of allowing walk-on players to try out for the football team

5. Temple

E. Before each game, the students sing the school song and then raise their right hands in a victory salute

6. Tennessee

F. This school's band is widely regarded as the most irreverent musical body in all of college sports, oftentimes eliciting disgust even from their own school administration

7. Texas

G. This school sports a flotilla of several hundred boats in their floating tailgate parties at every home game

1. Texas A & M

A. On the night before home games, as many as 20,000 fans gather on campus for Yell Practice

2. Texas Tech

B. Students gather around Spirit Rock for their pep rallies, then proceed to burn, paint, tar and feather it, though the painting can only take place during the twilight hours

3. Toledo

C. This school's marching band has traditionally used big-name entertainers such as Frank Sinatra and Glen Campbell to raise funds for uniforms and equipment

4. Tulsa

D. Each week this school produces a new video specifically for the team's entrance onto the field designed for that week's opponent

5. UNLV

E. The night before games, this school's all-male spirit group, the Saddle Tramps, covers the campus in red crepe paper

6. Vanderbilt

F. This school blares an old mechanical siren after each score

7. Virginia

G. This school has a tradition of no cursing on the football field

1. Wake Forest

   A. Each year the 1961 team hosts a party for all returning players during homecoming weekend

2. Washington

   B. Whenever a nearby train passes by, the public address announcer declares, "Here comes Amtrak!"

3. Washington State

   C. This school's fans walk the eight miles home if they lose their annual game with their nearby rival

4. West Virginia

   D. After each victory, students engage in "Rolling the Quad," covering the campus in toilet paper

5. Western Michigan

   E. This team's cheerleaders are brought onto the field riding Bucky Wagon, a restored fire engine

6. Wisconsin

   F. The football team enters the field by running through a man-made tunnel of band members

7. Columbia

   G. This school sounds an air raid siren after each score

CHAPTER 9

FROM WHENCE THEY CAME

Since 1936, the professional leagues have conducted league-wide organized drafts of the top players in college football. Before that it was chaos, with each team scrambling and scouting (and pulling dirty tricks to hide players from the other teams!) to sign their next stars. The next 11 games concern the NFL's #1 draft pick each year from 1936–2006. Can you match these #1 draft choices to their alma maters?

168

1. 1936: Jay Berwanger	A. Texas Christian
2. 1937: Sam Francis	B. Michigan
3. 1938: Corbett Davis	C. Chicago
4. 1939: Ki Aldrich	D. Indiana
5. 1940: George Cafego	E. Tennessee
6. 1941: Tom Harmon	F. Virginia
7. 1942: Bill Dudley	G. Nebraska

169

(Note: two schools in this game are the answers to two players each.)

1. 1943: Frank Sinkwich	A. Georgia
2. 1944: Angelo Bertelli	B. Alabama

3. 1945: Charley Trippi   C. Oklahoma A & M

4. 1946: Frank Dancewicz   D. Pennsylvania

5. 1947: Bob Fenimore   E. Notre Dame

6. 1948: Harry Gilmer

7. 1949: Chuck Bednarik

1. 1950: Leon Hart   A. Georgia

2. 1951: Kyle Rote   B. Notre Dame

3. 1952: Bill Wade   C. Stanford

4. 1953: Harry Babcock   D. Southern Methodist

5. 1954: Bobby Garrett   E. Oregon

6. 1955: George Shaw   F. Vanderbilt

7. 1956: Gary Glick   G. Colorado A & M

1. 1957: Paul Hornung   A. Rice

2. 1958: King Hill   B. North Carolina State

3. 1959: Randy Duncan   C. Auburn

4. 1960: Billy Cannon   D. Iowa

5. 1961 AFL: Ken Rice   E. Notre Dame

6. 1961 NFL: Tommy Mason   F. Tulane

7. 1962 AFL: Roman Gabriel G. Louisiana State

1. 1962 NFL: Ernie Davis   A. Boston College

2. 1963 AFL: Buck Buchanan   B. Grambling

3. 1963 NFL: Terry Baker   C. Auburn

4. 1964 AFL: Jack Concannon   D. Texas Tech

5. 1964 NFL: Dave Parks   E. Oregon State

6. 1965 AFL: Lawrence Elkins   F. Syracuse

7. 1965 NFL: Tucker Frederickson G. Baylor

(Note: one school in this game is the answer to two players.)

1. 1966 AFL: Jim Grabowski   A. Southern California

2. 1966 NFL: Tommy Nobis   B. Stanford

3. 1967: Bubba Smith   C. Michigan State

4. 1968: Ron Yary   D. Louisiana Tech

5. 1969: O.J. Simpson   E. Texas

6. 1970: Terry Bradshaw   F. Illinois

7. 1971: Jim Plunkett

1. 1972: Walt Patulski   A. Southern California

2. 1973: John Matuszak   B. Tampa

3. 1974: Ed Jones   C. Oklahoma

4. 1975: Steve Bartkowski   D. Notre Dame

5. 1976: Lee Roy Selmon   E. California

6. 1977: Ricky Bell   F. Texas

7. 1978: Earl Campbell   G. Tennessee State

1. 1979: Tom Cousineau   A. Oklahoma

2. 1980: Billy Sims   B. Stanford

3. 1981: George Rogers   C. Ohio State

4. 1982: Kenneth Sims   D. Texas

5. 1983: John Elway   E. Virginia Tech

6. 1984: Irving Fryar   F. South Carolina

7. 1985: Bruce Smith   G. Nebraska

(Note: two schools in this game are the answers to two players each.)

1. 1986: Bo Jackson   A. Illinois

2. 1987: Vinny Testaverde   B. Auburn

3. 1988: Aundray Bruce   C. Miami

4. 1989: Troy Aikman   D. Washington

5. 1990: Jeff George   E. UCLA

6. 1991: Russell Maryland

7. 1992: Steve Emtman

(Note: one school in this game is the answer to two players.)

1. 1993: Drew Bledsoe   A. Washington State

2. 1994: Dan Wilkinson   B. Southern California

3. 1995: Ki-Jana Carter   C. Ohio State

4. 1996: Keyshawn Johnson   D. Tennessee

5. 1997: Orlando Pace   E. Penn State

6. 1998: Peyton Manning   F. Kentucky

7. 1999: Tim Couch

1. 2000: Courtney Brown   A. Southern California

2. 2001: Michael Vick   B. Utah

3. 2002: David Carr   C. Penn State

4. 2003: Carson Palmer   D. Fresno State

5. 2004: Eli Manning   E. Mississippi

6. 2005: Alex Smith   F. North Carolina State

7. 2006: Mario Williams   G. Virginia Tech

Now it's time to identify the alma maters of significant players who weren't the NFL's #1 picks, although most were first rounders.

1. 1952: Ollie Matson   A. San Francisco

2. 1965: Joe Namath   B. Colorado

3. 1974: J.V. Cain   C. Georgia

4. 1979: Ottis Anderson   D. Oregon

5. 1993: Garrison Hearst   E. Alabama

6. 1982: Gerald Riggs   F. Miami

7. 1987: Chris Miller   G. Arizona State

1. 1989: Deion Sanders   A. Minnesota

2. 1996: Ray Lewis   B. Florida State

3. 2000: Jamal Lewis   C. Michigan State

4. 1964: Carl Eller   D. Miami

5. 1973: Joe DeLamielleure   E. Oklahoma State

6. 1988: Thurman Thomas   F. Tennessee

7. 1995: Kerry Collins   G. Penn State

181

1. 1983: Jim Kelly   A. Illinois

2. 1965: Dick Butkus   B. Notre Dame

3. 1948: Bobby Layne   C. Kansas

4. 1939: Sid Luckman   D. Texas

5. 1965: Gale Sayers   E. Miami

6. 1961: Mike Ditka   F. Pittsburgh

7. 1946: Johnny Lujack   G. Columbia

1. 1969: Rufus Mayes   A. Tennessee

2. 1975: Walter Payton   B. Jackson State

3. 1982: Jim McMahon   C. New Mexico

4. 1983: Willie Gault   D. Florida

5. 1984: Wilber Marshall   E. Brigham Young

6. 1985: William Perry   F. Ohio State

7. 2000: Brian Urlacher   G. Clemson

(Note: one school in this game is the answers to two players.)

1. 2003: Rex Grossman   A. Alabama

2. 1973: Isaac Curtis   B. Southern California

3. 1976: Archie Griffin   C. San Diego State

4. 1980: Anthony Munoz   D. Ohio State

5. 1957: Jim Brown   E. Syracuse

6. 1964: Paul Warfield   F. Florida

7. 1978: Ozzie Newsome

1. 1980: Charles White   A. California

2. 1989: Eric Metcalf   B. Texas

3. 2004: Kellen Winslow   C. Alabama

4. 1961: Bob Lilly   D. Southern California

5. 1963: Lee Roy Jordan   E. Texas Christian

6. 1965: Craig Morton   F. Yale

7. 1969: Calvin Hill   G. Miami

1. 1973: Billy Joe DuPree   A. Maryland

2. 1975: Randy White   B. West Texas State

3. 1977: Tony Dorsett   C. Michigan State

4. 1988: Michael Irvin   D. Miami

5. 1970: Duane Thomas   E. Utah State

6. 1990: Emmitt Smith   F. Pittsburgh

7. 1962: Merlin Olsen   G. Florida

1. 1963: Kermit Alexander   A. Louisiana State

2. 1967: Floyd Little   B. UCLA

3. 1974: Randy Gradishar   C. Ohio State

4. 1982: Gerald Willhite   D. Northwestern

5. 1944: Otto Graham   E. Iowa

6. 1948: Y.A. Tittle   F. Syracuse

7. 1958: Alex Karras   G. San Jose State

1. 1992: Tommy Maddox   A. UCLA

2. 1962: John Hadl   B. Houston

3. 1968: Greg Landry   C. Kansas

4. 1986: Chuck Long   D. Oklahoma State

5. 1970: Steve Owens   E. Massachusetts

6. 1989: Barry Sanders   F. Oklahoma

7. 1990: Andre Ware   G. Iowa

1. 1967: Mel Farr   A. Stanford

2. 2002: Joey Harrington   B. Michigan State

3. 1952: Babe Parilli   C. UCLA

4. 1978: James Lofton   D. Kentucky

5. 1988: Sterling Sharpe   E. South Carolina

6. 1961: Herb Adderley   F. Penn State

7. 1956: Lenny Moore   G. Oregon

1. 1989: Tony Mandarich
2. 1960: Ron Mix
3. 1961: Tom Matte
4. 1967: Jim Detwiler
5. 1973: Bert Jones
6. 1987: Cornelius Bennett
7. 1988: Chris Chandler

A. Michigan State
B. Ohio State
C. Louisiana State
D. Washington
E. Southern California
F. Michigan
G. Alabama

1. 1967: Bubba Smith
2. 1994: Marshall Faulk
3. 1999: Edgerrin James
4. 2004: Bob Sanders
5. 1960: Don Meredith
6. 1997: Tony Gonzalez
7. 1967: Bob Griese

A. Southern Methodist
B. Michigan State
C. Iowa
D. San Diego State
E. California
F. Miami
G. Purdue

1. 1989: Andre Rison
2. 1968: Larry Csonka
3. 1983: Dan Marino
4. 1964: Carl Eller

A. Syracuse
B. Pittsburgh
C. Southern California
D. Miami

5. 1965: Jack Snow

E. Michigan State

6. 1968: Ron Yary

F. Notre Dame

7. 1973: Chuck Foreman

G. Minnesota

1. 1967: Alan Page

A. Penn State

2. 1977: Tommy Kramer

B. Rice

3. 1987: D.J. Dozier

C. Central Florida

4. 1998: Randy Moss

D. Alabama

5. 1999: Daunte Culpepper

E. Marshall

6. 1973: John Hannah

F. Notre Dame

7. 1973: Sam Cunningham

G. Southern California

1. 1973: Darryl Stingley

A. South Carolina

2. 1975: Russ Francis

B. Michigan

3. 1977: Stanley Morgan

C. Oregon

4. 1995: Ty Law

D. California

5. 1971: Archie Manning

E. Mississippi

6. 1976: Chuck Muncie

F. Tennessee

7. 1981: George Rogers

G. Purdue

1. 1986: Jim Dombrowski   A. Ohio State

2. 2006: Reggie Bush   B. Southern California

3. 1979: Phil Simms   C. Miami

4. 1981: Lawrence Taylor   D. Virginia

5. 2002: Jeremy Shockey   E. North Carolina

6. 1964: Matt Snell   F. Kansas

7. 1971: John Riggins   G. Morehead State

1. 1952: Frank Gifford   A. Ohio State

2. 1988: Tim Brown   B. Texas A & I

3. 1975: Neal Colzie   C. Southern California

4. 1973: Ray Guy   D. Southern Mississippi

5. 1967: Gene Upshaw   E. Marshall

6. 2001: Santana Moss   F. Notre Dame

7. 2000: Chad Pennington   G. Miami

1. 1975: Anthony Davis   A. Oklahoma

2. 1971: Jack Tatum   B. Southern California

3. 2006: Michael Huff   C. Texas

4. 1944: Steve Van Buren   D. Purdue

5. 1969: Leroy Keyes   E. Syracuse

6. 1988: Keith Jackson   F. Ohio State

7. 1999: Donovan McNabb   G. Louisiana State

1. 1982: Marcus Allen   A. Southern California

2. 1946: Doc Blanchard   B. North Texas State

3. 1938: Byron White   C. Colorado

4. 1953: Ted Marchibroda   D. Utah

5. 1957: Len Dawson   E. St. Bonaventure

6. 1965: Roy Jefferson   F. Purdue

7. 1969: Mean Joe Greene   G. Army

1. 1972: Franco Harris   A. Purdue

2. 1974: Lynn Swann   B. Michigan State

3. 1984: Louis Lipps   C. Penn State

4. 1987: Rod Woodson   D. Southern Mississippi

5. 1998: Alan Faneca   E. Louisiana State

6. 2000: Plaxico Burress   F. Miami of Ohio

7. 2004: Ben Roethlisberger   G. Southern California

1. 2003: Troy Polamalu   A. Southern California

2. 1945: Elroy Hirsch   B. Wisconsin

3. 1959: Dick Bass   C. Michigan

4. 1962: Merlin Olsen   D. Penn State

5. 1966: Tom Mack   E. Pacific

6. 1971: Jack Youngblood   F. Utah State

7. 1974: John Cappelletti   G. Florida

1. 1983: Eric Dickerson   A. Nebraska

2. 1993: Jerome Bettis   B. Southern Methodist

3. 1999: Torry Holt   C. Missouri

4. 1973: Johnny Rodgers   D. Notre Dame

5. 1979: Kellen Winslow   E. Auburn

6. 1981: James Brooks   F. North Carolina State

7. 1988: Anthony Miller   G. Tennessee

1. 1990: Junior Seau   A. Texas Christian

2. 2001: LaDainian Tomlinson   B. Stanford

3. 1950: Leo Nomellini   C. Michigan State

4. 1952: Hugh McElhenny   D. Minnesota

5. 1956: Earl Morrall   E. Southern California

6. 1957: John Brodie   F. UCLA

7. 1961: Jimmy Johnson   G. Washington

1. 1962: Lance Alworth   A. North Texas State

2. 1963: Kermit Alexander   B. UCLA

3. 1967: Steve Spurrier   C. Mississippi Valley State

4. 1970: Cedric Hardman   D. Southern California

5. 1981: Ronnie Lott   E. Florida

6. 1983: Roger Craig   F. Arkansas

7. 1985: Jerry Rice   G. Nebraska

1. 1980: Jacob Green   A. Grambling

2. 1981: Ken Easley   B. Miami

3. 1983: Curt Warner   C. UCLA

4. 1990: Cortez Kennedy   D. Fresno State

5. 2000: Shaun Alexander   E. Alabama

6. 1978: Doug Williams   F. Penn State

7. 1994: Trent Dilfer   G. Texas A & M

1. 1995: Warren Sapp

2. 1997: Warrick Dunn

3. 1971: Dan Pastorini

4. 1975: Robert Brazile

5. 1976: Mike Barber

6. 1986: Jim Everett

7. 1988: Lorenzo White

A. Santa Clara

B. Florida State

C. Michigan State

D. Miami

E. Louisiana Tech

F. Jackson State

G. Purdue

1. 1987: Alonzo Highsmith

2. 1995: Steve McNair

3. 1996: Eddie George

4. 1937: Sammy Baugh

5. 1964: Charley Taylor

6. 1980: Art Monk

7. 1992: Desmond Howard

A. Alcorn State

B. Arizona State

C. Miami

D. Texas Christian

E. Syracuse

F. Ohio State

G. Michigan

And now for some Hall of Famers who weren't #1 picks, even though they are just as revered by their alma maters.

1. 1971: Dan Dierdorf

2. 1949: George Blanda

A. Southern University

B. Michigan

3. 1954: Raymond Berry   C. Southern Methodist

4. 1968: Elvin Bethea   D. Florida State

5. 1965: Fred Biletnikoff   E. Nebraska

6. 1970: Mel Blount   F. Kentucky

7. 1964: Bob Brown   G. North Carolina A & T

(Note: one school in this game is the answer to two players)

1. 1953: Roosevelt Brown   A. Morgan State

2. 1962: Nick Buoniconti   B. Oregon

3. 1976: Harry Carson   C. Notre Dame

4. 1974: Dave Casper   D. Colorado College

5. 1950: Art Donovan   E. South Carolina State

6. 1929: Earl "Dutch" Clark   F. Boston College

7. 1973: Dan Fouts

1. 1925: Red Grange   A. Penn State

2. 1956: Forrest Gregg   B. Miami

3. 1946: Lou Groza   C. Illinois

4. 1971: Jack Ham   D. Ohio State

5. 1976: Mike Haynes   E. Arizona State

6. 1969: Ted Hendricks   F. Prairie View A & M

7. 1967: Ken Houston   G. Southern Methodist

1. 1927: Cal Hubbard   A. Centenary; Geneva

2. 1935: Don Hutson   B. Alabama

3. 1953: John Henry Johnson   C. South Carolina State; Mississippi Vocational

4. 1969: Charlie Joiner   D. Iowa

5. 1961: Deacon Jones   E. St. Mary's; Arizona State

6. 1957: Sonny Jurgensen   F. Grambling

7. 1964: Paul Krause   G. Duke

1. 1974: Jack Lambert   A. Tulsa

2. 1952: Dick "Night Train" Lane   B. Kent State

3. 1967: Willie Lanier   C. Free agent; played at Bethune-Cookman College

4. 1976: Steve Largent   D. Free agent with some junior college experience

5. 1967: Larry Little   E. Villanova

6. 1981: Howie Long   F. Morgan State

7. 1963: John Mackey   G. Syracuse

1. 1952: Gino Marchetti   A. Texas Western

2. 1957: Don Maynard   B. Stanford

3. 1958: Bobby Mitchell   C. West L.A. Junior College; Washington

4. 1979: Joe Montana   D. Illinois

5. 1978: Warren Moon   E. San Francisco

6. 1930: Bronko Nagurski   F. Minnesota

7. 1925: Ernie Nevers   G. Notre Dame

1. 1941: Tony Canadeo   A. Miami

2. 1958: Ray Nitschke   B. Illinois

3. 1960: Jim Otto   C. Maryland State—Eastern Shore

4. 1924: Steve Owen   D. Oregon

5. 1964: Mel Renfro   E. Phillips University

6. 1946: George Connor   F. Gonzaga

7. 1968: Art Shell   G. Holy Cross; Notre Dame

1. 1981: Mike Singletary   A. Georgia

2. 1956: Bart Starr   B. Montana State

3. 1974: John Stallworth   C. Alabama

4. 1966: Jan Stenerud

5. 1944: Bob Waterfield

6. 1961: Fran Tarkenton

7. 1958: Jim Taylor

D. Louisiana State

E. UCLA

F. Alabama A & M

G. Baylor

1. 1912: Jim Thorpe

2. 1955: Johnny Unitas

3. 1949: Norm Van Brocklin

4. 1974: Mike Webster

5. 1984: Reggie White

6. 1960: Larry Wilson

7. 1984: Steve Young

A. Utah

B. Louisville

C. Tennessee

D. Carlisle

E. Wisconsin

F. Brigham Young

G. Oregon

CHAPTER 10

NAME THAT YEAR

How's your memory? If you're like me, you associate certain songs, personal events, or items to particular past years. Like lime-green leisure suits. I know that was 1976 because that's the year Wendy Jo and I . . . well, that was the year of Wendy Jo. Anyway, along the lines of lime-green leisure suits and Wendy Jo, each of the games in this chapter has seven clues that all refer to one *calendar* year in NFL history. Your objective is to guess the correct year in as few clues as possible.

1 Lloyd Nordstrom, president of the Seattle Seahawks, dies.

2 The New York Giants move into Giants Stadium in East Rutherford, New Jersey.

3 St. Louis defeats San Diego, 20–10, in Korakuen Stadium in Tokyo, Japan, the first NFL game ever played outside of North America.

4 The Pittsburgh Steelers defeat the College All Stars in Chicago in a storm-shortened game, the last ever in the annual series.

5 The Seattle Seahawks and Tampa Bay Buccaneers are each awarded eight extra selections for this year's draft.

6 The Dallas Cowboys become the first wild card team to play in the Super Bowl.

7 The Pittsburgh Steelers defeat the Dallas Cowboys, 21–17, in one of the most exciting Super Bowls ever played.

1 The Houston Oilers defeat the Los Angeles Chargers, 24–16, in the first AFL Championship Game on January 1.

2 Detroit defeats Cleveland, 17–16, in the first Playoff Bowl, or Bert Bell Benefit Bowl, between 2nd-place teams in each conference on January 7.

3 End Willard Dewveall of the Bears plays out his option and joins the Oilers on January 14, the first player to move deliberately from one league to the other.

4 Canton, Ohio, is chosen as the site of the Pro Football Hall of Fame on April 27.

5 A bill legalizing single-network television contracts by professional sports leagues is introduced in Congress. It passes the House and Senate and is signed into law by President John F. Kennedy on September 30.

6 Houston defeats San Diego, 10–3, for the AFL title on December 24. Green Bay wins its first NFL championship since 1944, defeating the New York Giants, 37–0, on December 31.

7 Jim Brown leads the NFL in rushing for the fifth consecutive year.

1 The Los Angeles Raiders defeat the Washington Redskins, 38–9, in the Super Bowl.

2 The Colts relocate to Indianapolis on March 28.

3 The New York Jets move their home games to Giants Stadium in East Rutherford, New Jersey.

4 Alex G. Spanos purchases the San Diego Chargers from Eugene V. Klein on August 28.

5 An investment group headed by H.R. Bright purchases the Dallas Cowboys from Clint Murchison, Jr. on March 20. Tex Schramm is designated as managing general partner.

6 Chicago's Walter Payton breaks Jim Brown's career rushing mark, finishing the season with 13,309 yards.

7 Dan Marino of Miami passes for 5,084 yards and 48 touchdowns; Eric Dickerson of the Los Angeles Rams rushes for 2,105 yards; Art Monk of Washington catches 106 passes.

1 San Francisco defeats Denver, 55–10, in the Super Bowl joining Pittsburgh as the NFL's only teams to win four Super Bowls.

2 The NFL announces that college juniors are now eligible for the draft, but must renounce their collegiate football eligibility before applying for the NFL Draft.

3 Commissioner Tagliabue announces that NFL teams will play their 16-game schedule over 17 weeks this year and next, and over 18 weeks in the following two years.

4 New four-year TV agreements were ratified for ABC, CBS, NBC, ESPN, and TNT at the NFL annual meeting on March 12. The contracts total $3.6 billion, the largest in television history.

5 NFL International Week was marked by four preseason games in seven days in Tokyo, London, Berlin, and Montreal.

6 The Super Bowl Most Valuable Player trophy is renamed the Pete Rozelle Trophy.

7 For the first time since 1957, every NFL club wins at least one of its first four games.

1 NFL clubs agreed to pool the visiting team share of gate receipts for all preseason and regular-season games and divide the pool equally starting next year.

2 The Baltimore Ravens win their first Super Bowl by defeating the NFC champion New York Giants, 34–7.

3 The Washington Redskins set an all-time NFL regular-season home paid attendance record with a total of 656,599 for eight games, breaking the record of 634,204 held by the 1980 Detroit Lions.

4 Heinz Field opens in Pittsburgh.

5 President George W. Bush becomes the first U.S. President to be involved in an NFL regular-season pregame coin toss as he helps kick off the season from the White House. Via satellite, President Bush tosses the coin for 10 regular-season games that start at 1:00 PM ET, September 9.

6 President Bush designates the Super Bowl as a "National Special Security Event," allowing all security for the game to be coordinated by the Secret Service.

7 The St. Louis Rams compile the best regular-season record at 14–2.

1 Vince Lombardi becomes head coach of the Green Bay Packers.

2 Lamar Hunt of Dallas announces his intentions to form a second pro football league.

3 Joe Foss is named AFL Commissioner.

4 Hunt's new league is named the American Football League (AFL).

5 The first AFL draft, lasting 33 rounds, is held on November 22.

6 NFL Commissioner Bert Bell dies of a heart attack while attending a game between the Eagles and the Steelers on October 11.

7 The Colts again defeat the Giants in the NFL Championship Game, 31–16.

1 According to a Harris Survey, sports fans choose professional football (41 percent) as their favorite sport, overtaking baseball (38 percent) for the first time.

2 NFL teams pledge not to sign college seniors until completion of all their games, including bowl games.

3 The NFL adds a sixth official, the line judge.

4 The color of the officials' penalty flags is changed from white to bright gold.

5 Field Judge Burl Toler becomes the first black official in NFL history.

6 In the AFL Championship Game, the Bills defeat the Chargers, 23–0.

7 Green Bay defeats Baltimore 13–10 in sudden-death overtime in a Western Conference playoff game when Don Chandler kicks a 25-yard field goal for the Packers after 13 minutes, 39 seconds of overtime.

1 The Boston Patriots change their name to the New England Patriots.

2 The NFC defeats the AFC, 27–6, in the first AFC-NFC Pro Bowl.

3 Baltimore defeats Dallas, 16–13, in the Super Bowl on Jim O'Brien's 32-yard field goal with five seconds to go.

4 The Philadelphia Eagles leave Franklin Field for their new home at Veterans Stadium.

5 The San Francisco 49ers leave Kezar Stadium for Candlestick Park.

6 The Dallas Cowboys move from the Cotton Bowl into their new home, Texas Stadium.

7 Miami defeats Kansas City, 27–24, after 22 minutes, 40 seconds of sudden-death overtime in an AFC Divisional Playoff Game, making it the longest game in NFL history.

1 Tex Schramm is named president of the new World League of American Football.

2 Jerry Jones purchases the Dallas Cowboys.

3 A strengthened policy regarding anabolic steroids and masking agents is announced by Commissioner Pete Rozelle.

4 San Francisco defeats Cincinnati, 20–16, in the Super Bowl.

5 Art Shell is named head coach of the Los Angeles Raiders, making him the NFL's first black head coach since Fritz Pollard coached the Akron Pros in 1921.

6 Paul Tagliabue becomes the seventh commissioner of the NFL.

7 NFL Charities donates $1 million through United Way to benefit Bay Area earthquake victims.

1 Bert Bell, co-owner of the Steelers, becomes the NFL's new commissioner.

2 The NFL's headquarters move from Chicago to the Philadelphia suburb of Bala-Cynwyd.

3 Free substitution was withdrawn and substitutions are limited to no more than three men at a time.

4 The Rams relocate from Cleveland to Los Angeles.

5 Halfback Kenny Washington and end Woody Strode become the first modern-era African-Americans to play in the NFL when they join the Rams.

6 The rival All-America Football Conference begins play with eight teams. The Cleveland Browns defeat the New York Yankees, 14–9, to win the AAFC's first championship.

7 Bill Dudley of the Steelers leads the NFL in rushing, interceptions, and punt returns, and cops the league's MVP Award.

1 The Super Bowl is held indoors for the first time.

2 A seventh official, the side judge, is added to the officiating crew.

3 An NFL game is played for the first time in Mexico City, with the Saints defeating the Eagles, 14–7, in a preseason game.

4 Dallas defeated Denver, 27–10, in the Super Bowl. It is the first victory for the NFC in six years.

5 The NFL continues its trend toward opening up the game. A rule change now permits a defender to maintain contact with a receiver within five yards of the line of scrimmage, but restricts contact beyond that point.

6 Rookie Earl Campbell leads the NFL in rushing with 1,450 yards.

7 Rookie Frank Corral leads the NFL in scoring with 118 points.

1 Atlanta Falcons owner Rankin Smith dies of heart failure.

2 Indianapolis Colts owner Robert Irsay dies from complications related to a stroke he suffered two years earlier.

3 Washington Redskins owner Jack Kent Cooke dies at his home in Washington, D.C.

4 The Green Bay Packers win their first NFL title in 29 years by defeating the New England Patriots, 35–21, in the Super Bowl.

5 Paul Allen buys the Seahawks from Ken Behring.

6 The Washington Redskins defeat the Arizona Cardinals, 19–13, in overtime to christen their new Jack Kent Cooke Stadium.

7 The Barcelona Dragons defeat the Rhein Fire, 38–24, to win the World Bowl in Barcelona, Spain.

1 The Pro Football Hall of Fame opens in Canton, Ohio.

2 The Dallas Texans relocate to Kansas City, becoming the Chiefs.

3 Commissioner Pete Rozelle suspends Green Bay halfback Paul Hornung and Detroit defensive tackle Alex Karras for placing bets on their own teams and on other NFL games.

4 The AFL allows the Jets and Raiders to select players from other franchises in hopes of giving the league more competitive balance.

5 The New York Titans are sold to a five-man syndicate headed by David (Sonny) Werblin, and the team changes its name to the Jets.

6 The U.S. Fourth Circuit Court of Appeals reaffirms a lower court's finding for the NFL in the $10-million suit brought by the AFL, ending nearly four years of litigation.

7 The Bears defeat the Giants in the NFL Championship Game, 14–10, winning a sixth and final title for George Halas, who is in his 36th year as head coach.

1 The NFL Players Association is founded.

2 Grabbing an opponent's facemask (other than the ball carrier) is now made illegal.

3 A natural leather ball with white end stripes replaces the white ball with black stripes for night games.

4 The Giants change stadiums, moving from the Polo Grounds to Yankee Stadium.

5 CBS becomes the first network to broadcast NFL regular-season games to selected television markets across the nation.

6 Rick Casares of the Bears leads the NFL in rushing with 1,126 yards, just 20 yards short of tying the all-time record.

7 The Giants defeat the Bears, 47–7, in the NFL Championship Game.

1 Legendary quarterback Johnny Unitas dies of a heart attack at the age of 69.

2 The NFL plays its first-ever Thursday game in prime time as the 49ers defeat the Giants, 16–13.

3 Seahawks Stadium opens in Seattle, Washington.

4 Dallas Cowboys running back Emmitt Smith becomes the NFL's all-time rushing leader, surpassing Walter Payton.

5 Gillette Stadium opens in Foxborough, Massachusetts.

6 Reliant Stadium opens in Houston, Texas.

7 For the first time in history, the Super Bowl is decided on the game's final play.

1 The NFL reaches agreement with ESPN, its first contract with a cable network.

2 A special payment program is adopted to benefit nearly 1,000 former NFL players who participated in the league before the current NFL Pension Plan was created and is made retroactive to the 1959 season.

3 In a three-team deal involving 10 players and/or draft choices, the Los Angeles Rams send disgruntled running back Eric Dickerson to the Indianapolis Colts for six draft choices and two players.

4 The season is reduced from a 16-game season to 15 as the result of a players' strike.

5 The New York Giants defeat Denver, 39–20, in the Super Bowl.

6 Games scheduled for the third weekend are canceled, but the games of weeks four, five, and six are played with replacement teams.

7 Eric Dickerson's replacement in Los Angeles, Charles White, leads the NFL in rushing with 1,374 yards.

1 The Portsmouth Spartans relocate to Detroit and change their name to the Lions.

2 The Chicago Bears are matched against the best college football players in the first Chicago College All-Star Game, which ends in a 0–0 tie in front of nearly 80,000 fans at Soldier Field.

3 Rookie Beattie Feathers of the Bears becomes the NFL's first 1,000-yard rusher, gaining 1,004 yards on 119 carries.

4 The Thanksgiving Day game between the Bears and the Lions is the first NFL game broadcast nationally.

5 The Cincinnati Reds lose their first eight games, and then are suspended by the league for defaulting on payments.

6 The St. Louis Gunners, an independent team, join the NFL when they buy the Cincinnati franchise, and go 1–2 the last three weeks.

7 In the Championship Game, on an extremely cold and icy day at the Polo Grounds, the Giants trail the Bears, 13–3, in the third quarter before changing into basketball shoes for better footing. The Giants win, 30–13, in what has come to be known as the Sneakers Game.

1 Ted Collins is granted a franchise for Boston, which becomes an active franchise the following season.

2 For the first time in league history, the NFL plays a 10-game schedule.

3 The Bears win the NFL title, defeating the Redskins, 41–21.

4 The NFL makes the wearing of helmets mandatory.

5 Philadelphia and Pittsburgh merge for one season. The team, known as Phil-Pitt, is called the Steagles by fans.

6 Sammy Baugh leads the league in passing, punting, and interceptions.

7 The Cleveland Rams are granted permission to suspend operations for one season because the team's two co-owners have both enlisted in the military.

1 Malcolm Glazer buys the Tampa Bay Buccaneers from the estate of the late Hugh Culverhouse.

2 The Los Angeles Rams relocate to St. Louis.

3 The Los Angeles Raiders relocate to Oakland.

4 The NFL becomes the first major sports league to establish an Internet site.

5 Carolina and Jacksonville begin play in the NFL.

6 San Francisco defeats San Diego in the Super Bowl, 49–26.

7 The Frankfurt Galaxy defeats the Amsterdam Admirals, 26–22, to win the World Bowl in front of 23,847 fans in Amsterdam's Olympic Stadium.

1 NFL Commissioner Pete Rozelle announces that all Super Bowl tickets are sold, and that the game will be telecast in Los Angeles, the site of the game, on an experimental basis.

2 The AFC defeats the NFC, 33–28, in the Pro Bowl in Dallas, the first time since 1942 that the game is played anywhere other than Los Angeles.

3 A jersey numbering system is adopted: 1–19 for quarterbacks and specialists, 20–49 for running backs and defensive backs, 50–59 for centers and linebackers, 60–79 for defensive linemen and interior offensive linemen other than centers, and 80–89 for wide receivers and tight ends. Players who were in the NFL the year before could continue to use their old numbers.

4 Congress adopts experimental legislation requiring any NFL game that is declared a sellout 72 hours prior to kickoff is to be made available for local televising.

5 A new rival league, the World Football League, is announced and intends to begin play the next season.

6 O.J. Simpson of Buffalo becomes the first player to rush for more than 2,000 yards in a season.

7 Miami defeats Washington in the Super Bowl, 14–7.

CHAPTER 11

AMAZING INDIVIDUAL COLLEGE PERFORMANCES

Over the years there have been many incredible performances on the field. Some even seem superhuman, like the quarterback who threw 41 passes—in one quarter! And the running back who rushed for eight touchdowns—in one game! As incredible as some of the following performances might seem, they all actually did take place. See if you can connect these college players to their amazing performances.

Quarterback performances.

1. Jason Davis, UNLV

A. Threw 56 passes in one half

2. Rusty LaRue, Wake Forest

B. Threw 719 passes in one season (13 games)

3. Timmy Chang, Hawaii

C. Threw 1,241 passes over two seasons

4. B.J. Symons, Texas Tech

D. Threw 41 passes in one quarter

5. David Klingler, Houston

E. Threw 2,436 passes in his 4-year career

6. Kliff Kingsbury, Texas Tech

F. Averaged 58.5 pass attempts per game for one season (643 passes in 11 games)

7. Drew Brees, Purdue

G. Threw 83 passes in one game

Only *freshmen* quarterbacks in this game.

1. Luke McCown, Louisiana Tech	A. Highest passing efficiency rating for a season—180.4
2. Jared Lorenzen, Kentucky	B. Threw 559 passes in one season
3. Grady Benton, Arizona State	C. First of only two freshmen ever to pass for six touchdowns in one game
4. David Neill, Nevada	D. Passed for 611 yards in one game
5. Mike Gundy, Oklahoma State	E. Attempted 138 passes without an interception to start his college career
6. Bob Hoernschemeyer, Indiana	F. Threw 72 passes in one game
7. Michael Vick, Virginia Tech	G. Completed 66.2% of his passes for a season (149 of 225)

More amazing quarterback performances.

1. Tim Couch, Kentucky	A. Completed 73.6% of his passes for a season (296 of 402)
2. Tim Rattay, Louisiana Tech	B. Completed 23 consecutive passes in one game
3. Tee Martin, Tennessee	C. Completed an average of 36.4 passes per game for a season (400 completions in 11 games)
4. Steve Sarkisian, BYU	D. Completed 68.2% of his passes for his career (766 of 1,123)

5. Daunte Culpepper, UCF

E. Completed 31 of 34 passes in one game

6. Bruce Gradkowski, Toledo

F. Completed an average of 30.8 passes per game for his career (1,015 completions in 33 games)

7. Matt Blundin, Virginia

G. Threw 224 passes in a season without an interception

Still more quarterbacks.

1. Matt Leinart, USC

A. Averaged 326.8 passing yards gained per game over his 4-year career

2. Timmy Chang, Hawaii

B. Passed for 517 yards in one half

3. Trent Dilfer, Fresno State

C. Passed for 347 yards in one quarter

4. Ty Detmer, BYU

D. Passed for 716 yards in one game

5. Jason Davis, UNLV

E. Threw only 23 interceptions in 1,245 passes for his career (1.85%)

6. Andre Ware, Houston

F. Threw 70 passes in one game without an interception

7. David Klingler, Houston

G. Threw 271 consecutive passes without an interception

Still more passing performances.

1. David Klingler, Houston

A. Passed for 6 touchdowns in one quarter

2. Ben Roethlisberger, Miami (Ohio)

B. Only college quarterback ever to pass for 200 or more yards in 14 consecutive games in one season

3. Ty Detmer, BYU

C. Most passing yards gained in the opening game of a season—590

4. Tim Rattay, Louisiana Tech

D. Completed 10.6% of his pass attempts in a season for touchdowns (47 TDs in 445 attempts)

5. Jim McMahon, BYU

E. Threw for six touchdowns on his first six pass completions of the game

6. Brooks Dawson, UTEP

F. Only college quarterback ever to pass for 300 or more yards for 12 straight games

7. Stu Rayburn, Kent State

G. Threw 266 passes in one season without a touchdown (had 125 completions)

Now it's time for six games of the most amazing rushing performances of all time.

1. Herschel Walker, Georgia

    A. Had 1,215 rushing attempts in his 4-year career

2. Marcus Allen, USC

    B. Had 58 rushing attempts in one game

3. Ed Marinaro, Cornell

    C. Had 403 rushing attempts in one season

4. Alex Smith, Indiana

    D. Had 22 rushing attempts in one quarter

5. Steve Bartalo, Colorado State

    E. Had 52 rushing attempts in one game as a freshman

6. Michael Turner, Northern Illinois

    F. Had 994 rushing attempts in his 3-year career

7. Tony Sands, Kansas

    G. Averaged 39.6 rushing attempts per game for a season (356 attempts in 9 games)

1. William Howard, Tennessee

    A. First of only two players ever to rush for 287 yards in one half

2. Lorenzo White, Michigan State

    B. Had 102 rushing attempts in two consecutive games

3. Travis Prentice, Miami (Ohio)

    C. Rushed for 406 yards in one game

4. Corey Dillon, Washington   D. Had 862 consecutive rushing attempts in his career without losing a fumble

5. Stacey Robinson, North. Illinois   E. Rushed for 2,628 yards in his 11-game season

6. LaDainian Tomlinson, TCU   F. Rushed for 222 yards—in one quarter!

7. Barry Sanders, Oklahoma State   G. Rushed 16 times on 16 consecutive plays

1. Ron Dayne, Wisconsin   A. Rushed for 6,397 yards in his 4-year career

2. Troy Davis, Iowa State   B. Rushed for 4,195 yards in two consecutive seasons

3. Marshall Faulk, San Diego State   C. Rushed for 5,259 yards in his 3-year career

4. Ed Marinaro, Cornell   D. Averaged 174.6 yards per game for his career, most in NCAA history

5. Adrian Peterson, Oklahoma   E. Averaged 180.1 yards rushing as a freshman

6. Jamario Thomas, North Texas   F. Rushed for 1,925 yards in his freshman season

7. Herschel Walker, Georgia   G. Rushed for 386 yards in a game as a freshman

1. Barry Sanders, Oklahoma State
2. Ricky Williams, Texas
3. Archie Griffin, Ohio State
4. Mark Malone, Arizona State
5. Beau Morgan, Air Force
6. Brad Smith, Missouri
7. Stacey Robinson, North. Illinois

A. Rushed for 1,494 yards in a season as a quarterback
B. Had four games in one season with 300+ yards
C. Rushed for 100+ yards in 31 straight games
D. Longest rush by a quarterback—98 yards
E. Rushed for 4,289 yards in his career as a quarterback
F. Had back-to-back games with 300+ yards
G. Rushed for 308 yards in a game as a quarterback

1. Morley Drury, USC
2. Ed Marinaro, Cornell
3. Emmitt Smith, Florida
4. Marcus Allen, USC

A. Only player to rush for 200+ yards eight times in one season
B. First freshman to reach 1,000 rushing yards in only his 7th game of the season
C. First player to reach 1,000 rushing yards in just five games of his season
D. Rushed for 937 yards over three consecutive games (312, 293, and 332)

5. Herschel Walker, Georgia

E. Rushed for 668 yards over two consecutive games (318 and 350)

6. Ricky Williams, Texas

F. First player to rush for at least 1,000 yards in a season

7. Barry Sanders, Oklahoma State

G. First freshman to rush for 200+ yards four times in one season

1. Tony Dorsett, Pittsburgh

A. Rushed for 8 touchdowns in one game

2. Chris McCoy, Navy

B. Scored 7 touchdowns in one game as a freshman

3. Greg Hill, Texas A & M

C. Had a career rushing average of 8.3 for his career (2,957 yards on 358 carries)

4. Jerald Sowell, Tulane

D. Had a 98-yard rush in the first game of his career as a freshman

5. Glenn Davis, Army

E. Rushed for 212 yards as a freshman in the first game of his career

6. Howard Griffith, Illinois

F. Rushed for 273 yards in the first game of his career

7. Marshall Faulk, San Diego State

G. First player with three seasons of 1,500+ rushing yards

Now let's move on to three games featuring the most amazing pass receiving performances of all time.

1. Randy Gatewood, UNLV

    A. Caught at least one pass in 51 straight games

2. Manny Hazard, Houston

    B. Caught 23 passes in one game

3. Howard Twilley, Tulsa

    C. First of only two tight ends to catch 17 passes in one game

4. Taurean Henderson, Texas Tech

    D. Caught 142 passes in one season

5. Taylor Stubblefield, Purdue

    E. Caught 316 passes in his career

6. Emilio Vallez, New Mexico

    F. Averaged 13.4 pass receptions per game for a season (134 catches in 10 games)

7. Mark Templeton, Long Beach St.

    G. Running back who caught 18 passes in one game

1. Richard Woodley, TCU

    A. Had 100+ receiving yards in 11 straight games in one season

2. Troy Edwards, Louisiana Tech

    B. Averaged 25.7 yards per reception for his career (2,206 yards on 86 receptions)

3. Trevor Insley, Nevada

    C. Caught 18 passes in a game as a freshman

4. Corey Alston, Western Michigan

    D. Caught at least one touchdown pass in 12 straight games in one season

5. Aaron Turner, Pacific

E. Had 263 receiving yards in a game as a freshman

6. Wesley Walker, California

F. Had 2,060 receiving yards for one season

7. Randy Moss, Marshall

G. Had 405 receiving yards in one game

248

1. Rashaun Woods, Oklahoma State

A. Caught 18 touchdown passes in one season as a tight end

2. Troy Edwards, Louisiana Tech

B. Scored at least one touchdown by pass reception in 27 different games of his career

3. Nate Burleson, Nevada

C. Had 326 receiving yards in one game, but didn't score a touchdown

4. Carlos Carson, LSU

D. Caught 7 touchdown passes in one game

5. Ryan Yarborough, Wyoming

E. Caught at least one touchdown pass in 18 consecutive games over two seasons

6. Larry Fitzgerald, Pittsburgh

F. Scored six touchdowns on the first six passes he caught in his career

7. Dennis Smith, Utah

G. Caught 27 touchdown passes in one season

Let's try one game of amazing punting performances.

1. Charlie Calhoun, Texas Tech

A. Had one punt that went for 99 yards

2. Jim Bailey, VMI

B. Had 13 punts one season that went for 60 yards or more

3. Pat Brady, Nevada

C. Punted 101 times in one season

4. Mark Mariscal, Colorado

D. Had 300 consecutive punts in his career without ever having one blocked

5. Nick Harris, California

E. Punted 36 times—in one game!

6. Tony DeLeone, Kent State

F. Had 7 punts in one game that went for more than 50 yards each

7. Ryan Plackemeier, Wake Forest

G. Punted 322 times in his career

It isn't just the offense that contributes amazing performances. Here's one game of amazing interception performances.

1. Dick Miller, Akron

A. Returned three interceptions for touchdowns in one game

2. Ashley Lee, Virginia Tech

B. Returned four interceptions for touchdowns in one season

3. Al Brosky, Illinois

C. Intercepted 6 passes in one game

4. Johnny Jackson, Houston

D. Intercepted 14 passes in one season

5. Deltha O'Neal, California

E. Had 302 interception return yards in one season

6. Al Worley, Washington

F. Intercepted at least one pass in 15 straight games

7. Charles Phillips, USC

G. Had 182 interception return yards in one game

251

Now for amazing punt return performances.

1. Vai Sikahema, BYU

A. Averaged 23.6 yards per punt return for his career (922 yards on 39 returns)

2. Wes Welker, Texas Tech

B. Returned 153 punts in his career

3. Antonio Perkins, Oklahoma

C. Returned 20 punts in one game

4. Chad Owens, Hawaii

D. Returned 57 punts in one season

5. David Allen, Kansas State

E. Returned a punt for a touchdown in three consecutive games

6. Milton Hill, Texas Tech

F. Had 277 punt return yards in one game

7. Jack Mitchell, Oklahoma

G. Returned 5 punts for touchdowns in one season

Amazing kickoff return performances.

1. Trevor Cobb, Rice   A. Had 11 kickoff returns in one game

2. Justin Miller, Clemson   B. Had 55 kickoff returns in one season

3. Ashlan Davis, Tulsa   C. Scored touchdowns on season-opening kickoffs in two consecutive seasons

4. William White, Army   D. Returned 5 kickoffs for touchdowns in one season

5. Raghib Ismail, Notre Dame   E. Had 123 kickoff returns in his career

6. Jeff Liggon, Tulane   F. Had 282 kickoff return yards in one game

7. Barry Sanders, Oklahoma State   G. Only collegian to *twice* score two touchdowns on kickoff returns in one game

One game of amazing kick blocking performances.

1. Ken Irvin, Memphis   A. Blocked 5 extra points in one season

2. James King, Central Michigan   B. First of only two players ever to block four punts in one game

3. Lonnell Dewalt, Kentucky   C. Blocked 6 field goals in one season

4. Joe Wessel, Florida State   D. Blocked 19 kicks in his career (5 punts, 8 field goals, and 6 PATs)

5. James Ferebee, New Mexico State   E. Scored 2 touchdowns in one game on blocked punts

6. Ray Farmer, Duke   F. Blocked 7 punts in one season

7. David Langner, Auburn   G. Scored 3 touchdowns in one season on blocked punts

Now for some amazing scoring performances.

1. Howard Griffith, Illinois   A. Only freshman to score 7 touchdowns in one game

2. Kelvin Bryant, North Carolina   B. Scored at least one touchdown in 27 consecutive games during his career

3. Travis Prentice, Miami (Ohio)   C. Most points scored in one game—48 (8 touchdowns)

4. Marshall Faulk, San Diego State   D. Most points scored in a career—468 (78 touchdowns)

5. Barry Sanders, Oklahoma State   E. Scored at least one touchdown in 37 games of his career

6. Cedric Benson, Texas   F. Most points scored in a season—234 (39 touchdowns)

7. Lee Suggs, Virginia Tech   G. Scored 15 touchdowns over a 3-consecutive game span

More amazing scoring performances.

1. John Becksvoort, Tennessee

A. Made all 161 extra points he attempted in his career for a perfect 100%

2. Terry Leiweke, Houston

B. Scored 141 kicking points in one season (24 field goals and 69 extra points)

3. Mario Danelo, USC

C. Attempted 14 extra points in one game

4. Mike Prindle, Western Michigan

D. Scored 423 kicking points in his career (70 field goals and 213 extra points)

5. Tyler Jones, Boise State

E. Made 83 extra points in one season

6. Roman Anderson, Houston

F. Threw 12 two-point conversion passes in one season (attempted 21)

7. John Hangartner, Arizona State

G. Scored 24 kicking points in one game (7 field goals and 3 extra points)

And now one game of amazing defensive performances.

1. Tyrone Carter, Minnesota

A. Forced 10 fumbles in one season

2. Paul Rivers, Rutgers

B. Returned 2 fumbles for touchdowns in one game

3. Paul McClendon, Texas Tech

C. Returned a fumble 100 yards for a touchdown

4. Terrell Suggs, Arizona State

D. Returned both a fumble and interception for touchdowns in the same game

5. Elvis Dumervil, Louisville

E. Had 23 solo sacks in one season

6. Tyrell Johnson, Arkansas State

F. Had 360 solo tackles in his career

7. Rod Davis, Southern Mississippi

G. Had 20 solo tackles in one game

Now for the little men of the gridiron. Let's see how well you know some of the amazing field goal performances in college history.

1. Mike Prindle, Western Michigan

A. Made 110 field goals in his career

2. Marc Primanti, North Carolina St.

B. Made 4 field goals in one quarter

3. Billy Bennett, Georgia

C. Was a perfect 7-for-7 on field goal kicks in one game

4. Jose Cortez, Oregon State

D. Made 30 consecutive field goals over two seasons

5. Dale Klein, Nebraska

E. Was a perfect 20-for-20 on field goal kicks one season

6. Jerry DePoyster, Wyoming

F. Attempted 38 field goals in one season

7. Chuck Nelson, Washington

G. Attempted 9 field goals in one game

More field goal performances.

1. Gary Gussman, Miami (Ohio)

   A. Kicked eight 50+ yard field goals in one season

2. Billy Bennett, Georgia

   B. Kicked twenty 50+ yard field goals in his career

3. Tony Franklin, Texas A & M

   C. Only kicker ever to kick two field goals in the same game longer than 60 yards (65 and 64)

4. Russell Erxleben, Texas

   D. Kicked at least one field goal in 40 different games during his career (played 44 games)

5. Jason Hanson, Washington State

   E. Won 6 games for his team in one season when his field goals provided the margin of victory

6. Henrik Mike-Mayer, Drake

   F. Kicked three 60+ yard field goals in one season

7. Fuad Reveiz, Tennessee

   G. Kicked at least one field goal in 24 consecutive games

CHAPTER 12

AMAZING COLLEGE TEAM PERFORMANCES

Unlike most NFL teams which typically play a more controlled, methodical offensive game, college teams have been known to occasionally play almost without restraint. It's that college spirit thing, I guess. In any event, some college teams have put up some extraordinary numbers compared to their NFL counterparts. In the first four games of this chapter, try your hand at correctly matching up some of the most amazing team performances ever with the schools that accomplished them.

259

1. Montana

2. Nevada

3. Houston

4. North Carolina State

5. Texas Tech

6. Wyoming

7. Syracuse

A. Ran 112 offensive plays in one game

B. Gained just 10 total yards in a game—and won!

C. Finished a game with *minus* 47 total yards!

D. Gained 791 yards in a game—and lost!

E. Gained 1,021 total yards in one game

F. Scored 15 touchdowns in a non-overtime game

G. Ran just 12 offensive plays in one game

1. Arkansas

2. Navy

3. Missouri

4. Houston

5. Oklahoma

6. Northern Illinois

7. Air Force

A. Had only 5 rushing attempts in one game

B. Scored 16 touchdowns in an overtime game

C. Rushed for 768 yards in one game

D. Once had a 94-yard drive that took 26 plays, using 14:26 in elapsed time

E. Once finished a game with *minus* 109 yards rushing

F. Had 99 rushing attempts in one game

G. Had 545 yards rushing in a game—and lost

1. UTEP

2. West Virginia

3. Ohio

4. North Carolina State

5. Wake Forest

6. Iowa

7. California

A. Completed 55 passes in one game

B. Played a game in 1997 in which they didn't attempt even one pass

C. Had 12 rushing touchdowns in one game

D. Most recent of only two teams ever to have 10 passes intercepted in one game (Ugh!)

E. Had 32 consecutive passing attempts in a game without a rushing attempt

F. Attempted 18 passes in a game without making even one completion

G. Had the best perfect passing game in college history (12-for-12) in a 2002 game

1. Houston

A. Scored 7 two-point conversions in one game

2. Texas Tech

B. Scored 63 points in a regulation game—and lost

3. Texas A & M

C. Returned three punts for touchdowns in one game

4. Notre Dame

D. Scored 76 points in one half

5. Wyoming

E. Had 319 punt return yards in one game

6. Rice

F. Scored 103 points in one game

7. Pacific

G. Returned 22 punts in one game

Now for a mixed bag of college football trivia.

1. Florida State

A. Had the highest winning percentage (.877) in the 1970s (on a record of 102–13–3)

2. Kent State

B. Won more games in the 1980s than any other major college team—103

3. Nebraska

C. Won more games in the 1970s than any other major college team—103

4. Temple

D. Won more games in the 1990s than any other major college team—114

5. Marshall

E. Had the highest winning percentage (.890) in the 1990s (on a record of 109–13–1)

6. Oklahoma

F. Won the second fewest games in the 1990s of all major college teams—22

7. Alabama

G. Won fewer games in the 1990s than any other major college team—15

This game is based on final Associated Press polls.

1. Oklahoma	A. Last school to win back-to-back national titles
2. Minnesota	B. Won only two national titles, and they were both in the 1990s
3. Army	C. Has won the most national championships (8)
4. Florida State	D. Won only two national titles, and they were both in the 1980s
5. Southern California	E. First school to win back-to-back national titles
6. Notre Dame	F. Has won the second most national championships (7)
7. Penn State	G. Won only two national titles, and they were in back-to-back seasons

Another game based on the Associated Press final polls.

1. Nebraska	A. Their only two national titles were separated by 47 years
2. Alabama	B. Won six national titles, including back-to-back years twice
3. Miami (Florida)	C. Their last national title was in 1976
4. Tennessee	D. Won four national titles, and they were in back-to-back years twice
5. Ohio State	E. Their only two national titles were separated by 49 years

6. Michigan

F. Three of their five national titles were in the 1980s

7. Pittsburgh

G. Only college ever to win a national title in the 1940s, 1950s, and 1960s

Now a game based on the Associated Press weekly polls.

1. Florida State

A. The 1981 season saw more different teams (7) ranked #1 during the season than any other year of the 1980s, and this team was the last

2. Alabama

B. During the 1993 season, this was the only team besides Florida State to be ranked #1 in a weekly poll

3. Notre Dame

C. During the 1990s, this was the only school to lead the AP rankings every week of one season

4. Miami (Florida)

D. During the 1985 season, this team was ranked #1 only twice, in the preseason poll and the final poll, the only time in the poll's 70+year history the oddity's occurred

5. Colorado

E. During the 1989 season, this school was ranked #1 only once—the final week

6. Clemson

F. The 1990 season saw more different teams (5) ranked #1 during the season than any other year of the 1990s, and this team was the last

7. Oklahoma

G. During the 1992 season, this school was ranked #1 only once—the final week

Another game based on the Associated Press weekly polls.

1. Nebraska

2. Southern California

3. Pittsburgh

4. Notre Dame

5. Oklahoma

6. Texas

7. Ohio State

A. #1 every week of the 2005 season except the last

B. #1 every week of the 1983 season except the last

C. Spent more weeks ranked #1 in the 1960s than any other team—23

D. Spent more weeks ranked #1 in the 1970s than any other team—31

E. Spent more weeks ranked #1 in the 1940s than any other team—30

F. Spent more weeks ranked #1 in the 1950s than any other team—24

G. Spent more weeks ranked #1 in the 1930s than any other team—8

Still another game based on the AP polls (since 1936 and through the 2006 season).

1. Notre Dame

2. Mississippi

3. Michigan

4. Texas

A. Holds the record for the most consecutive weeks spent at #1—33

B. The first team to be ranked #1 in the preseason poll but not be ranked #1 during the rest of the season (1964)

C. School which took the biggest jump to #1 from the previous week—8th to 1st from Sept. 30 to Oct. 7, 1952

D. 2nd most weeks ranked #1 all-time—86

5. Wisconsin

E. Most weeks ranked #1 all-time—89

6. Oklahoma

F. School with the longest active streak of consecutive weeks ranked in the AP poll—109 through 2006

7. Southern California

G. Team that has appeared in the most weekly AP polls all-time—741

269

See if you can match these poll-related events to their correct year of occurrence.

1. 1943

A. The most recent of only two years in history in which four different teams were ranked #1 on four consecutive weeks in the AP poll (the teams were: Ohio State, Oklahoma, Auburn, and Army)

2. 1971

B. The first of only two years in history that USC was ranked #1 every week of the season

3. 1958

C. The year there were seven different teams ranked #1 at some point in the season, the most ever (the teams were: Michigan, Notre Dame, USC, Texas, Penn State, Pittsburgh, and Clemson)

4. 1981

D. The only year in history in which Notre Dame was ranked #1 every week of the season

5. 1942

E. The only year in history in which Nebraska was ranked #1 every week of the season

6. 1945

F. The year unranked Holy Cross beat the #1 team in the country by 43 points, the largest margin of victory ever against a #1 team

7. 1972

G. The only year in history in which Army was ranked #1 every week of the season

Another mixed bag of interesting trivia.

1. Notre Dame

2. Penn State

3. Texas

4. Oklahoma

5. Iowa

6. Stanford

7. Michigan State

A. Holds the record for largest margin of victory by a *ranked* team over a #1—34 points (they were ranked #11 when they defeated #1 Pittsburgh, 48–14, in 1981)

B. This was the #1 ranked team who beat #2 Michigan, 12–10, in a classic 1985 contest

C. The unranked team with a 4–4 record who knocked off #1 Ohio State, 28–24, in 1998

D. Of the first 15 match-ups of #1 vs. #2 in college history, the #1s won 14, with this team being the only #2 in that stretch to win (they beat #1 Oklahoma 28–7 in 1963)

E. This team was ranked #1 in the AP preseason poll in 1985, 1986, and 1987, the only team in history to be a preseason #1 three straight years

F. The team with a 1–3 record who knocked off #1 Notre Dame, 36–31, in 1990

G. Has defeated the most #1 ranked teams in history—8

271

1. Washington

2. Yale

A. Team that ended college football's 2ⁿᵈ longest winning streak at 39 games, tying them at 0–0

B. Team that ended both 37-game winning streaks by the answer to Clue E

3. Notre Dame   C. Holds the NCAA record for most consecutive wins—47

4. Princeton   D. Won 39 games in a row, 2nd best all-time

5. Toledo   E. Team that has had two 37-game winning streaks, the 3rd and 4th longest winning streaks of all time

6. Oklahoma   F. Team that ended college football's record 47-game winning streak, defeating the record holder 7–0

7. Oregon State   G. Won 35 games in a row from 1969–1971, the 5th longest winning streak in college history

This game concerns match-ups of undefeated, untied teams that met in the last game of the season (since 1937 only).

1. 1938   A. The year Dartmouth beat Princeton, 28–14, in the season finale after both were 8–0 up to that game

2. 1940   B. The season Oklahoma (10–0 with eight shutouts) met Tennessee (10–0 with seven shutouts) in the Orange Bowl, won 17–0 by Tennessee

3. 1973   C. The season 12–0 Florida was drubbed by 11–0 Nebraska in the Fiesta Bowl, 62–24

4. 1965   D. The year Harvard and Yale played to a 29–29 tie in the season finale after both went 8–0 up to that game

5. 1995   E. The only season ever in which two perfect teams met in the season finale and needed two overtimes to settle the matter [Ohio State defeated Miami (Fla.), 31–24]

6. 2002

F. The season Boston College (10–0) met Tennessee (10–0) in the Sugar Bowl, won by Boston College, 19–13, the only time two perfect teams met in the 1940s in a season finale

7. 1968

G. The last year two teams with perfect records met in the regular season finale and played to a tie (Ohio State and Michigan, 10–10)

Another mixed bag of fun facts.

1. Maryland

A. This school holds the NCAA record for the longest unbeaten streak—63 (59 wins, 4 ties)

2. Pittsburgh

B. This perennial powerhouse had its 31-game winning streak snapped by the unlikely opponent Cleveland Naval Reserve, 10–9

3. Penn State

C. This school holds the NCAA record for the longest string of games without being held scoreless—361

4. Washington

D. This school holds the NCAA record for the longest home winning streak—58 games

5. Miami (Fla.)

E. This school holds the NCAA record for the most consecutive non-losing seasons—49

6. Northwestern

F. This school holds the NCAA record for the longest losing streak—34 games

7. Brigham Young

G. From the 1941 season through the 1964 season, there were only two season finales that pitted undefeated, untied teams, and this team played in both games

Now a game concerning two particular opponents (through the 2006 season).

1. Minnesota-Wisconsin

A. The two schools that have played each other the most consecutive times without missing a season—101

2. Notre Dame-Navy

B. The rivalry that saw one of the teams win 32 straight times from 1937–1968

3. Nebraska-Kansas

C. The two schools that have played each other the most times—116

4. Clemson-Virginia

D. The rivalry that has seen one of the teams win the last 43 straight times they've met

5. Oklahoma-Kansas State

E. The two schools that have played each other the 2nd most times—115

6. Kansas-Missouri

F. The rivalry that has seen one of the teams compile an incredible 83–16–2 record all time against the other

7. Iowa State-Nebraska

G. The rivalry that saw one of the teams win 29 straight times between 1955–1990 (they didn't play every year)

Another mixed bag of truly amazing and oddball trivia (through the 2006 season).

1. Missouri

A. Played seven games decided by three points or less in 1980

2. North Texas

B. Defeated Minnesota, 35–29, in a 1990 game when they scored on a 91-yard return of a blocked field goal on the last play of the game

3. Kansas

C. Since overtime play became mandatory in 1996, this school has played the most overtime games—11

4. Bowling Green

D. Defeated Western Michigan, 60–57, in a 2005 game that took five overtimes to play

5. UNLV

E. Played six games decided by two points or less in 1973

6. Utah

F. The last major college team to play in an overtime game once it became mandatory in 1996 (Oct. 7, 2006)

7. Ball State

G. Defeated Baylor, 27–24, in a 1999 game when they scored on a 100-yard fumble return on the last play of the game

More oddball trivia for the truly insatiable fanatic.

1. 1958

A. Year there were 28 tie games played, the most ever

2. 1991

B. Year that all college home teams compiled a .640 winning percentage, highest ever (387–215–13)

3. 1987

C. Year Nebraska suffered its first losing season in 43 years

4. 1999

D. Year Alabama's 57-game home winning streak ended

5. 1988

E. Year that San Diego State and BYU played to a 52–52 tie, the highest scoring tie game in college history

6. 2004

F. Year Hawaii set the NCAA record for best improvement from one year to the next (0–12 one year, 9–4 the next)

7. 1982   G. Year Penn State suffered its first losing
                                         season in 50 years

277

Still more oddball facts to beat your head against a wall with.

1. Rutgers   A. Has lost more college football games than
                          any 1-A school in history—605 through 2006

2. Michigan   B. Has won more college football games than
                          any 1-A school in history—860 through 2006

3. Northwestern   C. Winner of the first overtime game in college
                          history, played in 1981

4. Kansas   D. Has played more college football games
                          than any 1-A school in history—1,202
                          games through 2006

5. Yale   E. Has had more consensus All-Americans
                          than any other 1-A school in history—95
                          through 2006

6. Notre Dame   F. Has had more consensus All-Americans
                          than any other school in history—100
                          through 2006

7. Weber State   G. Has played more tie games than any 1-A
                          school in history—58 through 2006

CHAPTER 13

AMAZING INDIVIDUAL NFL PERFORMANCES

There are a number of benchmarks that identify individual achievement in the NFL. In the first 26 games in this chapter, there is a differentiation between a franchise's various cities. For example, there will be separate answers for the Cleveland Rams, Los Angeles Rams, and St. Louis Rams, even though they all represent the same franchise. If a team changed its name but stayed in the same city, however, as in the case of the Arizona Cardinals who were previously the Phoenix Cardinals, no distinction is made. Also, AFL teams that eventually merged into the NFL are considered to be NFL teams for their entire team history.

In these first five games, see if you can match each team to the player (and his yards) who was the first ever to crack the 1,000-yard mark for that team.

1. Arizona Cardinals

2. Atlanta Falcons

3. Baltimore Colts

4. Baltimore Ravens

5. Boston Patriots

6. Buffalo Bills

A. Beattie Feathers (1,004)

B. Anthony Johnson (1,120)

C. Jim Nance (1,458)

D. Ron Moore (1,018)

E. Dave Hampton (1,002)

F. Lydell Mitchell (1,193)

7. Carolina Panthers

G. Cookie Gilchrist (1,096)

8. Chicago Bears

H. Jamal Lewis (1,364)

1. Chicago Cardinals

A. Steve Owens (1,035)

2. Cincinnati Bengals

B. Floyd Little (1,133)

3. Cleveland Browns

C. No 1,000-yard rushers in their 8-year history

4. Cleveland Rams

D. Paul Robinson (1,023)

5. Dallas Cowboys

E. No 1,000-yard rushers in their 40-year history

6. Denver Broncos

F. Marshall Faulk (1,381)

7. Detroit Lions

G. Calvin Hill (1,036)

8. St. Louis Rams

H. Jim Brown (1,527)

1. Green Bay Packers

A. Charlie Tolar (1,012)

2. Houston Oilers

B. Domanick Davis (1,031)

3. Houston Texans

C. Mike Garrett (1,087)

4. Indianapolis Colts

D. Marcus Allen (1,014)

5. Jacksonville Jaguars

E. Dick Bass (1,033)

6. Kansas City Chiefs

F. Eric Dickerson (1,011)

7. Los Angeles Raiders

G. Fred Taylor (1,223)

8. Los Angeles Rams

H. Tony Canadeo (1,052)

1. Miami Dolphins	A. John Riggins (1,005)
2. Minnesota Vikings	B. Chuck Foreman (1,070)
3. New England Patriots	C. Ron Johnson (1,027)
4. New Orleans Saints	D. Steve Van Buren (1,008)
5. New York Giants	E. Sam Cunningham (1,015)
6. New York Jets	F. Clem Daniels (1,099)
7. Oakland Raiders	G. Chuck Muncie (1,198)
8. Philadelphia Eagles	H. Larry Csonka (1,051)

1. Pittsburgh Steelers	A. Curt Warner (1,449)
2. San Diego Chargers	B. Larry Brown (1,125)
3. San Francisco 49ers	C. Ricky Bell (1,263)
4. Seattle Seahawks	D. John Henry Johnson (1,141)
5. St. Louis Cardinals	E. Joe Perry (1,018)
6. Tampa Bay Buccaneers	F. Paul Lowe (1,010)
7. Tennessee Titans	G. Eddie George (1,294)
8. Washington Redskins	H. John David Crow (1,071)

Another benchmark performance is 200 yards rushing in one game. Can you connect each team to the first back to attain the coveted mark for them in these next five games?

1. Arizona Cardinals

2. Atlanta Falcons

3. Baltimore Colts

4. Baltimore Ravens

5. Boston Patriots

6. Buffalo Bills

7. Carolina Panthers

8. Chicago Bears

A. Jim Nance (208 yards on 38 carries)

B. Gale Sayers (205 yards on 24 carries)

C. No 200-yard rushers through the 2006 season

D. Cookie Gilchrist (243 yards on 36 carries)

E. No 200-yard rushers in their 31-year history

F. Gerald Riggs (202 yards on 35 carries)

G. LeShon Johnson (214 yards on 21 carries)

H. Priest Holmes (227 yards on 36 carries)

1. Chicago Cardinals

2. Cincinnati Bengals

3. Cleveland Browns

4. Cleveland Rams

A. Terrell Davis (215 yards on 27 carries)

B. Marshall Faulk (208 yards on 25 carries)

C. Barry Sanders (220 yards on 23 carries)

D. No 200-yard rushers in their 40-year history

5. Dallas Cowboys

E. James Brooks (201 yards on 20 carries)

6. Denver Broncos

F. No 200-yard rushers in their 8-year history

7. Detroit Lions

G. Jim Brown (237 yards on 31 carries)

8. St. Louis Rams

H. Tony Dorsett (206 yards on 23 carries)

1. Green Bay Packers

A. Bo Jackson (221 yards on 18 carries)

2. Houston Oilers

B. Barry Word (200 yards on 18 carries)

3. Houston Texans

C. Ahman Green (218 yards on 20 carries)

4. Indianapolis Colts

D. Fred Taylor (234 yards on 30 carries)

5. Jacksonville Jaguars

E. Billy Cannon (216 yards on 25 carries)

6. Kansas City Chiefs

F. Dan Towler (205 yards on 14 carries)

7. Los Angeles Raiders

G. No 200-yard rushers through 2006 season

8. Los Angeles Rams

H. Edgerrin James (219 yards on 38 carries)

1. Miami Dolphins

A. Clem Daniels (200 yards on 27 carries)

2. Minnesota Vikings

B. Steve Van Buren (205 yards on 27 carries)

3. New England Patriots

C. Curtis Martin (203 yards on 30 carries)

4. New Orleans Saints

D. Chuck Foreman (200 yards on 28 carries)

5. New York Giants

E. Ricky Williams (228 yards on 27 carries)

6. New York Jets

F. Gene Roberts (218 yards on 26 carries)

7. Oakland Raiders

G. George Rogers (206 yards on 24 carries)

8. Philadelphia Eagles

H. Tony Collins (212 yards on 23 carries)

1. Pittsburgh Steelers

A. John David Crow (203 yards on 24 carries)

2. San Diego Chargers

B. Eddie George (216 yards on 35 carries)

3. San Francisco 49ers

C. John Henry Johnson (200 yards on 30 carries)

4. Seattle Seahawks

D. James Wilder (219 yards on 31 carries)

5. St. Louis Cardinals

E. George Rogers (206 yards on 34 carries)

6. Tampa Bay Buccaneers

F. Gary Anderson (217 yards on 34 carries)

7. Tennessee Titans

G. Charlie Garner (201 yards on 36 carries)

8. Washington Redskins

H. Curt Warner (207 yards on 32 carries)

A benchmark figure for quarterbacks is 400 yards passing in one game, and it only happens a handful of times a season. See if you can correctly identify the quarterbacks who were the first to reach this mark for each team in these next five games.

(Note: Two teams in this game have never had a quarterback throw for 400 yards in a game through the 2006 season, and therefore have "A" as their answer.)

1. Arizona Cardinals

2. Atlanta Falcons

3. Baltimore Colts

4. Baltimore Ravens

5. Boston Patriots

6. Buffalo Bills

7. Carolina Panthers

8. Chicago Bears

A. No 400-yard passers in their team's history

B. Johnny Unitas (401 yards on 22 completions)

C. Sid Luckman (433 yards on 21 completions)

D. Joe Ferguson (419 yards on 38 completions)

E. Steve Bartkowski (416 yards on 33 completions)

F. Babe Parilli (422 yards on 25 completions)

G. Steve Beuerlein (431 yards on 34 completions)

(Note: Two teams in this game have never had a quarterback throw for 400 yards in a game through the 2006 season, and therefore have "A" as their answer.)

1. Chicago Cardinals

2. Cincinnati Bengals

3. Cleveland Browns

4. Cleveland Rams

5. Dallas Cowboys

6. Denver Broncos

7. Detroit Lions

8. St. Louis Rams

A. No 400-yard passers in their team's history

B. Otto Graham (401 yards on 21 completions)

C. Scott Mitchell (410 yards on 30 completions)

D. Ken Anderson (447 yards on 30 completions)

E. Frank Tripucka (447 yards on 29 completions)

F. Don Meredith (460 yards on 30 completions)

G. Tony Banks (401 yards on 23 completions)

1. Green Bay Packers

2. Houston Oilers

3. Houston Texans

4. Indianapolis Colts

A. No 400-yard passers in their team's history

B. Peyton Manning (404 yards on 29 completions)

C. Jeff Hostetler (424 yards on 20 completions)

D. Don Horn (410 yards on 22 completions)

5. Jacksonville Jaguars

E. Jim Hardy (406 yards on 28 completions)

6. Kansas City Chiefs

F. Jacky Lee (457 yards on 27 completions)

7. Los Angeles Raiders

G. Mark Brunell (432 yards on 23 completions)

8. Los Angeles Rams

H. Len Dawson (435 yards on 23 completions)

1. Miami Dolphins

A. Joe Namath (415 yards on 23 completions)

2. Minnesota Vikings

B. Fran Tarkenton (407 yards on 21 completions)

3. New England Patriots

C. Tom Flores (407 yards on 17 completions)

4. New Orleans Saints

D. Y.A. Tittle (505 yards on 27 completions)

5. New York Giants

E. David Woodley (408 yards on 21 completions)

6. New York Jets

F. Bobby Thomason (437 yards on 22 completions)

7. Oakland Raiders

G. Aaron Brooks (441 yards on 30 completions)

8. Philadelphia Eagles

H. Tony Eason (414 yards on 26 completions)

1. Pittsburgh Steelers

2. San Diego Chargers

3. San Francisco 49ers

4. Seattle Seahawks

5. St. Louis Cardinals

6. Tampa Bay Buccaneers

7. Tennessee Titans

8. Washington Redskins

A. Charley Johnson (428 yards on 20 completions)

B. Sammy Baugh (446 yards on 17 completions)

C. Doug Williams (486 yards on 30 completions)

D. Steve McNair (421 yards on 18 completions)

E. Joe Montana (408 yards on 26 completions)

F. Dave Krieg (418 yards on 31 completions)

G. Dan Fouts (444 yards on 26 completions)

H. Bobby Layne (409 yards on 23 completions)

Another benchmark figure for quarterbacks is 4,000 yards passing in a season. In the next three games, see if you can match the quarterbacks who were the first to reach this mark for each team, only about two-thirds of which have ever had a 4,000-yard passer.

1. St. Louis Rams

2. Carolina Panthers

3. Cleveland Browns

A. Scott Mitchell (4,338)

B. Kurt Warner (4,353)

C. John Elway (4,030)

4. Baltimore Ravens D. Drew Bledsoe (4,359)

5. Buffalo Bills E. Steve Beuerlein (4,436)

6. Denver Broncos F. Brian Sipe (4,132)

7. Detroit Lions G. Vinny Testaverde (4,177)

8. New Orleans Saints H. Drew Brees (4,418)

1. Green Bay Packers A. Jim Everett (4,310)

2. Houston Oilers B. Lynn Dickey (4,458)

3. San Diego Chargers C. Bill Kenney (4,348)

4. Indianapolis Colts D. Mark Brunell (4,367)

5. Jacksonville Jaguars E. Steve Young (4,023)

6. Kansas City Chiefs F. Warren Moon (4,689)

7. San Francisco 49ers G. Peyton Manning (4,135)

8. Los Angeles Rams H. Dan Fouts (4,082)

1. Miami Dolphins A. Joe Namath (4,007)

2. Minnesota Vikings B. Warren Moon (4,264)

3. New England Patriots C. Jay Schroeder (4,109)

4. St. Louis Cardinals D. Phil Simms (4,044)

5. New York Giants E. Dan Marino (5,084)

6. New York Jets F. Rich Gannon (4,689)

7. Cincinnati Bengals   G. Neil Lomax (4,614)

8. Washington Redskins   H. Drew Bledsoe (4,086)

9. Oakland Raiders   I. Carson Palmer (4,035)

One benchmark figure for receivers is 1,000 yards receiving in a season. In these next five games, see if you can match the receivers who were the first to reach this mark for each team.

1. Arizona Cardinals   A. Harlon Hill (1,124)

2. Atlanta Falcons   B. Rob Moore (1,016)

3. Baltimore Colts   C. Derrick Alexander (1,099)

4. Baltimore Ravens   D. Raghib Ismail (1,024)

5. Boston Patriots   E. Wallace Francis (1,013)

6. Buffalo Bills   F. No 1,000-yard receivers in their history

7. Carolina Panthers   G. Raymond Berry (1,298)

8. Chicago Bears   H. Elbert Dubenion (1,139)

1. Chicago Cardinals   A. Frank Clarke (1,043)

2. Cincinnati Bengals   B. Paul Warfield (1,067)

3. Cleveland Browns   C. Isaac Bruce (1,781)

4. Cleveland Rams   D. Bob Mann (1,014)

5. Dallas Cowboys   E. Cris Collinsworth (1,009)

6. Denver Broncos   F. Lionel Taylor (1,235)

7. Detroit Lions   G. Jim Benton (1,067)

8. St. Louis Rams   H. No 1,000-yard receivers in their history

1. Green Bay Packers   A. Otis Taylor (1,297)

2. Houston Oilers   B. Todd Christensen (1,247)

3. Houston Texans   C. Bill Groman (1,473)

4. Indianapolis Colts   D. Andre Johnson (1,142)

5. Jacksonville Jaguars   E. Tom Fears (1,013)

6. Kansas City Chiefs   F. Don Hutson (1,211)

7. Los Angeles Raiders   G. Keenan McCardell (1,129)

8. Los Angeles Rams   H. Bill Brooks (1,131)

1. Miami Dolphins   A. John Gilliam (1,035)

2. Minnesota Vikings   B. Del Shofner (1,125)

3. New England Patriots   C. Art Powell (1,304)

4. New Orleans Saints   D. Pete Pihos (1,049)

5. New York Giants   E. Stanley Morgan (1,002)

6. New York Jets   F. Dan Abramowicz (1,015)

7. Oakland Raiders   G. Mark Duper (1,003)

8. Philadelphia Eagles   H. Art Powell (1,167)

1. Pittsburgh Steelers	A. Dave Kocourek (1,055)
2. San Diego Chargers	B. Buddy Dial (1,047)
3. San Francisco 49ers	C. Kevin House (1,176)
4. Seattle Seahawks	D. Sonny Randle (1,158)
5. St. Louis Cardinals	E. Steve Largent (1,168)
6. Tampa Bay Buccaneers	F. Bobby Mitchell (1,384)
7. Tennessee Titans	G. R.C. Owens (1,032)
8. Washington Redskins	H. Derrick Mason (1,128)

An even more rare occurrence for receivers is to catch 100 passes in a season. See if you can match up each of these elite receivers who were the first to accomplish the feat for each of these teams in the next three games.

1. Denver Broncos	A. Jerry Rice (100)
2. Houston Oilers	B. Cris Carter (122)
3. Washington Redskins	C. Charley Hennigan (101)
4. San Francisco 49ers	D. Art Monk (106)
5. Green Bay Packers	E. Terance Mathis (111)
6. Atlanta Falcons	F. Lionel Taylor (100)
7. Minnesota Vikings	G. Sterling Sharpe (108)
8. San Diego Chargers	H. LaDainian Tomlinson (100)

1. Arizona Cardinals

2. Detroit Lions

3. Dallas Cowboys

4. St. Louis Rams

5. Cincinnati Bengals

6. Oakland Raiders

7. Indianapolis Colts

8. Kansas City Chiefs

A. Tony Gonzalez (102)

B. Carl Pickens (100)

C. Marvin Harrison (115)

D. Larry Centers (101)

E. Michael Irvin (111)

F. Isaac Bruce (119)

G. Tim Brown (104)

H. Brett Perriman (108) and Herman Moore (123)

1. Jacksonville Jaguars

2. Carolina Panthers

3. Chicago Bears

4. New England Patriots

5. Tampa Bay Buccaneers

6. Buffalo Bills

7. Pittsburgh Steelers

A. Troy Brown (101)

B. Jimmy Smith (116)

C. Eric Moulds (100)

D. Marty Booker (100)

E. Hines Ward (112)

F. Keyshawn Johnson (106)

G. Muhsin Muhammad (102)

An even more rare feat for receivers is to accumulate 250 yards pass receiving in one game, something that only happens about once every five years or so. See if you can match up these receivers and their extraordinary games.

1. Jim Benton   A. Holds the NFL record for the most receiving yards in a non-overtime game—309

2. Qadry Ismail   B. Only receiver during the 1970s to have a 250-yard game

3. Terrell Owens   C. Of all 250-yard receivers, he needed the most receptions to accomplish the feat—20

4. Willie Anderson   D. One of only two 250-yard receivers to score 4 TDs in his big game, he is the only one to crack 300 yards

5. Cloyce Box   E. First receiver ever to break the 250-yard mark, he also was the first to break 300 yards in a game

6. Stephone Paige   F. Of all 250-yard receivers, he accomplished the feat with the fewest number of passes—6

7. Jerry Butler   G. Still holds the NFL record for most pass receiving yards in one game—336

Now try your hand at these six games of amazing individual quarterback performances.

1. Sammy Baugh   A. Had 418 pass completions in one season

2. Steve Young   B. Led the NFL in passing four consecutive seasons

3. Peyton Manning   C. Had a 98.1 passer rating as a rookie

4. Ben Roethlisberger   D. Led the NFL in pass attempts five times

5. Dan Marino   E. Led the NFL in passing six times

6. Drew Bledsoe   F. Had a 121.1 passer rating for one season

7. Rich Gannon   G. One of only three quarterbacks to lead the
                            league in pass attempts three consecutive
                            seasons (Johnny Unitas and George Blanda
                            are the other two)

1. Steve Young   A. Attempted 575 passes as a rookie

2. Peyton Manning   B. Had a 96.8 career passer rating, highest ever
                            through the 2006 season

3. Drew Bledsoe   C. Attempted 69 passes in one regulation game

4. Vinny Testaverde   D. Had 24 consecutive pass completions

5. Brett Favre   E. Only quarterback to lead the NFL in pass
                            completion percentage eight times

6. Donovan McNabb   F. Only quarterback in NFL history to have
                            more than 5,000 pass completions

7. Len Dawson   G. Attempted 691 passes in one season

1. Ken Anderson   A. Led the NFL in passing yardage five times

2. Kurt Warner   B. Last quarterback to pass for 400+ yards in
                            two consecutive games

3. Sonny Jurgensen   C. Only NFL quarterback with 15 3,000-yard
                            seasons

4. Dan Fouts

D. Had a 70.55 pass completion percentage for a season

5. Peyton Manning

E. Led the NFL in passing yardage four consecutive years

6. Brett Favre

F. Passed for over 3,700 yards as a rookie

7. Billy Volek

G. NFL's career pass completion leader at over 65%

1. Dan Marino

A. Had a 99-yard TD pass

2. Norm Van Brocklin

B. Had 13 games of 400+ passing yards in his career

3. Rich Gannon

C. Passed for 554 yards in one game

4. Steve Young

D. Holds NFL record for highest average gain per pass attempt for a career—8.63 yards

5. Joe Montana

E. Had 10 games of 300+ passing yards in one season

6. Sonny Jurgensen

F. First quarterback in history to have six consecutive games of 300+ passing yards

7. Otto Graham

G. First quarterback in history to have five consecutive games of 300+ passing yards

1. Johnny Unitas

A. Last quarterback to throw for seven TDs in one game

2. Peyton Manning

B. Had 308 consecutive pass attempts without an interception

3. Dan Marino

C. Only quarterback to lead the NFL in TDs four consecutive years

4. Joe Kapp

D. Threw 49 TD passes in one season

5. Bernie Kosar

E. Only quarterback to be sacked more than 500 times in his career (516)

6. Jim Hardy

F. First quarterback to reach 400 career TD passes

7. John Elway

G. Only NFL quarterback to suffer eight interceptions in one game

1. Charlie Batch

A. Threw 70 passes in one game without an interception

2. Joe Ferguson

B. Lowest percentage of passes had intercepted in a career—2.11 (3,229 passes attempted, just 68 interceptions)

3. Bert Jones

C. Lowest percentage of passes had intercepted in a season—0.66 (151 passes, just one interception)

4. David Carr

D. Was sacked 76 times in one season

5. Warren Moon

E. Lowest percentage of passes had intercepted as a rookie—1.98 (303 passes, just six interceptions)

6. Neil O'Donnell

F. Most recent of only two quarterbacks to be sacked 12 times in one game

7. Drew Bledsoe

G. First quarterback to be sacked 12 times in one game

Now let's focus on four games of amazing individual running back performances.

1. Jim Brown	A. Last player to lead the NFL in rushing attempts four consecutive seasons
2. Emmitt Smith	B. Only player to lead the NFL in rushing eight times
3. Walter Payton	C. Second player ever to collect 15,000+ rushing yards
4. Jamal Anderson	D. Had 45 rushing attempts in one game
5. Eric Dickerson	E. Had 410 rushing attempts in one season
6. Jamie Morris	F. Last player to lead the NFL in rushing three consecutive seasons
7. Barry Sanders	G. Had 390 rushing attempts in his rookie season

1. Steve Van Buren	A. Only player with over 4,000 career rushing attempts (4,409)
2. Walter Payton	B. Rushed for 295 yards in one game
3. Curtis Martin	C. Rushed for an NFL-record 2,105 yards in one season
4. Barry Sanders	D. First player ever to lead the NFL in rushing attempts four consecutive seasons
5. Eric Dickerson	E. Only the second player ever to rush for 1,000+ yards in his first 10 seasons in the NFL

6. Jamal Lewis

F. First player ever to rush for 1,000+ yards in his first ten seasons in the NFL

7. Emmitt Smith

G. First player ever to collect 15,000+ rushing yards

1. Eric Dickerson

A. First player ever to rush for 275 yards in one game

2. O.J. Simpson

B. Rushed for 1,808 yards in his rookie season

3. Walter Payton

C. First of only two players to score a TD in 18 consecutive games

4. Marshall Faulk

D. Rushed for 28 TDs in one season

5. LaDainian Tomlinson

E. Had four games with 200+ rushing yards in one season

6. Lenny Moore

F. Only player with six games of 200+ yards rushing in his career

7. Earl Campbell

G. First of only two players ever to score four TDs in two consecutive games

1. Tony Dorsett

A. Only player in history with a 99-yard TD run

2. Emmitt Smith

B. First player ever to rush for a TD in 13 straight games

3. John Riggins

C. Scored 27 TDs in one season

4. Jim Brown

D. Had 14 consecutive games with at least 100 yards rushing

5. Priest Holmes

E. Scored 164 TDs in his career

6. Eric Dickerson   F. Scored five TDs in one game

7. Barry Sanders   G. Scored 18 TDs in his rookie season

The next three games deal with amazing individual receiving performances.

1. Don Hutson   A. Only player in history with more than 1,500 pass receptions (1,549)

2. Jerry Rice   B. Had 20 receptions in one game

3. Marvin Harrison   C. First rookie player to catch more than 100 passes in a season (101)

4. Anquan Boldin   D. Only player to lead the NFL in receiving for five consecutive seasons

5. Terrell Owens   E. Had 143 receptions in one season

6. Art Monk   F. 2nd on the career list in reception yards (14,934)

7. Tim Brown   G. First player to catch a pass in at least 183 consecutive games

1. Steve Largent   A. Only player to lead the NFL in receiving yards for four consecutive seasons

2. Bill Groman   B. Only player with three games of 200+ receiving yards in one season

3. Jerry Rice   C. First player with eight seasons of 1,000+ receiving yards

4. Don Hutson

D. Only player with five career games of 200+ yards receiving

5. Lance Alworth

E. Had 11 games of 100+ yards receiving in one season

6. Charley Hennigan

F. Had 1,848 receiving yards in one season

7. Michael Irvin

G. Had 1,473 receiving yards in his rookie season

1. Andy Farkas

A. Scored 17 receiving TDs in his rookie season

2. Bobby Moore

B. Scored 22 receiving TDs in one season, the most ever

3. Homer Jones

C. First receiver to score 5 TDs in one game

4. Randy Moss

D. Had a 98-yard pass reception, but didn't score a TD!

5. Jerry Rice

E. Averaged 22.26 yards per reception for his career, the most in NFL history

6. Bob Shaw

F. First player to score pass reception TDs in 11 consecutive games

7. Elroy Hirsch

G. First player to have a 99-yard pass reception for a TD

The next two games feature amazing placekicking performances.

1. Gary Anderson

A. Only kicker to lead the NFL in field goals for five seasons

2. Jim Bakken   B. Made 40 field goals in one season

3. Bruce Gossett   C. Only kicker ever to attempt nine field goals in one game

4. Neil Rackers   D. Last player to make seven field goals in a regulation game

5. Ali Haji-Sheikh   E. Made 35 field goals in his rookie season

6. Lou Groza   F. First of only two kickers ever to attempt 49 field goals in one season

7. Chris Boniol   G. Made more field goals (538) than any kicker in NFL history

1. Matt Stover   A. 2nd kicker to make a field goal from at least 60 yards

2. Mike Vanderjagt   B. First kicker to make seven field goals in seven attempts in one game

3. Garo Yepremian   C. Made the most field goals of 50 or more yards in his career—40

4. Jason Elam   D. 2nd of only two kickers ever to make a 63-yard field goal (Tom Dempsey was the first)

5. Steve Cox   E. First kicker to make four field goals in one quarter

6. Rich Karlis   F. Kicked at least one field goal in 38 consecutive games

7. Morten Andersen   G. Kicked 42 consecutive field goals

Here's one game of amazing punt return performances.

1. Brian Mitchell   A. Returned 70 punts in one season

2. Danny Reece   B. Returned 10 punts for TDs in his career

3. Eddie Brown   C. Returned 463 punts in his career

4. Lew Barnes   D. Returned 57 punts in his rookie season

5. Desmond Howard E. Returned a punt 103 yards for a TD

6. Robert Bailey   F. Returned 11 punts in one game

7. Eric Metcalf   G. Had 875 yards on punt returns in one season

Here is a game of amazing kickoff return performances.

1. MarTay Jenkins   A. Returned four kickoffs for TDs in one season

2. Desmond Howard B. Returned 82 kickoffs in one season

3. Tyrone Hughes   C. First player to return 10 kickoffs in one game

4. Roy Green   D. Most recent of only three players to return a kickoff 106 yards for a TD (Al Carmichael and Noland Smith were the others)

5. Brian Mitchell   E. Highest average return for a career—30.56 yards

6. Gale Sayers   F. Had 304 kickoff return yards in one game

7. Travis Williams   G. Returned 607 kickoffs during his career

This game features amazing punting performances.

1. Sammy Baugh	A. Placed eight punts inside the 20-yard line in one game
2. Jeff Feagles	B. Had six punts blocked in one season
3. Leo Araguz	C. Only player ever to lead the NFL in punting four consecutive seasons
4. Bob Parsons	D. In 1,177 punts over his first 15 years in the NFL, he never had a punt blocked
5. Steve O'Neal	E. Punted 16 times in one game
6. Chris Gardocki	F. Had one punt go an NFL-record 98 yards
7. Harry Newsome	G. Only NFL punter with more than 1,500 career punts
8. Bryan Barker	H. Punted 114 times in one season

Now for the defense. Let's start with one game of amazing interception performances.

1. Paul Krause	A. Returned an interception 106 yards for a TD
2. Dick (Night Train) Lane	B. Had 177 interception return yards in one game
3. Sammy Baugh	C. Intercepted at least one pass in eight consecutive games
4. Tom Morrow	D. Had 81 interceptions in his career
5. Charlie McNeil	E. First player to intercept four passes in one game

6. Ed Reed   F. Returned 12 interceptions for TDs in his career

7. Rod Woodson   G. Had 14 interceptions in one season

Here are some amazing sack performances.

1. Bruce Smith   A. Had 22.5 sacks in one season

2. Michael Strahan   B. First of only two players to lead the NFL in sacks in back-to-back seasons

3. Mark Gastineau   C. Had seven sacks in one game

4. Derrick Thomas   D. Had 14.5 sacks in his rookie season

5. Reggie White   E. Had at least one sack in 10 consecutive games

6. Simon Fletcher   F. Had 200 sacks in his career, the most ever

7. Jevon Kearse   G. Had nine consecutive seasons with at least 10 sacks

Now for the butter fingers performances—fumbles.

1. Warren Moon   A. Recovered four fumbles in one game

2. Len Dawson   B. Fumbled 23 times in one season

3. Kerry Collins   C. Had 161 fumbles in his career

4. David Carr   D. Fumbled seven times in one game

5. Randall Cunningham   E. Recovered 12 fumbles in one season

6. Dave Krieg   F. Recovered 47 of his own fumbles in his career

7. John Elway   G. Most fumbles by one player who played his entire career with one team—137

From butter fingers to sticky fingers—most opponents' fumbles recovered.

1. Don Hultz   A. Recovered 29 opponents' fumbles in his career

2. Corwin Clatt   B. First player to recover three opponents' fumbles in one game

3. Jack Tatum   C. 2nd of two players to return a fumble 104 yards for a TD

4. Jim Marshall   D. 1st of two players to return a fumble 104 yards for a TD

5. Aeneas Williams   E. Returned two fumbles for TDs in one game

6. Jessie Tuggle   F. Recovered 9 opponents' fumbles in one season

7. Fred Evans   G. Returned five fumbles for TDs in his career

And one final game of miscellaneous amazing individual performances.

1. Nathan Vasher   A. Only player ever to have four two-point conversions in one season

2. Fred Dryer   B. Returned a missed field goal 108 yards for a TD

3. Doug English

C. Only player in NFL history to have two safeties in one game

4. George Blanda

D. Played 20 years for the same team

5. Darrell Green

E. Only player in NFL history to have played in more than 300 consecutive games

6. Jeff Feagles

F. Played in the NFL for 26 seasons

7. Todd Heap

G. One of only two players with four safeties in their careers (Ted Hendricks is the other)

CHAPTER 14

AMAZING NFL TEAM PERFORMANCES

While not on a level with the colleges when it comes to amazing team or individual performances, there have been some pretty spectacular NFL accomplishments on the gridiron over the years. Like the NFL team that went through an entire season without attempting even one field goal! Or the team that lost only three fumbles all season. Try your hand at these 20 games of amazing all-time NFL performances.

1. Green Bay Packers

2. New York Giants

3. Los Angeles Rams

4. Dallas Cowboys

5. Buffalo Bills

6. Chicago Bears

7. San Francisco 49ers

A. Won the most consecutive divisional titles—7

B. Made the most consecutive trips to the Super Bowl—4

C. Most seasons leading the league in scoring—10

D. Won the most divisional titles—21

E. Had the most consecutive winning seasons—20

F. Most consecutive seasons leading the league in scoring—4

G. Won the most league titles—12

1. Minnesota Vikings   A. Most points scored in one season—556

2. Chicago Bears   B. Most touchdowns scored in one season—70

3. Green Bay Packers   C. Most recent of only three teams ever to score 31 points in the 4th quarter

4. Los Angeles Rams   D. Most points scored in the first half—49

5. Atlanta Falcons   E. Scored in 370 consecutive games (streak ran from 1977 to October 1, 2006 before it ended)

6. San Francisco 49ers   F. Most recent of only two teams ever to score 41 points in one quarter

7. Miami Dolphins   G. Most points scored in one game—73

1. Cincinnati Reds   A. Only team ever to go through an entire season and not attempt even one field goal

2. Philadelphia Eagles   B. First of only three teams ever to score 10 touchdowns in one game

3. Cleveland Browns   C. Fewest touchdowns scored in a season—3

4. St. Louis Rams   D. Most two-point conversions in one game—4

5. Minnesota Vikings   E. Attempted 49 field goals in one season

6. Washington Redskins   F. Most recent of only two teams to score six two-point conversions in one season (Miami was the other)

7. Chicago Bears   G. Most consecutive games scoring a touchdown—166

1. New York Jets

2. Dallas Cowboys

3. Baltimore Ravens

4. Tennessee Titans

5. Los Angeles Rams

6. New England Patriots

7. Chicago Bears

A. Last team to attempt eight field goals in one game

B. 2nd longest regular-season winning streak—17

C. Most consecutive games with at least one field goal—38

D. Longest regular-season winning streak—18

E. Last team to make four safeties in one season

F. Last team to make seven field goals in one game

G. Only team to make three safeties in one game

1. Canton Bulldogs

2. San Francisco 49ers

3. Chicago Bears

4. Pittsburgh Steelers

5. Miami Dolphins

6. Pottsville Maroons

7. Cleveland Browns

A. Last team to win 18 games in a season (regular season and postseason combined)

B. Most recent of only three teams ever to go through the regular season without a loss

C. First team to win six consecutive Conference titles

D. First team to record 10 shutouts in one season

E. First team to win 18 games in a season (regular season and postseason combined)

F. Most recent of only two teams ever to win 14 consecutive games in one regular season

G. Most consecutive games without suffering a defeat—25 (22 wins, 3 ties)

1. Miami Dolphins

A. Longest home unbeaten streak—30 (27 wins, 3 ties)

2. Green Bay Packers

B. First team to lose 15 games in one season

3. San Francisco 49ers

C. Had 10 shutouts in one season (9 wins, 1 tie)

4. New York Giants

D. Lost 26 consecutive games

5. Tampa Bay Buccaneers

E. Only team to lose 15 consecutive games in one season

6. New Orleans Saints

F. Won 27 consecutive home games

7. Carolina Panthers

G. Won 18 consecutive road games

1. Buffalo Bills

A. Played three consecutive tie games in one season

2. San Francisco 49ers

B. Lost 23 consecutive road games

3. Dallas Cowboys

C. Trailed 35–3 in the 3rd quarter and came back to win, 41–38, the largest comeback in NFL history (it was a playoff game)

4. Houston Oilers

D. Trailed 35–7 in the 3rd quarter and came back to win, 38–35, the largest regular-season comeback in NFL history

5. Brooklyn Dodgers

E. Lost 14 consecutive home games

6. Chicago Bears

F. Have the best overall record (353–213–2) since the AFL-NFL merger in 1970

7. Miami Dolphins

G. Lost eight games by shutout in one season

1. Jacksonville Jaguars
2. San Francisco 49ers
3. St. Louis Rams
4. Los Angeles Rams
5. Seattle Seahawks
6. San Diego Chargers
7. Minnesota Vikings

A. Most yards gained in one game—735

B. Fewest yards gained in one game—(-7)

C. Most yards gained in one season—7,075

D. Most consecutive games with at least 400 yards—11

E. Of all 32 current NFL teams, this one has the best winning percentage for opening day games (.750)

F. Team with the best road record (150-133-1) since the AFL-NFL merger in 1970

G. Most consecutive games with at least 300 yards—30

1. Chicago Bears
2. Minnesota Vikings
3. Cleveland Browns
4. Pittsburgh Steelers
5. San Francisco 49ers
6. Buffalo Bills
7. New England Patriots

A. Most seasons leading the league in rushing—16

B. Most passes completed in one season—432

C. Most passes completed in one game—45

D. Most passes attempted in one season—709

E. Last team to attempt zero passes in one game

F. Only team to attempt zero passes in a game twice

G. Last team to complete zero passes in a game

1. San Diego Chargers

2. Chicago Cardinals

3. Denver Broncos

4. Miami Dolphins

5. Philadelphia Eagles

6. Houston Oilers

7. Pittsburgh Steelers

A. Most times sacked in one season—104

B. Fewest passing yards gained in one season—302

C. Fewest times sacked in one season—7

D. Most recent of only two teams ever to go through an entire season without throwing a TD pass

E. Most recent team to suffer 12 sacks in one game

F. Fewest passing yards gained in one game—(-53)

G. Most seasons leading the league in passing yards—10

1. San Diego Chargers

2. Houston Oilers

3. Kansas City Chiefs

4. Pittsburgh Steelers

5. Oakland Raiders

6. Philadelphia Eagles

7. Chicago Bears

A. One of only four teams ever to have only five passes intercepted all season

B. Had 72 rushing attempts in one game

C. Had 681 rushing attempts in one season

D. Suffered 48 pass interceptions in one season

E. Most recent of seven teams to throw seven TD passes in one game

F. Had nine passes intercepted in one game

G. Had only 211 rushing attempts in one season, lowest ever

1. New England Patriots

2. Detroit Lions

3. Cleveland Browns

4. Philadelphia Eagles

5. Green Bay Packers

6. Miami Dolphins

7. New York Jets

A. Had the most first downs in a season—387

B. Only team to make 39 first downs in a regulation game

C. Had the highest average gain per rushing attempt for a season—5.74

D. Had only six rushing attempts in one game

E. Had 36 rushing TDs in one season

F. Had the lowest average gain per rushing attempt for a season—0.94

G. Had 426 yards rushing in one game

1. Denver Broncos

2. New England Patriots

3. New York Giants

4. Cleveland Browns

5. Detroit Lions

6. Chicago Bears

7. Atlanta Falcons

A. Allowed the fewest points in a season (129) since the 14-game schedule was adopted

B. Made 11 first downs by penalty in one game

C. Had 3,165 yards rushing in one season, the most ever

D. Had (-53) yards rushing in one game, the lowest ever

E. Allowed only 44 points in one season

F. Led the league in fewest points allowed five consecutive seasons

G. Led the league 11 times in fewest points allowed

1. Baltimore Ravens

A. Only team since 1937 to lead the league in fewest yards allowed for three consecutive seasons

2. Baltimore Colts

B. Allowed 3,228 yards rushing in one season

3. Kansas City Chiefs

C. Only team to lead the league in fewest passing yards allowed for five consecutive seasons

4. Chicago Bears

D. Allowed the most points in one season—533

5. Dallas Cowboys

E. Allowed 56 first downs by penalty in one season

6. Buffalo Bills

F. Allowed the fewest points in a season (165) since the 16-game schedule was adopted

7. Green Bay Packers

G. Only team ever to lead the NFL in fewest rushing yards allowed four consecutive seasons

1. Atlanta Falcons

A. Had 72 sacks in one season

2. Denver Broncos

B. Allowed 4,541 yards passing in one season

3. Philadelphia Eagles

C. Only team to lead the NFL in sacks three consecutive seasons

4. Oakland Raiders

D. Punted only 23 times one season

5. Chicago Bears

E. Allowed 40 passing touchdowns in one season

6. Washington Redskins

F. Had one season in which they allowed only one passing touchdown against them all year

7. San Diego

G. Only team to lead the NFL in punting four consecutive seasons

1. Chicago Bears

A. Had the highest average punting distance for a season—47.6

2. Detroit Lions

B. Most recent of only five teams ever to go through an entire season without making a fair catch

3. Pittsburgh Steelers

C. Had 12 punt returns in one game

4. San Diego Chargers

D. Most recent of only two teams ever to return just 12 punts in one season

5. Philadelphia Eagles

E. Only team ever to return five punts for TDs in one season

6. Dallas Cowboys

F. First of only three teams to return 71 punts in one season

7. Chicago Cardinals

G. One of only two teams ever to punt 17 times in one game

1. Atlanta Falcons

A. Had a kickoff return average of just 14.7 for one season

2. Washington Redskins

B. One of only two teams ever to allow four TDs on punt returns in one season (New York Giants the other)

3. Denver Broncos

C. Had 89 kickoff returns in one season

4. Cleveland Browns

D. Had 12 kickoff returns in one game

5. New York Giants

E. Led the league in kickoff return average eight times

6. Baltimore Ravens

F. Only team to lead the league in kickoff return average for three consecutive seasons

7. New York Jets

G. Had 367 kickoff return yards in one game

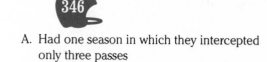

345

1. Buffalo Bills

A. Had the lowest average kickoff return against (14.3) in a season

2. Minnesota Vikings

B. First team to fumble 56 times in one season

3. Cleveland Browns

C. Returned six kickoffs for TDs in one season

4. San Francisco 49ers

D. Only team to allow four TDs on kickoff returns in a season

5. Pittsburgh Steelers

E. Committed 63 turnovers in one season

6. Chicago Bears

F. Committed 12 turnovers in one game

7. Kansas City Chiefs

G. Fumbled 10 times in one game

346

1. Cleveland Browns

A. Had one season in which they intercepted only three passes

2. Minnesota Vikings

B. Led the NFL in interceptions for five consecutive seasons

3. New York Giants

C. Led the NFL in interceptions 10 seasons

4. Kansas City Chiefs

D. Returned nine interceptions for TDs in one season

5. Houston Oilers   E. Had one season in which they fumbled only eight times

6. Seattle Seahawks   F. Had one season in which they lost only three fumbles

7. San Diego Chargers   G. Returned four interceptions for TDs in one game

1. Miami Dolphins   A. Team with the worst winning percentage one season (.188) to reach the NFC championship game the next season

2. Chicago Bears   B. Suffered the most penalty yards against in one game—212

3. Detroit Lions   C. Most recent of only three teams to be assessed 22 penalties against them in one game

4. Kansas City Chiefs   D. Set an NFL record with 158 penalties in one season

5. San Francisco 49ers   E. 16 times they led the NFL in most penalties against

6. Tennessee Titans   F. Led the NFL in fewest penalties for nine consecutive seasons

7. New Orleans Saints   G. Had one season in which they were penalized only 19 times

CHAPTER 15

NFL POTPOURRI

Okay, now we're really going to scramble it up, just like a team going through a two-minute drill. This chapter contains a mixed but fun bag of NFL trivia. Everything from nicknames to books, referee signals, careers outside the NFL, the USFL, and more. That's right, *the USFL*. Quit whining and answer the questions. And be glad I didn't ask you any questions about the Arena Football League.

Match the monikers with the teams they were attributed to.

1. Killer B's   A. Miami Dolphins

2. Steel Curtain   B. Dallas Cowboys

3. Fearsome Foursome   C. Pittsburgh Steelers

4. Sack Exchange   D. Los Angeles Rams

5. Doomsday Defense   E. Minnesota Vikings

6. Purple People Eaters   F. Washington Redskins

7. The Hogs   G. New York Jets

349

Each of the current teams in the left column played previously in one of the cities from the right column. Can you correctly connect their lineage?

1. Chicago Bears   A. Boston

2. Washington Redskins   B. Portsmouth

3. St. Louis Rams   C. Cleveland

4. Arizona Cardinals   D. Baltimore

5. Detroit Lions   E. St. Louis

6. Tennessee Titans   F. Decatur

7. Indianapolis Colts   G. Houston

350

Each of the players listed was a two-sport player. Match the player to his career.

1. Bo Jackson   A. NFL (Steelers), MLB (Pirates)

2. John Brodie   B. NFL (Browns), NBA (Royals)

3. Deion Sanders   C. NFL (Raiders), MLB (Royals)

4. George Halas   D. NFL (49ers), PGA golfer

5. Otto Graham   E. NFL (Giants), MLB (Giants, Reds)

6. Rex Johnston   F. NFL (Bears), MLB (Yankees)

7. Steve Filipowicz   G. NFL (Falcons), MLB (Yankees)

More two-sport *personnel.*

1. Ed Jones

2. Bronko Nagurski

3. Brian Jordan

4. Hugo Bezdek

5. Bud Grant

6. Herschel Walker

7. Tom Brown

A. NFL (Falcons), MLB (Cardinals, Braves)

B. NFL (Cowboys), pro boxer

C. NFL (Rams), MLB (Pirates)

D. NFL (Packers), MLB (Senators)

E. NFL (Cowboys), Olympic bobsledder

F. NFL (Bears), pro wrestler

G. NFL (Vikings), NBA (Lakers)

How well do you know your NFL referee's signals?

1. Fourth Down

2. Safety

3. Delay of Game

4. First Down

5. Illegal Contact

6. Loss of Down

7. Ineligible Receiver

A. Arm pointed toward defensive team's goal

B. One arm above head with fist closed

C. One open hand extended forward

D. Right hand touching top of cap

E. Palms together above head

F. Both hands held behind head

G. Folded arms

353

See if you can connect the book to its (supposed, alleged) author.

1. Keyshawn Johnson

2. George Plimpton

3. Joe Theismann

4. Vince Lombardi

5. Reggie White

6. John Madden

7. Alex Karras

A. *My Life in Football, Television, and the Movies*

B. *Paper Lion*

C. *In the Trenches*

D. *Quarterbacking*

E. *Run to Daylight*

F. *Just Give Me the Damn Ball*

G. *Hey! Wait a Minute! I Wrote a Book!*

354

Each of these famous players had a real first name that most people aren't aware of. Are you?

1. Bryan

2. Christian

3. Charles

4. Harold

5. David

6. Elroy

7. Eugene

A. Mean Joe Greene

B. Crazylegs Hirsch

C. Mercury Morris

D. Red Grange

E. Sonny Jurgensen

F. Bart Starr

G. Deacon Jones

Each of the players in this game was affectionately known by one of the listed nicknames. Can you match them up?

1. White Shoes

2. Ironhead

3. Big Daddy

4. Whizzer

5. Slash

6. Sweetness

7. Prime Time

A. Billy Johnson

B. Deion Sanders

C. Eugene Lipscomb

D. Craig Heyward

E. Walter Payton

F. Kordell Stewart

G. Byron White

More nicknames.

1. The Mad Stork

2. The Dutchman

3. The Jet

4. The Tyler Rose

5. The Hammer

6. The Galloping Ghost

7. The Chief

A. Joe Perry

B. Earl Campbell

C. Ted Hendricks

D. Red Grange

E. Norm Van Brocklin

F. Art Rooney

G. Fred Williamson

From 1983–1985, a competing league to the NFL played. It was called the United States Football League (USFL). In the next three games, see if you can match each team that played for the USFL with its nickname.

1. Arizona (1st team)   A. Gold

2. Baltimore   B. Gamblers

3. Birmingham   C. Breakers

4. Boston   D. Wranglers

5. Chicago   E. Blitz

6. Denver   F. Stallions

7. Houston   G. Stars

1. Jacksonville   A. Breakers (relocated franchise)

2. Los Angeles   B. Showboats

3. Memphis   C. Bulls

4. Arizona (2nd team)   D. Federals

5. Michigan   E. Express

6. New Jersey   F. Generals

7. New Orleans   G. Outlaws

8. Washington   H. Panthers

1. Oakland   A. Bandits

2. Oklahoma   B. Renegades

3. Orlando   C. Breakers (relocated franchise)

4. Philadelphia   D. Outlaws (merged franchise)

5. Pittsburgh   E. Invaders

6. Portland   F. Gunslingers

7. San Antonio   G. Maulers

8. Tampa Bay   H. Stars

More USFL trivia.

1. Philadelphia Stars

2. Oakland Invaders

3. New Jersey Generals

4. Michigan Panthers

5. Houston Gamblers

6. Baltimore Stars

7. Los Angeles Express

A. Team 1985 MVP Herschel Walker played for

B. Won the last USFL Championship (1985)

C. Won the second USFL Championship (1984)

D. Won the first USFL Championship (1983)

E. Lost the final USFL Championship game

F. Team with the worst record in the league (3–15) in the USFL's final season

G. Team 1984 MVP Jim Kelly played for

Each of the players listed below also was known for another occupation. Can you put them together?

1. Steve Largent

2. Byron White

3. Jack Kemp

4. Ed Marinaro

5. Rolf Benirschke

6. Alan Page

7. Jerry Richardson

A. U.S. Supreme Court justice

B. Host of *Wheel of Fortune* (albeit briefly)

C. State of Minnesota Supreme Court justice

D. Secretary of HUD (Housing and Urban Development)

E. Owner of an NFL team (Carolina)

F. U.S. Congressman

G. Actor on *Hill Street Blues*

CHAPTER 16

FROM THE HALLOWED HALLS

Every player's dream—besides winning the Super Bowl—is to wind up in the Hall of Fame in Canton, Ohio. Because the Hall of Fame contains only a relatively small number of the greatest players who've ever stepped onto the gridiron, this should be an easy category for you, right? Well, we're about to find out. In this chapter, match the Hall of Fame player to his career . . . if you can.

The first four games are all quarterbacks.

1. Troy Aikman

2. John Elway

3. Jim Kelly

4. Dan Marino

5. Warren Moon

6. Steve Young

A. Inducted in 2005; passed for 61,361 yards and 420 touchdowns

B. Inducted in 2002; led his team to four Super Bowls; mastered the no-huddle offense

C. Inducted in 2000; three-time Super Bowl MVP

D. Inducted in 2006; passed for 49,325 yards and 291 touchdowns in his 17 NFL seasons; elected to eight straight Pro Bowls and nine overall

E. Inducted in 2005; led NFL in passing six times; passed for more than 33,000 yards

F. Inducted in 2006; his 90 wins in the 1990s make him the winningest quarterback of any decade in history

7. Joe Montana

G. Passed for 25,092 yards and 192 touchdowns; led team to two Super Bowl victories

8. Bob Griese

H. Inducted in 2004; passed for 300 touchdowns and 51,475 yards

363

1. Sammy Baugh

A. Charter enshrinee; led NFL in passing six times; led the NFL in passing and punting in the same season

2. George Blanda

B. Had longest career in NFL history: 26 seasons and 340 games

3. Earl "Dutch" Clark

C. Player-coach of four NFL teams; coached the Cardinals to the NFL title one year

4. Jimmy Conzelman

D. All-NFL five times; passed for 137 touchdowns; NFL MVP in 1943

5. John "Paddy" Driscoll

E. Was named All-NFL seven times; dropkicked a record four field goals in one game

6. Benny Friedman

F. Three-time NFL passing leader; came out of retirement to lead the Giants to the NFL Eastern title

7. Arnie Herber

G. Charter enshrinee; NFL scoring champ three times; led the Lions to the NFL title one year

8. Sid Luckman

H. The NFL's first great passer; led NFL in touchdown passes in each of his first four seasons

1. Terry Bradshaw

A. Upon his retirement, he held the NFL career record for passing yards (47,003) and touchdowns (342); threw for four touchdowns in his first NFL game

2. Len Dawson

B. Led his team to five NFL titles; two-time Super Bowl MVP

3. Dan Fouts

C. Passed for 32,224 yards and 255 touchdowns; had five 3,000+-yard seasons

4. Sonny Jurgensen

D. Passed for 28,711 yards and 239 touchdowns; won four AFL passing crowns; a Super Bowl MVP

5. Joe Namath

E. Led his team to four NFC titles and two Super Bowl wins; his 83.4 career passer rating at his retirement was the best of all time

6. Bart Starr

F. First quarterback ever to pass for more than 4,000 yards in a season

7. Roger Staubach

G. Passed for 43,040 yards and 254 touchdowns; named to six Pro Bowls; was the NFL MVP in 1982

8. Fran Tarkenton

H. Passed for 27,989 yards and 212 touchdowns; was a two-time Super Bowl MVP

365

1. Norm Van Brocklin

A. Passed for 554 yards in a season opening game; led his team to the NFL title in his MVP season

2. Bob Waterfield

B. Passed for 33,070 yards and 242 touchdowns; was a two-time NFL MVP

3. Johnny Unitas

C. Passed for 23,584 yards and 174 touchdowns; led his team to 10 division or league titles in 10 seasons

4. Y.A. Tittle

D. Passed for 40,239 yards and 290 touchdowns, including at least one TD in 47 consecutive games

5. Clarence Parker

E. Played defense as well as quarterback; a two-time All-NFL performer and one-time league MVP

6. Bobby Lane

F. Won the NFL MVP Award in his rookie season, the same year he led his team to the NFL title

7. Otto Graham

G. Passed for 26,768 yards and 196 touchdowns; won an NFL title game with a late pass

Now it's time to match the Hall of Fame running backs to their careers in the next six games.

1. Jim Brown

A. Charter enshrinee; the first "name" player in pro football who helped draw large crowds

2. Earl Campbell

B. First running back in history to collect 10,000 yards rushing and 5,000 yards in pass receptions

3. Tony Dorsett

C. Rushed for 9,407 yards; had four 200-yard games in one season

4. Charley Taylor

D. Won Rookie of the Year Award as a running back, then, two years later, switched to receiver and led the NFL in receiving two years in a row

5. Red Grange

E. Led the NFL in rushing twice; first running back ever to rush for more than 200 yards in a game

6. Cliff Battles

F. Rushed for 12,312 yards; led the NFL in rushing eight seasons

7. Marcus Allen

G. Rushed for 12,739 yards; had 398 receptions and a record 99-yard touchdown run

1. Jim Taylor

A. Played for four different teams; was once traded for nine players

2. Joe Perry

B. Three-time Pro Bowl MVP who led the league with 22 touchdowns his rookie season

3. Gale Sayers

C. Starred on both offense and defense; named to seven Pro Bowls; Player of the Year in 1956

4. Bobby Mitchell

D. Had 14,078 combined yards; scored 91 touchdowns, including eight on kickoff and punt returns

5. Lenny Moore

E. Rushed for 8,597 yards; led the NFL in rushing and scoring (19 touchdowns) in 1962

6. Ollie Matson

F. Scored 113 touchdowns in his career, including TDs in a record 18 straight games in the mid-1960s

7. Frank Gifford

G. First player in NFL history to gain 1,000 yards rushing in back-to-back seasons

1. Joe Guyon

A. Led the NFL in rushing as a rookie in 1936

2. Bill Dudley

B. Longtime halfback-end of the Rams who had 7,000+ receiving yards; part of the team's revolutionary "three-end" offense

3. Tuffy Leemans

C. Charter enshrinee; still holds the NFL record for most points scored in one game with 40; allowed two of Babe Ruth's 60 home runs in 1927 season during brief baseball career

4. Clarke Hinkle

D. Three-time All-NFL player who played both offense and defense; had an incredible year in 1946, winning the league's rushing, interception, and punt return titles

5. Elroy Hirsch

E. Green Bay star of the 1930s and early 1940s who was a fullback on offense and a linebacker on defense

6. Ernie Nevers

F. Charter enshrinee; played for five teams over 14 seasons, including the Milwaukee Badgers, Duluth Eskimos, Pottsville Maroons, Green Bay Packers, and Pittsburgh Pirates

7. Johnny McNally

G. His TD pass gave the Giants the win over the Bears in the 1927 NFL title game

1. Hugh McElhenny

A. Four-time rushing champion; won 1944 punt return title and 1945 kickoff return title

2. George McAfee

B. NFL's leading scorer in 1933; scored 17 points in the famous "Sneakers" NFL title game of 1934

3. Marion Motley

C. All-time rushing leader of the All-America Football Conference (rival pro league to the NFL in 1946–1949 until it merged with the NFL in 1950); led the NFL in rushing his first season in the league

4. Fritz Pollard

D. Had 11,369 total combined yards for four teams, including the 49ers, Vikings, Giants, and Lions

5. Ken Strong

E. Charter enshrinee; first president (commissioner, essentially) of the American Professional Football Association

6. Jim Thorpe

F. One of two African-American players in the NFL in 1920; NFL's first black head coach in 1921

7. Steve Van Buren

G. Starred on both offense and defense for the Bears; career punt-return average of 12.78 yards

370

1. Doak Walker

A. Won two NFL scoring titles; scored the winning touchdown of the 1952 title game on a 67-yard run

2. Charley Trippi

B. Rushed for 6,803 yards; member of San Francisco's famous "Million Dollar Backfield"

3. Bronko Nagurski

C. Rushed for 7,274 yards and 90 touchdowns; rushed for more than 1,000 yards each of his first three seasons as a starter; won the punt return title one season

4. John Henry Johnson

D. Charter enshrinee; All-NFL five times for the Bears

5. Tony Canadeo

E. Rushed for 8,081 yards and 68 touchdowns; committed only 21 fumbles in 1,997 rushing attempts and pass receptions

6. Leroy Kelly

F. Versatile player—played halfback for five years, quarterback for two, and defense for two for Cardinals

7. Larry Csonka

G. Played both offense and defense; third player in NFL history to rush for more than 1,000 yards in a season

1. O.J. Simpson

A. Rushed for 12,120 yards; 100 touchdowns; 1,556 rushing yards in 19 postseason games; Super Bowl MVP

2. John Riggins

B. First player ever to rush for 2,000 yards in a season

3. Barry Sanders

C. Rushed for 15,269 yards; 99 touchdowns; rushed for at least 1,000 yards in all ten of his NFL seasons

4. Walter Payton

D. Rushed for 13,259 yards, including an NFL record 2,105 one season

5. Eric Dickerson

E. Three-time NFL scoring leader; 760 career points, including then-record 176 points one season

6. Franco Harris

F. Rushed for 11,352 yards; had 116 touchdowns; Super Bowl MVP with 166 yards rushing, including 43-yard game-winning score

7. Paul Hornung

G. Retired as the NFL's all-time leading rusher with 16,726 yards and combined yardage with 21,803

Now for four games of Hall of Fame receivers and their careers.

1. Lance Alworth

2. Raymond Berry

3. Fred Biletnikoff

4. Dave Casper

5. Charlie Joiner

6. Lynn Swann

7. Steve Largent

A. 631 receptions for 9,275 yards and 68 TDs; set a record with 12 catches and 178 yards in an NFL title game

B. 750 receptions for 12,146 yards and 65 TDs; at time of his retirement, he had played the most games (239) of any wide receiver in history

C. 819 receptions for 13,089 yards and 100 TDs; had a pass reception in 177 straight games

D. 542 receptions for 10,266 yards and 85 TDs; named to the All-AFL team seven times

E. 589 receptions for 8,974 yards and 76 TDs; had at least 40 catches in 10 consecutive years; Super Bowl MVP

F. 378 receptions for 5,216 yards and 52 TDs; named to five straight Pro Bowls as a tight end

G. 336 receptions for 5,462 yards and 51 TDs; three-time Pro Bowler and a Super Bowl MVP

1. Guy Chamberlin

2. Morris Badgro

3. Tom Fears

A. Player-coach of four NFL championship teams

B. 427 receptions for 5,812 yards and 43 TDs; first tight end ever selected to the Hall of Fame

C. Scored the first touchdown in NFL Championship Game series

4. George Halas

D. First receiver ever to be named All-NFL with two different teams (Bears and Eagles)

5. Mike Ditka

E. 400 receptions for 5,397 yards and 38 TDs; set a then-record with 18 receptions in one game; led all NFL receivers his first three seasons in the league

6. Bill Hewitt

F. Charter enshrinee; achieved more fame as a head coach; in the NFL for 50 years

1. Don Hutson

A. Redskins' all-time receptions leader when he retired; had two long touchdown receptions (55 and 78 yards) in an NFL title game

2. Dante Lavelli

B. Charter enshrinee; 488 receptions for 7,991 yards and 99 TDs; two-time NFL MVP who won eight receiving championships

3. Pete Pihos

C. 495 receptions for 8,410 yards and 84 TDs with five different teams, mostly Philadelphia

4. Wayne Millner

D. 386 receptions for 6,488 yards and 62 TDs; 24 catches in six title games with Cleveland

5. Tommy McDonald

E. 331 receptions for 5,236 yards and 38 TDs; second tight end to enter the Hall of Fame

6. John Mackey

F. Three-time NFL receiving champion with Eagles; caught winning TD in 1949 NFL title game

1. John Stallworth

A. 480 receptions for 7,918 yards and 40 TDs; third tight end to be inducted into the Hall of Fame

2. Jackie Smith

B. 662 receptions for 7,980 yards, both all-time records for tight ends when he retired

3. Paul Warfield

C. 764 receptions for 14,004 yards and 75 TDs; eight-time Pro Bowler

4. Kellen Winslow

D. 541 receptions for 6,741 yards and 45 TDs; had 13 receptions and a blocked field goal in a 1981 playoff win over the Dolphins

5. Ozzie Newsome

E. 537 receptions for 8,723 yards and 63 TDs; scored critical, go-ahead 73-yard TD in Super Bowl

6. James Lofton

F. 427 receptions for 8,565 yards and 85 TDs; eight-time Pro Bowl selection

7. Don Maynard

G. 633 receptions for 11,834 yards and 88 TDs; had at least 50 receptions and 1,000 yards in five different seasons

Now for a couple games of Hall of Fame safeties and cornerbacks.

1. Herb Adderly

A. 56 interceptions, 11 TDs; played in seven Pro Bowls in his 11 seasons, all with the same team

2. Mike Haynes

B. 48 interceptions, 7 TDs; played in four Super Bowls and five Pro Bowls in his 12 seasons for two teams

3. Lem Barney

C. 63 interceptions; 10 Pro Bowls; member of the NFL's 75th Anniversary Team

4. Ken Houston

D. 54 interceptions, including a 75-yard return in the Super Bowl; played for two teams in his 16-year NFL career

5. Willie Brown

E. 49 interceptions, 9 TDs; 12 Pro Bowls in 14 seasons

6. Paul Krause

F. 57 interceptions; was the NFL's defensive MVP in one of his 14 seasons, all spent with the same team

7. Mel Blount

G. 46 interceptions, including one in a Super Bowl; was the NFL's Defensive Rookie of the Year; nine Pro Bowls

8. Ronnie Lott

H. NFL's all-time leader with 81 interceptions; played in four Super Bowls and eight Pro Bowls

1. Mel Renfro

A. 52 interceptions; named to the Pro Bowl the first 10 seasons of his 14-year career, all spent with one team; had 842 punt return yards and 2,246 kickoff return yards

2. Emlen Tunnell

B. 52 interceptions, including at least one interception in seven consecutive games one year; made the safety blitz famous

3. Willie Wood

C. 47 interceptions; 16 seasons all with the same team; five Pro Bowls; so good that opposing passers avoided throwing to his area of the field

4. Jack Christiansen

D. 79 interceptions; actually had more yards gained from interception, punt, and kickoff returns one season than the NFL's leading rusher had in rushing yards

5. Larry Wilson   E. 68 interceptions, including an NFL record 14 as a rookie; played in seven Pro Bowls

6. Dick "Night Train" Lane   F. 46 interceptions; led NFL twice; returned 8 punt returns for touchdowns in his eight seasons, all with one team

7. Jimmy Johnson   G. 48 interceptions; played in six NFL Championship Games and two Super Bowls

Time for two games of Hall of Fame linebackers.

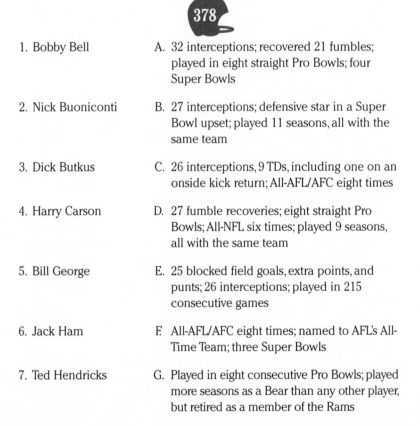

1. Bobby Bell   A. 32 interceptions; recovered 21 fumbles; played in eight straight Pro Bowls; four Super Bowls

2. Nick Buoniconti   B. 27 interceptions; defensive star in a Super Bowl upset; played 11 seasons, all with the same team

3. Dick Butkus   C. 26 interceptions, 9 TDs, including one on an onside kick return; All-AFL/AFC eight times

4. Harry Carson   D. 27 fumble recoveries; eight straight Pro Bowls; All-NFL six times; played 9 seasons, all with the same team

5. Bill George   E. 25 blocked field goals, extra points, and punts; 26 interceptions; played in 215 consecutive games

6. Jack Ham   F. All-AFL/AFC eight times; named to AFL's All-Time Team; three Super Bowls

7. Ted Hendricks   G. Played in eight consecutive Pro Bowls; played more seasons as a Bear than any other player, but retired as a member of the Rams

8. Willie Lanier

H. 11 interceptions; named to nine Pro Bowls; inducted in 2006

1. Sam Huff

A. 50 interceptions; also won three NFL punting titles; played in nine Pro Bowls

2. Jack Lambert

B. 15 years, all with the same team; won the MVP Award in one year's NFL title game; voted in a poll as the NFL's all-time best linebacker

3. Yale Lary

C. 11 seasons, all with one team, and missed only one game due to injury; seven Pro Bowls; All-NFL five times

4. Ray Nitschke

D. 24 interceptions; team captain for nine years; refined the position of middle linebacker that evolved into what it is today

5. Mike Singletary

E. Played in 9 Pro Bowls in his 11-year career, all with the same team; voted NFL Defensive Player of the Year one season

6. Lawrence Taylor

F. Played in 10 Pro Bowls in his 12-year career, all with the same team

7. Joe Schmidt

G. 30 interceptions; played in six NFL title games and five Pro Bowls; later became a player-coach for Washington

8. Dave Wilcox

H. 10 Pro Bowls; won the NFL MVP Award one season

Let's try four games of defensive linemen enshrined in the Hall of Fame.

1. Doug Atkins

A. Eight Pro Bowls and four All-NFL selections in his 17-year, 205 game career with three teams

2. Elvin Bethea

B. Played 16 seasons for two teams; six Pro Bowls; retired as a member of the Seattle Seahawks

3. Willie Davis

C. Played 11 seasons with three teams; All-NFL five times; four Pro Bowls; recovered 20 fumbles; inducted in 1976

4. Carl Eller

D. Played 12 years for two teams and never missed a game; five Pro Bowls and five All-NFL selections

5. Len Ford

E. Played 12 seasons for four teams, including a different team in each of his first four years in the NFL; five Pro Bowls

6. Art Donovan

F. Eight Pro Bowls in his 16 seasons, all with the same team; led his team in sacks six times

7. Buck Buchanan

G. Played 13 years, all for the same team and didn't miss a game; two Super Bowls

1. Joe Greene

A. Played 13 seasons, all with the same *franchise*; eight Pro Bowls, All-AFC four times

2. Henry Jordan

B. Played 13 seasons, all for the same team; 10 Pro Bowls; twice named NFL Defensive Player of the Year; four Super Bowls

3. Stan Jones

C. Played 14 seasons, all for the same team; 11 Pro Bowls and two Super Bowls; played 196 consecutive games

4. Howie Long

D. Played 12 seasons, all for the same team; earned all-pro honors at both defensive end and defensive tackle; four Pro Bowls

5. Bob Lilly

E. Played 13 seasons for two teams; seven consecutive Pro Bowl appearances; early pioneer in use of weightlifting to prepare for the season

6. Dan Hampton

F. Played 13 seasons for two teams; four Pro Bowls, seven NFL title games, and two Super Bowls

1. Gino Marchetti

A. Played 14 seasons, all for the same team; only member of this team to have his number retired; nine Pro Bowls; one award for NFL's Best Lineman of the Year

2. Leo Nomellini

B. Played 16 seasons for two teams, including 218 consecutive games; four Super Bowls; league MVP one season

3. Alan Page

C. Played nine seasons, all for the same team; 78$^1/_2$ sacks;   six consecutive Pro Bowls

4. Lee Roy Selmon

D. Played 13 seasons for three teams; 10 consecutive ProBowls; All-NFL seven times; named the top defensive end of the NFL's first 50 years

5. Ernie Stautner

E. Played 14 seasons, all for the same team, and never missed a game; 10 Pro Bowls

6. Merlin Olsen

F. Played 15 seasons, all for the same team; named to 14 consecutive Pro Bowls; he was "fearsome"

1. Deacon Jones

A. Played 14 seasons for two teams; played in eight NFL title games; named the NFL's player of the year in 1962

2. Andy Robustelli

B. Played 14 seasons, all for the same team, and missed only one game; nine Pro Bowls; Super Bowl MVP

3. Arnie Weinmeister

C. Played 14 seasons for three teams; unanimous selection as All-NFL five straight seasons; coined the phrase "quarterback sack"

4. Randy White

D. Played 14 seasons, all for the same team, including 201 consecutive games; named to seven consecutive Pro Bowls; one Super Bowl

5. Reggie White

E. Played for three teams in his 15 seasons; retired as the NFL's all-time sack leader with 198; named to 13 consecutive Pro Bowls

6. Jack Youngblood

F. Played six seasons for two teams; four Pro Bowls and four All-NFL selections

Next are two games of Hall of Fame centers.

1. Dwight Stephenson

A. Played eight seasons, all for the same team; five Pro Bowls

2. Mike Webster   B. Played 14 seasons, all with the same team; eight Pro Bowls; named the NFL's all-time center in 1969

3. Jim Langer   C. Played in 11 title games in 12 seasons with two teams; never missed a game in high school, college, or pro ball

4. Mel Hein   D. Played 12 seasons for two teams; six Pro Bowls; played every offensive down of his team's 17–0 season

5. Frank Gatski   E. Played 245 games over 17 seasons with two teams; nine Pro Bowls and four Super Bowls

6. Chuck Bednarik   F. Charter enshrinee; All-NFL eight consecutive years; a true iron man who was a starter on offense, defense, and special teams for 15 seasons

1. Alex Wojciechowicz   A. Played 13 seasons, all with the same team, including four NFL championship teams

2. Clyde Turner   B. Played 14 seasons for two teams, including both on offense and defense for eight years with Detroit

3. George Trafton   C. Played 15 seasons for two teams; 10 Pro Bowls; seven time selection as All-NFL; set a then-record by starting in 182 consecutive games

4. Jim Ringo   D. Played 15 seasons, all for the same team; played in 12 Pro Bowls or AFL All-Star games; was named as the AFL's all-time center

5. Jim Otto   E. NFL's top center of the 1920s, he was the first to snap the ball with one hand

The next five games concern Hall of Fame offensive linemen.

1. Bob Brown

    A. Played eight seasons, all for the same team; played in NFL's first four Pro Bowls; named to the All-NFL team at three different positions: linebacker, defensive tackle, and tackle

2. Roosevelt Brown

    B. Played 9 seasons for three teams; first player ever to be chosen both All-NFL and All-AAFC

3. George Connor

    C. Played 10 seasons, all for the same team; eight Pro Bowls; played on three NFL championship teams

4. Lou Creekmur

    D. Played 21 seasons, all for the same team; NFL Player of the Year in 1954; was also a kicker who scored 1,608 points

5. Forrest Gregg

    E. Played 10 seasons for three teams; six Pro Bowls and seven All-NFL selections; named a member of the 1960s All Decade Team

6. Walt Kiesling

    F. Played 15 seasons for two teams; nine Pro Bowls; played on six NFL championship teams, including three Super Bowls; played in 188 consecutive games

7. Frank Kinard

    G. Played 13 seasons, all for the same team; nine Pro Bowls; NFL's Lineman of the Year in 1956

8. Lou Groza

    H. Played 13 seasons for six teams; later became a head coach who led the Steelers to their first winning season

1. Dan Dierdorf

    A. Played 13 seasons, all with the same team; selected to 11 consecutive Pro Bowls; inducted in 1998

2. Joe DeLamielleure

    B. Played 185 games over 13 seasons with two teams; six Pro Bowls; All-AFC six consecutive years

3. Mike Munchak

    C. Played 13 seasons, all with the same team; six Pro Bowls; named the NFL's best blocker three times

4. Larry Little

    D. Played 13 seasons, all with the same team; named to 11 Pro Bowl teams; never missed a game in his entire 184-game career

5. Tom Mack

    E. Played 12 seasons, all with the same team; selected to nine Pro Bowls; named All-AFC seven times

6. Anthony Munoz

    F. Played 14 seasons with two teams; selected to five Pro Bowls; three Super Bowls

7. John Hannah

    G. Played 13 seasons, all with the same team; nine Pro Bowls; 10 All-Pro selections; considered the top guard of his era

1. Albert "Turk" Edwards

    A. Charter enshrinee; played nine seasons for three teams; the largest player (255 pounds) of the 1920s

2. Dan Fortmann

    B. Played for two teams in 10 seasons; six Pro Bowls; was the main player involved in a 15-player deal while he was away for two years of military service

3. Ed Healey

C. Played for four teams in 13 NFL seasons; considered the player who initiated the defensive shifting style of play

4. Wilbur Henry

D. Played eight seasons, all with the same team; named All-NFL every year of his career; though just six feet tall and 210 pounds, he was the top lineman of his era; earned his medical degree while playing with the Bears

5. Robert "Cal" Hubbard

E. A devastating tackler and blocker who was an eight-time All-NFL selection in his nine seasons; suffered a career-ending injury in a … (gulp!) … coin toss ceremony

6. William Lyman

F. Charter enshrinee; All-NFL six times in the 1920s and 1930s; considered the most feared lineman of his era

7. Mike McCormack

G. Played nine seasons for two teams; two-way star for the Bears in the 1920s

1. Mike Michalske

A. Played for two teams in 11 seasons; All-AFL selection nine times; was only called for two holding penalties in ten years with the Chargers

2. Ron Mix

B. Played nine seasons, all with the same team; named All-NFL five consecutive seasons; often played without a helmet; played on three NFL title teams; later became a coach for Rams and Cardinals

3. George Musso

C. Played 12 seasons, all with the same team; was the first player ever to be named All-NFL at two different positions: guard and tackle

4. Joe Stydahar

D. Played nine years, all with the same team; first player who played his entire career in the AFL to be named to the Hall of Fame; eight-time AFL All-Star

5. Billy Shaw

E. Played 11 seasons, all with the same team; first full-time offensive lineman to be elected to the Hall of Fame; eight Pro Bowls; eight selections as All-NFL

6. Bob St. Clair

F. Played 11 seasons for two teams; first guard enshrined in Hall of Fame; seven times selected as All-NFL; made the blitz popular

7. Jim Parker

G. Played 11 seasons, all with the same team; also played on special teams; had one season in which he blocked ten field goals; five Pro Bowls; All-NFL four times

1. Art Shell

A. Played 15 seasons, all with the same team; eight Pro Bowls; 23 postseason games; later became a head coach

2. Steve Owen

B. Played 13 seasons, all for the same team; six Pro Bowls; five Super Bowls; named to the NFL's 1970s All Decade Team

3. Rayfield Wright

C. Played eight seasons, all with the same team; three Pro Bowls; four times named All-NFL; two-way player

4. Ron Yary

D. Played 20 seasons, all for the same team; seven Pro Bowls; his 259 games played were the most in NFL history by an offensive lineman at the time he retired

5. Gene Upshaw

E. Played 15 seasons, all with the same team; played in seven Pro Bowls, three Super Bowls, and ten AFL/AFC title games

6. Bill Willis

F. Played for two teams in 15 seasons; six-time All Pro; seven Pro Bowls; played in four Super Bowls

7. Jackie Slater

G. Played nine years for three teams; later became a longtime head coach who won 155 games, eight divisional titles, and two NFL championships

The next two games are Hall of Fame coaches.

1. George Allen

A. 80 career wins; introduced the screen pass and platoon system

2. Paul Brown

B. 222 career wins; four AAFC championships; three NFL championships; great innovator with many firsts to his credit, including film study, intelligence tests, and the isolation of his team before home and road games

3. Weeb Ewbank

C. 270 career wins; had 20 consecutive winning seasons

4. Ray Flaherty

D. Charter enshrinee; 229 career wins; six NFL titles; founded the pre-NFL Packers

5. Joe Gibbs

E. 124 career wins plus 16 more in postseason; 3–1 Super Bowl record

6. Sid Gillman

F. 168 career wins; led his team to 11 division titles and four Super Bowls (0–4 record)

7. Bud Grant

G. 123 career wins; first coach to win a divisional title in both the AFL and NFL

8. Earl Lambeau

H. 130 career wins; only coach ever to win a championship in both the AFL and NFL; 1–0 Super Bowl record

9. Tom Landry

I. 118 career wins; never had a losing season; twice named NFL Coach of the Year; 0–1 Super Bowl record

1. Marv Levy

A. 154 career wins; only coach to take his team to four consecutive Super Bowls

2. Vince Lombardi

B. 347 career wins, more than any coach in NFL history; 2–3 Super Bowl record

3. John Madden

C. 63 career wins; two NFL titles; only coach ever to win back-to-back NFL titles by shutouts; also played major league baseball, hitting .357 in the 1919 Black Sox World Series as a member of the Cincinnati Reds

4. Earle "Greasy" Neale

D. 102 career wins; 3–0 Super Bowl record

5. Chuck Noll

E. 136 career wins; winningest coach in AFL history; 1–1 Super Bowl record

6. Don Shula

F. 105 career wins; five NFL titles; 2–0 Super Bowl record

7. Hank Stram

G. 209 career wins; only coach to win four Super Bowls

8. Bill Walsh

H. 112 career wins; 1–0 Super Bowl record; has the best regular season career winning percentage (.742) of all coaches with at least 100 career wins

The next two games concern Hall of Fame team owners, officials, and other non-players and coaches.

1. Bert Bell

    A. Key NFL executive for many years; on the board of directors for the NFL Trust Fund, NFL Films, and the Scheduling Committee; key labor negotiator; owner of the Steelers for 20 years

2. Charles Bidwill Sr.

    B. The driving force behind the formation of the AFL; one of the driving forces behind the merger of the AFL and NFL

3. Dan Rooney

    C. Charter enshrinee; team owner, including Eagles and Steelers; NFL Commissioner for 14 years

4. Al Davis

    D. Longtime owner of the Cardinals; his optimism and faith in the NFL kept the league going during the depression years of the 1930s

5. Jim Finks

    E. Charter enshrinee; initiated many progressive rules changes; pioneer of halftime shows and team band; 38-year owner of Redskins

6. Lamar Hunt

    F. Only person ever in pro history to serve in all of the following positions: personnel assistant, scout, assistant coach, head coach, general manager, team owner, and commissioner

7. Tim Mara

    G. Charter enshrinee; founder of the New York Giants who oversaw their 10 divisional titles and four NFL championships

8. George Marshall

    H. A top-flight team administrator who took three losing teams (Vikings, Saints, Bears) and turned them all into winners

1. Wellington Mara	A. Charter enshrinee; NFL president and co-organizer in 1920; introduced the standard player contract
2. Joe Carr	B. 40-year team owner who played prominent role in the merger of the AFL and NFL; chairman of the NFL's Competition Committee for 23 years
3. Hugh (Shorty) Ray	C. First pure placekicker enshrined in the Hall of Fame
4. Dan Reeves	D. Generally considered the premiere commissioner in all of sports history
5. Art Rooney	E. Supervisor of Officials who streamlined the NFL's rules to improve the game's tempo and provide for player safety
6. Pete Rozelle	F. 56-year team owner who didn't realize his first NFL title until his 42nd season
7. Tex Schramm	G. 31-year owner of the Rams; opened up West Coast to the NFL when he moved his team to L.A. from Cleveland; first post-WWII owner to sign a black player
8. Jan Stenerud	H. Started as ballboy for New York Giants, eventually came to own the team; president of the NFC for more than 20 years

See if you can match the NFL Hall of Famer to his country of birth.

1. Jan Stenerud	A. Bavaria
2. Bronko Nagurski	B. Italy

3. Ernie Stautner	C. Mexico
4. Leo Nomellini	D. Canada
5. Ted Hendricks	E. Norway
6. Steve Van Buren	F. Guatemala
7. Tom Fears	G. Honduras

The next 13 games concern the states various Hall of Famers were born in.

Match the state to the fact about it.

1. Texas	A. State whose only Hall of Famer is linebacker Dave Wilcox
2. Iowa	B. State with the 2nd most Hall of Famers—25
3. Pennsylvania	C. State whose only Hall of Famer is QB Norm Van Brocklin
4. South Dakota	D. State whose only Hall of Famer is QB Earl (Dutch) Clark
5. Idaho	E. State whose only Hall of Famer is safety Larry Wilson
6. Colorado	F. State with no Hall of Famers by birth
7. Oregon	G. State with the most Hall of Famers—26

Each of these states proudly boasts two Hall of Famers. Can you connect them?

1. South Carolina   A. Weeb Ewbank and Bob Griese

2. New Mexico   B. Paul Hornung and George McAfee

3. Kentucky   C. Ronnie Lott and Tommy McDonald

4. Indiana   D. Andy Robustelli and Ken Strong

5. Utah   E. Merlin Olsen and Steve Young

6. Connecticut   F. Guy Chamberlin and William Lyman

7. Nebraska   G. Harry Carson and Art Shell

Do you know where all these mighty Steelers of the 1970s were born?

1. Texas   A. Terry Bradshaw

2. Louisiana   B. Lynn Swann

3. Georgia   C. John Stallworth

4. Alabama   D. Franco Harris

5. Pennsylvania   E. Mean Joe Greene

6. New Jersey   F. Jack Ham

7. Ohio   G. Jack Lambert

8. Tennessee   H. Mel Blount

Which states claim these legendary quarterbacks?

1. California	A. Y.A. Tittle
2. Illinois	B. Troy Aikman
3. North Carolina	C. Sonny Jurgensen
4. Ohio	D. Joe Montana
5. Texas	E. Otto Graham
6. Washington	F. Fran Tarkenton
7. Virginia	G. Roger Staubach
8. Pennsylvania	H. John Elway

Running back native sons.

1. Georgia	A. Tony Dorsett
2. Ohio	B. Joe Perry
3. California	C. Jim Brown
4. Pennsylvania	D. Jim Thorpe
5. Illinois	E. Larry Csonka
6. Oklahoma	F. O.J. Simpson
7. Arkansas	G. Tony Canadeo

More Hall of Fame running backs.

1. Kansas

2. Mississippi

3. Texas

4. Minnesota

5. Wisconsin

6. Pennsylvania

7. Louisiana

A. Earl Campbell

B. Elroy Hirsch

C. Walter Payton

D. Barry Sanders

E. Leroy Kelly

F. Jim Taylor

G. Ernie Nevers

Try your hand at these legendary defensive players and their states of birth.

1. Florida

2. California

3. Georgia

4. Ohio

5. Oklahoma

6. Illinois

7. Alabama

A. Deacon Jones

B. John Hannah

C. Lee Roy Selmon

D. Buck Buchanan

E. Anthony Munoz

F. Alan Page

G. Dick Butkus

More defensive players.

1. Illinois	A. Randy White
2. Pennsylvania	B. Reggie White
3. Tennessee	C. Willie Lanier
4. Virginia	D. Carl Eller
5. Texas	E. Bob Lilly
6. North Carolina	F. Ray Nitschke
7. Massachusetts	G. Nick Buoniconti

Now for Hall of Fame tight ends and wide receivers and their birth states.

1. Florida	A. Dave Casper
2. Ohio	B. Steve Largent
3. Texas	C. Fred Biletnikoff
4. Louisiana	D. Charlie Joiner
5. Minnesota	E. Paul Warfield
6. Pennsylvania	F. Michael Irvin
7. Oklahoma	G. Lance Alworth

More native son tight ends and wide receivers.

1. Alabama	A. Lem Barney
2. Mississippi	B. Don Maynard
3. Missouri	C. Ozzie Newsome
4. Texas	D. James Lofton
5. New York	E. John Mackey
6. North Carolina	F. Kellen Winslow
7. California	G. Charlie Sanders

Do you know where these Hall of Fame coaches were born?

1. Illinois	A. Art Shell
2. Pennsylvania	B. Paul Brown
3. South Carolina	C. John Madden
4. Michigan	D. George Halas
5. Minnesota	E. Mike Ditka
6. Indiana	F. Weeb Ewbank
7. Ohio	G. George Allen

More coaches.

1. Illinois	A. Vince Lombardi
2. New York	B. Joe Gibbs
3. Ohio	C. Earle (Greasy) Neale
4. North Carolina	D. Bud Grant
5. Texas	E. Chuck Noll
6. Wisconsin	F. Tom Landry
7. West Virginia	G. Hank Stram

See if you can match these states to their group of native sons.

1. California	A. Sammy Baugh, Eric Dickerson, and Thurman Thomas
2. Ohio	B. Lawrence Taylor, Roosevelt Brown, and Clarence Parker
3. Pennsylvania	C. Marcus Allen, Dan Fouts, and Pete Rozelle
4. Texas	D. Jim Otto, Mike Webster, and Earl Lambeau
5. Kansas	E. Len Dawson, Dan Dierdorf, and Lou Groza
6. Wisconsin	F. Dan Marino, Johnny Unitas, and Red Grange
7. Virginia	G. Gale Sayers, John Riggins, and Jack Christiansen

CHAPTER 17

AND THE AWARD GOES TO . . .

Some of those who suit up in pads and helmets do so because they love the game of football, the fierce and sometimes brutal competition, or the pure athleticism of the sport. Others do so for big bucks and to get girls. In any event, in addition to big bucks and girls, sometimes a player receives an award or trophy for his accomplishments on the field.

In the first three games, see if you can identify each of the initial winners of the listed college awards.

409

1. Jay Berwanger	A. John Outland Trophy
2. O.J. Simpson	B. Walter Camp Award
3. Jim Stillwagon	C. Heisman Memorial Trophy
4. Earl Campbell	D. Vince Lombardi Rotary Award
5. George Connor	E. O'Brien Memorial Trophy
6. Jim McMahon	F. Maxwell Award
7. Clint Frank	G. Davey O'Brien National Quarterback Award
8. Matt Leinart	H. Manning Award

1. Joe Allison
2. Brian Bosworth
3. Rob Waldrop
4. Bobby Engram
5. Greg Lewis
6. Don McPherson
7. Thomas Everett
8. David Pollack

A. Ronnie Lott Trophy
B. Jim Thorpe Award
C. Johnny Unitas Golden Arm Award
D. Doak Walker Award
E. Lou Groza Award
F. Bronko Nagurski Award
G. Fred Biletnikoff Award
H. Dick Butkus Award

1. Pat Fitzgerald
2. Jason Wright
3. Dominic Raiola
4. Brock Olivo
5. Tim Stratton
6. Terrell Suggs
7. Kevin Stemke

A. Bobby Bowden Award
B. Mosi Tatupu Award
C. Ray Guy Award
D. John Mackey Award
E. Dave Rimington Trophy
F. Ted Hendricks Award
G. Chuck Bednarik Award

Now that you know who the initial winners of each of the awards were, can you identify who each of the awards goes to in the next three games?

1. Maxwell Award

A. Honors the country's top college player

2. Ronnie Lott Trophy

B. The top special teams player in the country

3. Bobby Bowden Award

C. The nation's top collegiate punter

4. Ted Hendricks Award

D. The nation's top collegiate defensive end

5. Dave Rimington Trophy

E. The player who best epitomizes the term student-athlete

6. John Mackey Award

F. The nation's top collegiate tight end

7. Ray Guy Award

G. Recognizes the defensive player of the year who has been successful on and off the field

8. Mosi Tatupu Award

H. The nation's top collegiate offensive center

1. Chuck Bednarik Award

A. Honors the country's top college player

2. Fred Biletnikoff Award

B. The nation's top junior or senior running back who combines top achievements on the field, in the classroom, and in the community

3. Bronko Nagurski Award

C. The nation's top defensive player

4. Lou Groza Award

D. Honors college football's defensive player of the year

5. Doak Walker Award

E. The nation's top collegiate pass receiver

6. Johnny Unitas Golden Arm Award

F. The nation's top place-kicker

7. Walter Camp Award

G. The nation's top senior quarterback

414

1. Dick Butkus Award

A. The outstanding player in the Southwest (the award was discontinued after the 1980 season)

2. Heisman Trophy

B. Honors the country's top lineman or linebacker

3. Manning Award

C. The nation's top collegiate defensive back

4. John Outland Trophy

D. The nation's top collegiate quarterback

5. Jim Thorpe Award

E. Originally awarded to the best college player east of the Mississippi River, it is now given to the outstanding player in the country

6. Vince Lombardi Rotary Award

F. The nation's top interior lineman

7. O'Brien Memorial Trophy

G. The nation's top collegiate linebacker

Now for two games of oddities regarding all the college awards.

1. Archie Griffin

2. Johnny Lattner

3. Dave Rimington

4. O.J. Simpson

5. Orlando Pace

6. Mike Singletary

7. Danny Wuerffel

A. Only player to win the John Outland Trophy twice

B. Only player to win the O'Brien Memorial Trophy twice

C. Only player to win the Maxwell Award twice

D. Only player to win the Vince Lombardi Rotary Award twice

E. Only player to win the Heisman Trophy twice

F. First player to win the Davey O'Brien National Quarterback Award twice

G. First player to win the Walter Camp Award twice

1. Brian Bosworth

2. Ricky Williams

3. Sebastian Janikowski

4. Pat Fitzgerald

5. David Pollack

A. First player to win the Heisman Trophy, Maxwell Award, Walter Camp Award, and Doak Walker Award all in the same season

B. Only player to win the Ted Hendricks Award twice

C. Only player to win the Lou Groza Award twice

D. Only player to win the Dick Butkus Award twice

E. Only player to win the Doak Walker Award twice

6. Archie Griffin   F. Only player to win the Bronko Nagurski Award twice

7. Eddie George   G. Second of only two players to win the Walter Camp Award twice

Now let's see if you can identify who gives out each of the awards named in the next two games.

1. Chuck Bednarik Award

     A. Football Writers Association of America and the Charlotte, North Carolina Touchdown Club

2. Fred Biletnikoff Award

     B. Quarterback Club of Tallahassee, Florida

3. Bronko Nagurski Award

     C. Football Writers Association of America

4. Doak Walker Award

     D. Maxwell Memorial Football Club of Philadelphia, Pa.

5. Lou Groza Award

     E. Palm Beach County Sports Commission

6. Dick Butkus Award

     F. Downtown Athletic Club of Orlando, Florida

7. John Outland Trophy

     G. GTE/SMU Athletic Forum in Dallas, Texas

1. Heisman Trophy

2. Ray Guy Award

3. Dave Rimington Trophy

4. Ted Hendricks Award

5. Manning Award

6. Ronnie Lott Trophy

7. Bobby Bowden Award

A. Pacific Club of Newport Beach, California

B. Boomer Esiason Foundation

C. Miami, Florida Touchdown Club

D. Greater Augusta, Georgia Sports Council

E. Downtown Athletic Club of New York City

F. Fellowship of Christian Athletes

G. Nokia Sugar Bowl

CHAPTER 18

COLLEGE BOWL GAMES

Okay, fans, we're building to a climax here. Just like the regular college football season culminates in a gazillion bowl games, this is your last chapter of college football trivia, and it's ALL bowl games. By the time you're through with this chapter, you'll be able to beat all your buddies in those barroom football trivia games in which the loser buys the drinks. (Now *there's* something to look forward to.)

In the first four games, see if you can match these once major but now defunct bowl games to the city in which they were played.

1. Presidential Cup

2. Christmas Festival

3. Cherry Bowl

4. Salad Bowl

5. Raisin Bowl

6. Shrine Bowl

7. Aviation Bowl

A. Fresno, California

B. Pontiac, Michigan

C. Dayton, Ohio

D. College Park, Maryland

E. Little Rock, Arkansas

F. Phoenix, Arizona

G. Los Angeles, California

1. Alamo Bowl   A. San Antonio, Texas

2. Oahu Classic   B. Havana, Cuba

3. Aloha Bowl   C. San Diego, California

4. Bacardi Bowl   D. Lafayette, Louisiana

5. East-West Christmas Classic   E. Seattle, Washington

6. Silicon Valley Football Classic   F. San Jose, California

7. Camellia Bowl   G. Honolulu, Hawaii

1. Freedom Bowl   A. Dallas, Texas

2. Dixie Classic   B. Anaheim, California

3. Dixie Bowl   C. Memphis, Tennessee

4. Delta Bowl   D. Los Angeles, California

5. Bayou City Bowl   E. Houston, Texas

6. Mercy Bowl   F. Birmingham, Alabama

7. Harbor Bowl   G. San Diego, California

1. Bluegrass Bowl   A. Birmingham, Alabama

2. Bluebonnet Bowl   B. Fresno, California

3. Hall of Fame Classic   C. Pasadena, California

4. Garden State Bowl   D. New York, New York

5. Gotham Bowl	E. Louisville, Kentucky
6. Junior Rose Bowl	F. East Rutherford, New Jersey
7. California Bowl	G. Houston, Texas

Those were too easy, you say? Okay, in the next six games let's try some incredibly obscure defunct bowl games, all of which were in existence *for only one year*.

1. Aluminum Bowl, 1956	A. Richmond, Virginia
2. Angel Bowl, 1956	B. Abilene, Texas
3. Azalea Bowl, 1946	C. Allentown, Pennsylvania
4. Beaver Bowl, 1958	D. Corry, Pennsylvania
5. Bicentennial Bowl, 1976	E. Little Rock, Arkansas
6. Boy's Ranch Bowl, 1947	F. Orlando, Florida
7. Cement Bowl, 1962	G. Los Angeles, California

1. Charity Bowl, 1937	A. Allentown, Pennsylvania
2. Cosmopolitan Bowl, 1951	B. Corpus Christi, Texas
3. Doll & Toy Charity Game, 1937	C. Los Angeles, California
4. Eastern Bowl, 1963	D. Alexandria, Louisiana
5. Fish Bowl, 1948	E. Brunswick, Georgia
6. Gate City Bowl, 1974	F. Gulfport, Mississippi
7. Golden Isles Bowl, 1962	G. Atlanta, Georgia

1. Great Lakes Bowl, 1947
2. Great Southwest Bowl, 1960
3. Kickapoo Bowl, 1947
4. Lions Bowl, 1952
5. Mercy Bowl II, 1971
6. Mirza Shrine Bowl, 1950
7. Missouri-Kansas Bowl, 1948

A. Grand Prairie, Texas
B. Wichita Falls, Texas
C. Pittsburg, Kansas
D. Cleveland, Ohio
E. Kansas City, Missouri
F. Anaheim, California
G. Salisbury, North Carolina

1. National Classic, 1954
2. Fort Worth Classic, 1921
3. Oleander Bowl, 1948
4. Palmetto Shrine, 1955
5. Peanut Bowl, 1968
6. Peninsula Bowl, 1950
7. Phillips Field Bowl, 1951

A. Tampa, Florida
B. Columbia, South Carolina
C. Greensboro, North Carolina
D. Charleston, South Carolina
E. Dothan, Alabama
F. Galveston, Texas
G. Fort Worth, Texas

1. Optimist Bowl, 1946
2. Piedmont Tobacco Bowl, 1946
3. Pretzel Bowl, 1951
4. Rocket Bowl, 1960

A. Reading, Pennsylvania
B. Houston, Texas
C. Pasadena, Texas
D. Galveston, Texas

5. San Jacinto Shrine Bowl, 1976   E. Knoxville, Tennessee

6. Share Bowl, 1971   F. Fayetteville, North Carolina

7. Shrimp Bowl, 1952   G. Huntsville, Alabama

1. Shrine Bowl, 1972   A. Spartanburg, South Carolina

2. Smoky Mountain Bowl, 1949   B. Lexington, Kentucky

3. Sugar Cup Classic, 1964   C. Evansville, Indiana

4. Textile Bowl, 1974   D. Oklahoma City, Oklahoma

5. Tobacco Bowl, 1946   E. New Orleans, Louisiana

6. Turkey Bowl, 1946   F. Bristol, Tennessee

7. Will Rogers Bowl, 1947   G. Ardmore, Oklahoma

Now for six games of obscure bowl games that managed to last more than just one year.

1. All-Sports Bowl, 1961–64   A. Tampa, Florida

2. Boot Hill Bowl, 1970–80   B. Oklahoma City, Oklahoma

3. Burley Bowl, 1946–56   C. Miami, Florida

4. Cattle Bowl, 1947–48   D. Dodge City, Kansas

5. Christmas Bowl, 1958–59   E. Fort Worth, Texas

6. Cigar Bowl, 1947–54   F. Johnson City, Tennessee

7. Coconut Bowl, 1942, 1946–1947   G. Natchitoches, Louisiana

1. Corn Bowl, 1947–55	A. Jacksonville, Florida
2. Cotton-Tobacco Bowl, 1946–47	B. San Francisco, California
3. Cowboy Bowl, 1971–72	C. Greensboro, North Carolina
4. Elks Bowl, 1953–54	D. Greenville and Raleigh, North Carolina
5. Flower Bowl, 1942–48	E. Lawton, Oklahoma
6. Fruit Bowl, 1947–48	F. Bloomington, Illinois
7. Glass Bowl, 1946–1949	G. Toledo, Ohio

1. Gold Bowl, 1977–80	A. Honolulu, Hawaii
2. Grape Bowl, 1947–48	B. St. Petersburg, Florida
3. Holiday Bowl, 1957–60	C. Richmond, Virginia
4. Iodine Bowl, 1949–53	D. St. Joseph, Missouri
5. Lions Bowl*, 1946–1952	E. Charleston, South Carolina
6. Moila Shrine Classic, 1979–80	F. Lodi, California
7. New Year's Classic, 1934–35	G. Ruston, Louisiana

---

* *(Different bowl game than the one of the same name used in an earlier game)*

1. Orchid Bowl, 1942/1946   A. Medford, Oregon

2. Palm Festival, 1933–34   B. Macon, Georgia

3. Paper Bowl, 1948–50   C. Pensacola, Florida

4. Peach Blossom Classic, 1939–42   D. Mexico City, Mexico

5. Peach Bowl, 1946–49   E. Orangeburg, South Carolina

6. Pear Bowl, 1946–1951   F. Atlanta, Georgia

7. Pecan Bowl, 1946–47   G. Miami, Florida

1. Pelican Bowl, 1972–75   A. Gainesville, Georgia

2. Pineapple Bowl, 1940–41/1947–52   B. Stuggart, Arkansas

3. Poultry Bowl, 1973–74   C. Honolulu, Hawaii

4. Pythian Bowl, 1949–51   D. Evansville, Indiana

5. Refrigerator Bowl, 1948–56   E. New Orleans, Louisiana

6. Rice Bowl, 1957–58/1960   F. Salisbury, North Carolina

7. Vulcan Bowl, 1942–49   G. Birmingham, Alabama

1. Poi Bowl, 1936–39   A. Clarksburg, West Virginia (duh!)

2. Space City Bowl, 1966–67   B. Mexico City, Mexico

3. Steel Bowl, 1941–42/1952   C. Huntsville, Alabama

4. Texhoma Bowl, 1948–49   D. Birmingham, Alabama

5. Silver Bowl, 1947–49 E. Dallas, Texas

6. West Virginia Bowl, 1960–61 F. Honolulu, Hawaii

7. Yam Bowl, 1946–47 G. Denison, Texas

Each of the bowl games in the next five games was the setting for one of the all-time NCAA single-game bowl records listed. See if you can match them up.

1. Holiday Bowl, 1989

A. Most yards rushing by two backs in the same game with at least 100 yards each—373

2. Freedom Bowl, 1984

B. One of only two bowl games ever to feature a receiver with 20 receptions

3. Sun Bowl, 2001

C. Most touchdown passes by a quarterback—6

4. Rose Bowl, 2006

D. Only bowl game ever in which a running back rushed for more than 300 yards (307)

5. Fiesta Bowl, 1972

E. Most yards rushing by a quarterback—200

6. Humanitarian Bowl, 2004

F. Most passing attempts by a quarterback—74

7. Hall of Fame Bowl, 1982

G. Most total yards offense by one player—594

1. Freedom Bowl, 1991

2. Sun Bowl, 2001

3. Cotton Bowl, 1954

4. Freedom Bowl, 1984

5. Holiday Bowl, 1988

6. Rose Bowl, 1902

7. California Bowl, 1981

A. Most recent of only two times in history when one player rushed for 5 TDs

B. First of only two times in history when one player rushed for 5 TDs

C. Most offensive plays by one player—83

D. Most TD passes in one game by one player—6

E. Most pass completions in one bowl game—43

F. Most rushing attempts by one player—46

G. Highest average gain per play by one player—24.1 yards (11 plays, 265 yards)

1. Outback Bowl, 1998

2. Fiesta Bowl, 1991

3. GMAC Bowl, 2001

4. Sun Bowl, 1968

A. Highest average yards per pass attempt—21.3 (277 yards on 13 attempts)

B. Most passing yards in one quarter—223

C. Most pass receiving yards by one player in one bowl game—299

D. Most recent of only two bowl games to feature 576 net passing yards by one team

5. Aloha Bowl, 1996

E. First of only three times ever in which a receiver had 4 TD receptions

6. Silicon Valley Bowl, 2001

F. Only bowl game ever to feature a quarterback who threw 6 interceptions

7. Camellia Bowl, 1948

G. Most consecutive pass completions—19

1. Cotton Bowl, 1946

A. Only bowl game ever to feature a player who was responsible for 40 points (he rushed for 3 TDs, passed for 2 TDs, caught 1 TD pass, & kicked 4 PATs)

2. Florida Citrus Bowl, 1983

B. First of only four times in history a kicker made 9 extra points in a game

3. Holiday Bowl, 1988

C. First of only two bowl games ever to feature 9 punt returns by one player

4. Fort Worth Classic, 1921

D. Last bowl game to feature a player who rushed for 5 TDs

5. GMAC Bowl, 2001

E. Most punts by one player in a bowl game—21

6. Rose Bowl, 1902

F. First bowl game ever to feature a kicker who made 5 field goals

7. Rose Bowl, 1919

G. Most points in a game by a kicker—19 (4 FGs, 7 PATs)

1. Orange Bowl, 2006

A. Most kickoff return yards—221

2. Salad Bowl, 1950

B. Most punt return yards by a player—180

3. Presidential Cup, 1950

C. Highest kickoff return average—60.5 (2 returns for 121 yards)

4. Rose Bowl, 1925

D. Most tackles made in one bowl game by one player—31

5. Orange Bowl, 1963

E. Only time ever one player sacked the quarterback 6 times

6. Rose Bowl, 2005

F. First of only two bowl games ever to feature 4 interceptions by one player

7. Cotton Bowl, 1997

G. Most interception return yards—148

The next seven games concern record-setting bowl game performances by teams.

1. Sun Bowl, 2001

A. Most yards gained by both teams—1,211

2. Hawaii Bowl, 2003

B. Only bowl game ever to feature a team with negative yards gained—(-21)

3. Fiesta Bowl, 1972

C. Most total plays by one team—107

4. Insight Bowl, 2005

D. Most yards gained by one team—718

5. Cotton Bowl, 1953

E. Fewest total plays by one team—35

6. Sun Bowl, 1945

F. Fewest yards gained by both teams in a bowl game—260

7. Cotton Bowl, 1944

G. Most total plays by both teams—180

1. Sugar Bowl, 1972

A. Most rushing attempts by one team—87

2. Bluebonnet Bowl, 1977

B. Most net rushing yards gained by one team—524

3. Fiesta Bowl, 1996

C. Highest rushing average by one team—9.3 (361 yards on 39 rushing attempts)

4. Sun Bowl, 1974

D. Fewest rushing attempts by both teams—51

5. Copper Bowl, 1995

E. Most net rushing yards gained by both teams—864

6. Hall of Fame Bowl, 1982

F. First of only two times ever in which both teams combined for 122 rushing attempts

7. Insight Bowl, 2004

G. Fewest rushing attempts by one team—12

1. Aloha Bowl, 1994

A. Most pass completions by one team—43

2. Freedom Bowl, 1994

B. Fewest rushing yards in a game by one team—(-61 on 23 attempts)

3. Sun Bowl, 2001

C. Most passing yards by both teams—907

4. California Bowl, 1981

D. Fewest rushing yards in a game by both teams—51

5. Silicon Valley Bowl, 2001

E. Only bowl game ever to feature 12 interceptions

6. Sun Bowl, 1968

F. Most passing attempts by both teams—116

7. Holiday Bowl, 2004

G. Most passes attempted by one team without suffering an interception—60

1. Humanitarian Bowl, 1998

A. Fewest pass attempts by both teams—9

2. Cotton Bowl, 1946

B. Most yards gained per attempt by one team—21.7 (282 yards on 13 pass attempts)

3. Rose Bowl, 1930

C. Most passes attempted by both teams without suffering an interception—93

4. Liberty Bowl, 1991

D. Fewest pass completions by both teams—3

5. Sugar Bowl, 1942

E. Most recent of only three bowl games ever to feature a team which attempted only 2 passes

6. Sun Bowl, 1940

F. Highest completion percentage by one team—.929 (13-for-14, 234 yards)

7. Sun Bowl, 1988

G. Most recent bowl game to feature a team which didn't complete a pass

1. Sun Bowl, 1945

2. Cotton Bowl, 1947

3. Alamo Bowl, 2000

4. GMAC Bowl, 2001

5. Fort Worth Classic, 1921

6. Copper Bowl, 1995

7. GMAC Bowl, 2004

A. Most rushing TDs by one team—8

B. Most passing TDs by both teams—9

C. Most TDs by one team—10

D. Fewest passing yards by one team—(-50)

E. Most rushing TDs by both teams—12

F. Most TDs by both teams—16

G. Most recent of only two bowl games in which both teams combined for only 16 passing yards

1. Peach Bowl, 1995

2. Alamo Bowl, 2000

3. GMAC Bowl, 2001

4. Orange Bowl, 1953

5. Sugar Bowl, 1942

6. Cotton Bowl, 1959

7. Insight.com Bowl, 1999

A. First bowl game to feature 7 field goals

B. Most points scored by a winning team—66

C. Most points scored by a losing team—61

D. Fewest points by a winning team—2

E. Most recent of only two bowl games ever in which a team scored 45 points in one half

F. Most recent of only four bowl games ever to end in a 0–0 tie

G. Game with the largest margin of victory—55 points (61–6)

1. Gator Bowl, 2005

A. Fewest first downs by passing by both teams—1

2. Tangerine Bowl, 2003

B. Most punts by one team in a bowl game—17

3. Cotton Bowl, 1944

C. Most first downs in a game by both teams—62

4. Sugar Bowl, 1962

D. Highest punting average by one team in a bowl game—53.9 (431 yards on 8 punts)

5. Rose Bowl, 1939

E. Most fumbles by both teams—17

6. Rose Bowl, 1953

F. Most first downs by penalty by both teams—12

7. Sugar Bowl, 1964

G. Fewest first downs by both teams—10

Now let's switch gears to the longest plays in college bowl history. See if you can match the record-setting play to the bowl game that featured it.

1. Liberty Bowl, 1962

A. Longest field goal—62 yards

2. Gator Bowl, 1965

B. Longest pass play—95 yards

3. Sun Bowl, 1977

C. Longest interception return—99 yards

4. Cotton Bowl, 1949

D. Longest kickoff return—103 yards

5. MPC Computers Bowl, 2005

E. Longest punt return—92 yards

6. Rose Bowl, 1947

F. Longest punt—84 yards

7. Independence Bowl, 2005

G. Longest run from scrimmage—99 yards

Now let's try some bowl games played overseas by service personnel. And as some of these answers will suggest, once upon a time there was no such thing as political correctness in American sports.

1. Spaghetti Bowl, 1945–1953   A. Nagasaki, Japan

2. Tea Bowl, 1944 (2 games)   B. Dutch Guiana

3. Potato Bowl, 1944   C. Florence, Italy

4. Atom Bowl, 1945   D. Belfast, Ireland

5. Rice Bowl, 1946–58   E. Oran, Africa

6. Arab Bowl, 1944   F. Tokyo, Japan

7. Chigger Bowl, 1945   G. London, England

Now for some NCAA-certified college all-star games. Do you know where they were played?

(Note: games listed without years played are current bowl games.)

1. East-West Shrine Classic   A. San Antonio, Texas (currently, although most of the games since 1925 have been played in the San Francisco Bay area)

2. Senior Bowl   B. Las Vegas, Nevada

3. All-American Classic   C. Maui, Hawaii

4. Magnolia Gridiron All-Star Classic   D. Tampa, Florida

5. Hula Bowl   E. Mobile, Alabama

6. All-American Bowl, 1969–77

F. Jackson, Mississippi

7. American College All-Star Game, 1948

G. Los Angeles, California

More college all-star games, all of which have been discontinued.

1. Black College All-Star Bowl, 1979–82

A. (Played in three sites: Buffalo, New York, Atlanta, Georgia, & Lubbock, Texas)

2. Blue-Gray All-Star Classic, 1939–2001

B. (Played in two sites: New Orleans, Louisiana & Jackson, Mississippi)

3. Canadian-American Bowl, 1978–79

C. Montgomery, Alabama

4. Challenge Bowl, 1978–79

D. Tampa, Florida

5. College All-Star Football Game, 1934–76

E. Seattle, Washington

6. Christian Bowl, 1955

F. Chicago, Illinois

7. Coaches All-American Game, 1961–76

G. Murfreesboro, Tennessee

More defunct all-star games.

1. Copper Bowl, 1958–60

A. Los Angeles, California

2. Crusade Bowl, 1963

B. Houston, Texas

3. Dixie Classic, 1928–31

C. Tempe, Arizona

4. East-West Black All-Star Game, 1971

D. (Played in two sites: San Jose, California & St. Petersburg, Florida)

5. East-West College All-Star Game, 1932

E. Dallas, Texas

6. Martin Luther King All-American Classic, 1990–91

F. Baltimore, Maryland

7. Olympia Gold Bowl, 1982

G. San Diego, California

One last round of defunct college all-star games.

1. Olympic Game, 1933

A. Washington, D.C.

2. Optimist All-America Bowl, 1958–62

B. Richmond, Virginia

3. U.S. Bowl, 1962

C. Bakersfield, California

4. Smoke Bowl, 1941

D. Denver, Colorado

5. Salad Bowl All-Star Game, 1955

E. Tucson, Arizona

6. Elks Charity Bowl, 1930

F. Chicago, Illinois

7. Potato Bowl, 1967

G. Phoenix, Arizona

While not technically bowl games, the contests listed below were special in that they were regular season games played overseas. See if you can match the site with the teams that played there.

1. Osaka, Japan (1978)

A. Utah State defeated Idaho State, 10–0

2. Dublin, Ireland (1996)

B. Notre Dame defeated Navy, 54–27

3. Hamilton, Bermuda (1995)   C. Clemson defeated Duke, 33–21

4. Tokyo, Japan (1991)   D. BYU defeated Colorado State, 30–26

5. Melbourne, Australia   E. Richmond defeated Boston University,
   (1987)   20–17

6. Milan, Italy (1989)   F. Fordham defeated Holy Cross, 17–10

7. London, England (1988)   G. Villanova defeated Rhode Island, 28–25

Now we're going to turn our attention to specific bowl games. See if you can identify each of the events listed to their correct year of occurrence. (Reminder: when the term "year" is used, it means calendar year; when the term "season" is used, it refers to the season connected with that bowl game. For example, if a bowl game was played on January 1, 1994, for the purposes of this book, it is considered to have been played in the year 1994 or was a part of the 1993 season. Pay close attention to the wording of the clue.)

The Rose Bowl.

1. 1942   A. Year the Rose Bowl was played in Durham, North Carolina

2. 1923   B. First season in which a #1 ranked team played in the Rose Bowl (Ohio State)

3. 1981   C. Last season in which the Rose Bowl featured two unranked teams (Alabama and Southern California)

4. 1950   D. First year the Rose Bowl was actually played in the Rose Bowl

5. 1968   E. Last season in which neither Rose Bowl team was ranked in the nation's top 10 (#12 Washington defeated #13 Iowa, 28–0)

6. 1954   F. First season of only two in history in which the country's #1 and #2 teams met in the Rose Bowl (2005 was the other when Texas defeated USC)

7. 1945   G. First year the Rose Bowl attendance topped 100,000 fans

More Rose Bowl.

1. 1927   A. The Rose Bowl record for largest shutout is 49–0, and it's been done twice, both times by Michigan; this was the most recent of the two seasons it was accomplished

2. 1922   B. The season unranked UCLA destroyed #4 Illinois, 45–9

3. 1983   C. Last time the Rose Bowl ended in a tie (7–7, Stanford and Alabama)

4. 1947   D. The season Washington won its second consecutive Rose Bowl as the underdog (#6 Washington upset #1 Minnesota, 17–7)

5. 1979   E. Last season in which the Rose Bowl attendance was below 90,000 (86,848)

6. 1960   F. Only year the Rose Bowl was played to a 0–0 tie (California and Washington & Jefferson)

7. 2002   G. Before #2 Texas' upset of #1 USC in 2005, this was the last season a #1 team was knocked off in the Rose Bowl (USC nipped Ohio State, 17–16)

And one game of particularly memorable Rose Bowls, by _year_.

1. 1966

    A. Trailing 7–6 at the half, #7 Illinois explodes for 27 points in the 4ᵗʰ quarter to trounce #4 Stanford, 40–7

2. 1963

    B. #5 UCLA holds off a furious 4ᵗʰ quarter rally by #1 Michigan State to win, 14–12, as the Spartans twice fail on two-point conversion attempts

3. 1967

    C. Georgia Tech beat California, 8–7, in the fourth straight Rose Bowl to be either decided by one point or end in a tie

4. 1952

    D. Trailing #1 USC 42–14 in the 4ᵗʰ quarter, #2 Wisconsin stages an incredible comeback, scoring 23 unanswered points before finally losing, 42–37

5. 2005

    E. In a nail-biting, see-saw battle, #6 Texas holds on to beat #13 Michigan, 38–37, on a 37-yard field goal as time expired

6. 1929

    F. #7 Purdue nips unranked USC, 14–13, when the Trojans fail to convert a two-point conversion attempt after a 4ᵗʰ quarter touchdown

7. 1925

    G. Though greatly dominated by Stanford, Notre Dame wins the game, 27–10, thanks to interception returns for TDs from 70 and 78 yards, and a 20-yard fumble return for a score

The Orange Bowl.

1. 1938

    A. First year the Orange Bowl featured two ranked opponents (#2 Tennessee defeated #4 Oklahoma, 17–0)

2. 1972

    B. Last year the Orange Bowl featured two unranked teams (Miami of Florida defeated Holy Cross, 13–6)

3. 1939   C. First time a #1 ranked team (Maryland) played in the Orange Bowl

4. 1946   D. First year the Orange Bowl featured a ranked team (#14 Duquesne defeated unranked Mississippi State, 13–12)

5. 1967   E. First year the Orange Bowl was actually played in the Orange Bowl

6. 1954   F. Last year the Orange Bowl featured only one ranked team (#8 Georgia Tech was upset by unranked Florida, 27–12)

7. 1937   G. First Orange Bowl to feature the country's #1 and #2 schools against each other

More Orange Bowl.

1. 2005   A. First year Federal Express had their name attached to the Orange Bowl

2. 1989   B. Calendar year in which no Orange Bowl game was played

3. 2001   C. Last year the Orange Bowl featured the country's #1 and #2 teams against each other

4. 1994   D. Year #1 Florida State defeated #2 Nebraska, 18–16

5. 1998   E. Year #1 Oklahoma defeated #3 Florida State, 13–2

6. 1995   F. Year #1 Nebraska defeated #3 Miami of Florida, 24–17

7. 1997   G. Year #2 Nebraska defeated #3 Tennessee, 42–17

One more game of Orange Bowl.

1. 1995   A. The highest scoring Orange Bowl (Florida defeated Maryland, 56–23)

2. 1938   B. The Orange Bowl which saw the most points scored by one team (61 by Alabama)

3. 1953   C. The first Orange Bowl to go into overtime (Michigan defeated Alabama, 35–34)

4. 2002   D. Before the 2007 Orange Bowl which featured #15 Wake Forest, this was the only Orange Bowl since 1960 to feature a team ranked lower than #13

5. 2000   E. The Orange Bowl which took three overtimes to settle (Penn State defeated Florida State, 26–23)

6. 2006   F. The lowest scoring Orange Bowl (Auburn defeated Michigan State, 6–0)

7. 1999   G. Year the Orange Bowl set its attendance record (81,753)

The Sugar Bowl.

1. 1974   A. Last year the Sugar Bowl was played in Tulane Stadium

2. 1987   B. Last Sugar Bowl to feature the country's #1 and #2 teams against each other

3. 1946   C. Last year the Sugar Bowl didn't have an advertising name attached

4. 1991   D. First year the Sugar Bowl had the Nokia name attached

5. 1976   E. Last year the Sugar Bowl featured two unranked teams (Oklahoma State and St. Mary's of California)

6. 1996 F. Last Sugar Bowl to feature only one ranked team (#10 Tennessee defeated unranked Virginia, 23–22)

7. 2000 G. Calendar year in which there was no Sugar Bowl

More Sugar Bowl.

1. 1979 A. Only Sugar Bowl to go into overtime (West Virginia defeated Georgia, 38–35)

2. 1984 B. First Sugar Bowl to feature a match-up of the country's #1 and #2 teams (#2 Alabama defeated #1 Penn State, 14–7)

3. 1972 C. Only Sugar Bowl since 1959 in which both teams scored less than 10 points (Auburn defeated Michigan, 9–7)

4. 2006 D. The highest scoring Sugar Bowl (LSU defeated Illinois, 47–34)

5. 1997 E. Sugar Bowl which featured the most points by one team (52 by Florida)

6. 2002 F. Last season to feature a Sugar Bowl in which one of the teams suffered a shutout (Oklahoma beat Penn State, 14–0)

7. 1988 G. The only Sugar Bowl ever to end in a tie (Auburn and Syracuse played to a 16–16 draw)

One more Sugar Bowl.

1. 1942   A. The lowest scoring Sugar Bowl (Fordham defeated Missouri, 2–0)

2. 1936   B. Year Santa Clara won its second straight Sugar Bowl, defeating #8 LSU, 6–0

3. 1950   C. Sugar Bowl in which Arkansas defeated Georgia, 16–2

4. 1969   D. Sugar Bowl in which TCU defeated LSU, 3–2

5. 1973   E. First Sugar Bowl to feature an MVP selection (Bobby Layne)

6. 1938   F. Season which featured #3 Notre Dame upsetting #1 Alabama in the Sugar Bowl, 24–23

7. 1948   G. Sugar Bowl which featured the largest shutout (Oklahoma defeated LSU, 35–0)

The Sun Bowl.

1. 1963   A. Last year the Sun Bowl was officially known as The John Hancock Bowl (no "Sun" in the name)

2. 1985   B. First year the Sun Bowl was actually played in the Sun Bowl

3. 2002   C. Last year the Sun Bowl featured two unranked teams (Purdue defeated Washington, 34–24)

4. 1990   D. Last year the Sun Bowl featured two ranked teams (#22 Michigan State defeated #21 Southern California, 17–16)

5. 1993   E. Sun Bowl in which UCLA defeated Illinois, 6–3

6. 1983 F. Sun Bowl featuring the highest ranked team ever to play in it (#6 SMU lost to unranked Alabama, 28–7)

7. 1991 G. Last year there was no advertising name attached to the Sun Bowl

More Sun Bowl.

1. 1957 A. Sun Bowl in which Alabama defeated Army, 29–28

2. 2005 B. Sun Bowl in which UTEP crushed Florida State, 47–20

3. 1940 C. The season UTEP played in its third Sun Bowl in four years

4. 1985 D. Only Sun Bowl in the first 26 years of its existence to feature a ranked team (#17 George Washington)

5. 1956 E. The last Sun Bowl to end in a tie (Arizona and Georgia played to a 13–13 draw) was also the Sun Bowl with the highest attendance (52,203)

6. 1955 F. The highest scoring Sun Bowl ever (UCLA defeated Northwestern, 50–38)

7. 1988 G. The lowest scoring Sun Bowl ever (Arizona State and Catholic University played to a 0–0 tie)

The Cotton Bowl.

1. 1937 A. Last year the Cotton Bowl ended in a tie (#6 Air Force tied #10 TCU, 0–0)

2. 1989 B. Only year the Cotton Bowl was played somewhere other than the Cotton Bowl

3. 1946   C. The year Texas played in its sixth consecutive Cotton Bowl (#12 Nebraska defeated #8 Texas, 19–3)

4. 1963   D. The only Cotton Bowl to feature the country's top two teams (#1 Texas defeated #2 Navy, 28–6)

5. 1959   E. Last year the Cotton Bowl featured a shutout (#7 LSU defeated #4 Texas, 13–0)

6. 1964   F. Last year the Cotton Bowl featured two unranked teams (Texas defeated Missouri, 40–27)

7. 1974   G. Year "Mobil" was added to the Cotton Bowl name

More Cotton Bowl.

1. 1994   A. Cotton Bowl in which unranked LSU shocked #2 Arkansas, 14–7, and vaulted all the way to #8 in the final AP poll)

2. 1978   B. First year the Cotton Bowl ended in a 0-0 tie (#8 LSU and #16 Arkansas were the opponents)

3. 1947   C. Last Cotton Bowl to feature an unranked team defeating a ranked team (Texas A & M upset #9 Alabama, 20–16)

4. 1966   D. Calendar year in which no Cotton Bowl was held

5. 1968   E. The highest scoring Cotton Bowl ever (Boston College defeated Houston, 45–28)

6. 1967   F. Last Cotton Bowl to feature two teams ranked in the Top 10 (#4 Notre Dame defeated #7 Texas A & M, 24–21)

7. 1985   G. Last Cotton Bowl to feature a #1 ranked team (#1 Texas was drubbed by #5 Notre Dame, 38–10)

One more Cotton Bowl.

1. 1979

2. 1948

3. 1986

4. 1991

5. 1984

6. 1995

7. 1960

A. The Cotton Bowl with the lowest attendance since WWII (32,500) was one of the best; trailing 34–12, Notre Dame rallies with 23 4th quarter points to defeat Houston, 35–34

B. Texas A & M plays in the first of six Cotton Bowls in a nine-year stretch, defeating Auburn, 36–16

C. #7 Georgia upsets #2 Texas, 10–9, scoring the game's only touchdown in the 4th quarter

D. #3 SMU and #4 Penn State play to a 13–13 tie, the second straight Cotton Bowl to end in a deadlock

E. #1 Syracuse defeats #4 Texas, 23–14

F. #4 Miami of Florida shows #3 Texas that they don't belong on the same field together, thrashing the Longhorns, 46–3

G. #21 USC takes a 28–0 lead in the 1st quarter, and cruises to a 55–14 rout of unranked Texas Tech

The Gator Bowl.

1. 1986

2. 1993

3. 1998

4. 2007

A. Last year the Gator Bowl featured a Top 10 team (#7 North Carolina crushed unranked Virginia Tech, 42–3)

B. Year the name Mazda was attached to the Gator Bowl

C. Calendar year in which there was no Gator Bowl

D. Season which featured the Gator Bowl with the highest attendance (82,911—#14 Clemson defeated #17 West Virginia, 27–7)

5. 1980   E. Last year the Gator Bowl was actually played in the Gator Bowl

6. 1989   F. Gator Bowl which featured the highest ranked team to play (#3 Pittsburgh defeated #18 South Carolina, 37–9)

7. 1990   G. Highest scoring Gator Bowl ever (#13 West Virginia defeated unranked Georgia Tech, 38–35)

More Gator Bowl.

1. 1966   A. Lowest scoring Gator Bowl ever (#13 Tennessee defeated #9 Texas A & M, 3–0)

2. 1996   B. Last 20th century Gator Bowl to feature two unranked teams (Tennessee defeated Syracuse, 18–12)

3. 1946   C. Gator Bowl with the lowest attendance ever (7,362— Wake Forest defeated South Carolina, 26–14)

4. 1987   D. First Gator Bowl to feature two Top 10 teams (#9 Oklahoma State defeated #7 South Carolina, 21–14)

5. 1984   E. Last Gator Bowl to feature two Top 10 teams (#7 LSU defeated #9 South Carolina, 30–13)

6. 1957   F. Last Gator Bowl to end in a tie (#10 Penn State was played to a 17–17 draw by unranked Florida State)

7. 1967   G. Last Gator Bowl to feature a shutout (unranked Syracuse embarrassed #23 Clemson, 41–0)

The Capital One Bowl (originated as the Tangerine Bowl in 1946, and has had numerous names since).

1. 1982

    A. Only Capital One Bowl ever to feature two teams from the Top 19 (Tennessee defeated Ohio State, 20–14, when both teams came into the game tied for 4th in the A.P. poll)

2. 1968

    B. Last year a Top 10 team appeared in the Capital One Bowl (#6 Wisconsin defeated #12 Arkansas, 17–14)

3. 2007

    C. First year a Top 10 team appeared in the Capital One Bowl (#2 Georgia Tech defeated #19 Nebraska, 45–21)

4. 1991

    D. Last year the game was known as the Tangerine Bowl

5. 1996

    E. Last year the game ended in a tie (#15 Florida State and unranked Georgia played to a 17–17 draw)

6. 2005

    F. First year a ranked team was featured (#15 Ohio University was upset by unranked Richmond, 49–42, which was also the highest scoring game in the history of the bowl)

7. 1984

    G. Capital One Bowl in which #11 Iowa defeated #12 LSU, 30–25

More Capital One Bowl.

1. 1958

    A. Lowest attendance (4,000) of any game in the series (East Texas State defeated Missouri Valley, 26–7)

2. 1998

    B. Lowest scoring game in the series (Catawba defeated Marshall, 7–0)

3. 1949

    C. First year the game ended in a tie (Murray State and Sul Ross State played to a 21–21 draw)

4. 1948   D. Capital One Bowl in which Peyton Manning was named the game's MVP for leading his #9 Tennessee team to a 48–28 victory over #11 Northwestern

5. 1997   E. The calendar year in which no Capital One Bowl game was played

6. 2000   F. Highest attendance (72,940) of any game in the series (#6 Florida defeated #11 Penn State, 21–6)

7. 1986   G. Capital One Bowl in which Plaxico Burress was named the game's MVP for leading his #9 Michigan State team to a 37–34 victory over #10 Florida

The Liberty Bowl.

1. 1993   A. Lowest scoring Liberty Bowl ever (Oregon State defeated Villanova, 6–0)

2. 2003   B. First year the game was known as St. Jude Liberty Bowl

3. 1965   C. Highest scoring Liberty Bowl ever (#7 Louisville defeated #10 Boise State, 44–40)

4. 2004   D. Liberty Bowl in which #15 Syracuse defeated unranked Miami of Florida, 15–14

5. 1962   E. Last year the game was known as the AXA Liberty Bowl

6. 1975   F. First year the Liberty Bowl was actually played in the Liberty Bowl

7. 1961   G. Liberty Bowl which featured the highest ranked team (#2 Texas A&M was embarrassed by unranked USC, 20–0)

More Liberty Bowl.

1. 1984   A. Last Liberty Bowl in which both teams scored under 10 points (unranked Penn State upset #15 Tulane, 9–6)

2. 1983   B. The most one-sided Liberty Bowl ever (#22 Southern Mississippi defeated unranked Pittsburgh, 41–7)

3. 1991   C. Liberty Bowl in which Doug Flutie was named the game's MVP, even though his #13 Boston College team was upset by unranked Notre Dame, 19–18

4. 1964   D. Liberty Bowl in which Bo Jackson was named the game's MVP after leading his #16 Auburn team to a victory over unranked Arkansas, 21–15

5. 1959   E. Lowest attendance (6,059) of any Liberty Bowl (Utah defeated West Virginia, 32–6)

6. 1997   F. First Liberty Bowl to feature a Top 10 team (#10 Alabama lost to #12 Penn State, 7–0)

7. 1979   G. Liberty Bowl in which quarterback Rob Perez won his second straight Liberty Bowl MVP Award for leading his Air Force team to a 38–15 trouncing of Mississippi State

The Peach Bowl.

1. 1971   A. Only Peach Bowl ever to feature a Top 10 team, and *both* teams were Top 10 teams (#10 LSU crushed #9 Miami of Florida, 40–3)

2. 1993   B. Last Peach Bowl to feature two unranked teams (Clemson defeated Tennessee, 27–14)

3. 2005   C. First year the Peach Bowl was played in Atlanta-Fulton County Stadium

4. 2004   D. Lowest scoring Peach Bowl ever was also the only time
           the game ended in a tie (Texas Tech and Vanderbilt,
           6–6)

5. 1997   E. Highest scoring Peach Bowl ever (unranked Arizona
           State defeated unranked North Carolina, 48–26)

6. 1974   F. First year the game was known as Chick-fil-A Peach
           Bowl

7. 1970   G. First year the Peach Bowl was played in the Georgia
           Dome

The Fiesta Bowl.

1. 1971   A. Only Fiesta Bowl ever to feature two unranked teams
           (Oklahoma State defeated BYU, 16–6)

2. 1975   B. First year the Fiesta Bowl was played in Sun Devil
           Stadium

3. 1974   C. Fiesta Bowl in which #14 UCLA defeated #13 Miami of
           Florida, 39–37)

4. 1994   D. First Fiesta Bowl to feature the country's #1 and #2
           teams (#2 Penn State upset #1 Miami of Florida, 14–10)

5. 1987   E. Highest scoring Fiesta Bowl ever (#1 Nebraska defeated
           #2 Florida, 62–24)

6. 1996   F. Only Fiesta Bowl ever to feature a shutout (#16 Arizona
           upset #10 Miami of Florida, 29–0)

7. 1985   G. First Fiesta Bowl to feature two Top 10 teams (#7
           Arizona State upset #6 Nebraska, 17–14)

More Fiesta Bowl.

1. 2007   A. Fiesta Bowl with lowest attendance (48,174) ever (#8 Oklahoma crushed unranked Wyoming, 41–7)

2. 2003   B. Fiesta Bowl in which #2 Oregon beat #3 Colorado, 38–16

3. 1978   C. Last Fiesta Bowl to go into overtime (#9 Boise State defeated #7 Oklahoma, 43–42)

4. 1976   D. Last Fiesta Bowl to feature the country's two top teams (#2 Ohio State upset #1 Miami of Florida, 31–24 in two overtimes)

5. 1999   E. Last Fiesta Bowl to feature an unranked team (#4 Colorado defeated unranked Notre Dame, 41–24)

6. 1995   F. Fiesta Bowl with highest attendance (80,470) ever (#1 Tennessee defeated #2 Florida State, 23–16)

7. 2002   G. Only Fiesta Bowl to end in a tie (#8 Arkansas and #15 UCLA played to a 10–10 draw)

The Independence Bowl.

1. 1991   A. Last Independence Bowl to feature a ranked team (#15 LSU defeated unranked Notre Dame, 27–9)

2. 1997   B. Only Independence Bowl to go into overtime (Mississippi State defeated Texas A & M, 43–41)

3. 1993   C. Only Independence Bowl ever to feature two ranked teams (#22 Virginia Tech defeated #21 Indiana, 45–20)

4. 2000   D. Only Independence Bowl ever to end in a tie (Louisiana Tech and Maryland played to a 34–34 draw)

5. 1983   E. First year the Independence Bowl was played in Independence Stadium

6. 1976   F. Lowest scoring Independence Bowl ever (#16 Air Force defeated unranked Mississippi, 9–3) also was the first one to feature a ranked team

7. 1990   G. First year the game became known as the Poulan/Weed Eater Independence Bowl

The Holiday Bowl.

1. 1992   A. Highest scoring Holiday Bowl ever (#14 BYU defeated #19 SMU, 46–45)

2. 1984   B. Second highest scoring Holiday Bowl ever (#9 Texas defeated #21 Washington, 47–43)

3. 1980   C. Only Holiday Bowl ever to end in a tie (#7 Iowa and unranked BYU played to a 13–13 draw) was also the lowest scoring game in the series

4. 1991   D. Holiday Bowl which featured the most points by one team (unranked Texas A & M smashed #13 BYU, 65–14)

5. 2001   E. Year BYU played in its first of seven consecutive Holiday Bowls (lost to Navy, 23–16)

6. 1978   F. Last Holiday Bowl to feature two unranked teams (Hawaii defeated Illinois, 27–17)

7. 1990   G. Only Holiday Bowl ever to feature the country's #1 team (#1 BYU defeated unranked Michigan, 24–17)

The Outback Bowl (previously called the Hall of Fame Bowl).

1. 1996

A. Only game in the series to feature a shutout (#14 Clemson defeated #16 Illinois, 30–0)

2. 1988

B. Only game in the series to feature two unranked teams (Michigan defeated Alabama, 28–24)

3. 2000

C. Outback Bowl which featured the highest ranked team (#8 Georgia defeated #16 Wisconsin 24–21)

4. 2005

D. First year the game was called the Outback Bowl.

5. 2003

E. Only Outback Bowl to go into overtime (#21 Georgia upset #19 Purdue, 28–25)

6. 1991

F. Only year the game was played in December (Unranked Boston College upset #17 Georgia, 27–24)

7. 1986

G. Highest scoring Outback Bowl ever (#12 Michigan defeated #22 Florida, 38–30)

The Insight Bowl (previously called the Copper Bowl).

1. 1991

A. Insight Bowl which featured the most points by one team (unranked Colorado shocked #25 Boston College, 62–28)

2. 1996

B. Only Insight Bowl ever to go into overtime (Texas Tech defeated Minnesota, 44–41)

3. 2003

C. The first year Domino's Pizza had its name attached to the game (California defeated Wyoming, 17–15)

4. 2006

D. Last year the Copper Bowl did not have an advertising name attached to it (Wisconsin defeated Utah, 38–10)

5. 2002   E. Only year the game featured a shutout (Indiana blanked Baylor, 24–0)

6. 1990   F. Last Insight Bowl to feature a ranked team (#24 Pittsburgh defeated Oregon State, 38–13)

7. 1999   G. Highest scoring Insight Bowl ever (California nipped Virginia Tech, 52–49)

The Champs Sports Bowl (previously known by five other names).

1. 1990   A. Only year the game featured two Top 10 teams (#6 Florida State defeated #7 Penn State, 24–17, the first year the game was called the Blockbuster Bowl)

2. 1999   B. The year Pittsburgh defeated North Carolina State, 34–19 (only year it was called the Visit Florida Tangerine Bowl)

3. 1993   C. Lowest scoring game in the series (#13 Stanford defeated #21 Penn State, 24–3, the last year the game was called the Blockbuster Bowl)

4. 2002   D. The year North Carolina State and Kansas combined for an incredible 62 first downs and over 1,100 yards of offense (NC State won, 56–26)

5. 1997   E. The year Georgia Tech defeated West Virginia, 35–30 (the last year it was called the Carquest Bowl)

6. 2001   F. The year Texas Tech defeated Clemson, 55–15 (the first year it was called the Mazda Tangerine Bowl)

7. 2003   G. Highest scoring game in the series (Illinois trounced Virginia, 63–21, when it was called the Micron PC Bowl)

The Las Vegas Bowl.

1. 1995

A. First year the game was known as the Pioneer PureVision Las Vegas Bowl (Wyoming defeated UCLA, 24–21)

2. 2001

B. Only Las Vegas Bowl to go into overtime, which was also the first overtime game played in NCAA 1–A history (#25 Toledo defeated Nevada, 40–37)

3. 1992

C. Last year the game was known as the Sega Sports Las Vegas Bowl (UCLA defeated New Mexico, 27–13)

4. 2004

D. Lowest scoring Las Vegas Bowl ever (Utah defeated Southern California, 10–6)

5. 2003

E. First Las Vegas Bowl played at Sam Boyd Stadium (Bowling Green defeated Nevada, 35–34)

6. 2002

F. Only year the game was known as the EA Sports Las Vegas Bowl (Utah defeated Fresno State, 17–16)

7. 1999

G. Las Vegas Bowl featuring the most points by one team (Oregon State defeated New Mexico, 55–14)

The Alamo Bowl.

1. 2006

A. Only Alamo Bowl game to go into overtime (unranked Wisconsin upset #14 Colorado, 31–28)

2. 1993

B. Last year the game was known as the Sylvania Alamo Bowl (Iowa defeated Texas Tech, 19–16)

3. 2002

C. Year the game's attendance (65,875) set not only an Alamo Bowl record, but an Alamodome facility record (#18 Texas defeated unranked Iowa, 26–24)

4. 1998   D. Alamo Bowl which ended with one of the most contro-
versial plays in college football history, similar to 1982's
"The Play" (unranked Nebraska defeated #20 Michigan,
32–28)

5. 2000   E. Alamo Bowl featuring the highest ranked team (Purdue
shocked #4 Kansas State, 37–34)

6. 2001   F. First year the Alamo Bowl was played in the
Alamodome (California defeated Iowa, 37–3)

7. 2005   G. Alamo Bowl which featured the most points by one
team and which was the highest scoring ever (#9
Nebraska trounced #18 Northwestern, 66–17)

The Motor City Bowl.

1. 2003   A. Motor City Bowl which featured the highest ranked
team (#11 Marshall defeated unranked BYU, 21–3)

2. 1999   B. Although the game is intended to pit a team from the
Mid-American Conference against one from the Big Ten,
this is the only one in which a Big Ten team played
(Bowling Green defeated Northwestern, 28–24)

3. 1998   C. First Motor City Bowl that didn't feature Marshall as one
of the opponents (#25 Toledo defeated Cincinnati, 23–16)

4. 2001   D. Highest scoring Motor City Bowl ever (Marshall defeated Louisville, 48–29)

5. 1997   E. Motor City Bowl with the highest attendance (54,113) ever
(Central Michigan defeated Middle Tennessee, 31–14)

6. 2002   F. First Motor City Bowl played in the Pontiac Silverdome
(Mississippi defeated Marshall, 34–31)

7. 2006   G. First Motor City Bowl played at Ford Field (Boston
College thumped Toledo, 51–25)

The MPC Computers Bowl (previously known by several other names).

1. 2007

A. Highest scoring MPC Computers Bowl game ever (Idaho defeated Southern Mississippi, 42–35)

2. 1997

B. Only MPC Computers Bowl game to go into overtime (Fresno State defeated Virginia, 37–34)

3. 2004

C. First year the game was played at Bronco Stadium (Cincinnati defeated Utah State, 35–19)

4. 2006

D. Last season the game was named Crucial.com Humanitarian Bowl (Georgia Tech crushed Tulsa, 52–10)

5. 1998

E. Year the game's name changed to the Roady's Truck Stops Humanitarian Bowl (eesh!)

6. 2003

F. Lowest scoring MPC Computers Bowl game ever (Miami of Florida defeated Nevada, 21–20)

7. 2002

G. MPC Computers Bowl featuring the highest ranked team (#18 Boise State defeated Iowa State, 34–16)

The Music City Bowl.

1. 2002

A. Only year the game was played at Vanderbilt Stadium (Virginia Tech crushed Alabama, 38–7)

2. 1998

B. Only year the game was known as the HomePoint.com Music City Bowl (Syracuse defeated Kentucky, 20–13)

3. 2000

C. Year Kentucky defeated Clemson, 28–20

4. 2003

D. Music City Bowl featuring the highest ranked team ever (unranked Boston College upset #16 Georgia, 20–16)

5. 2006   E. Year the game became known as the Gaylord Hotels Music City Bowl presented by Bridgestone (Auburn defeated Wisconsin, 28–14)

6. 1999   F. Highest scoring Music City Bowl game ever (West Virginia defeated Mississippi, 49–38)

7. 2001   G. Year the game became known as the Gaylord Hotels Music City Bowl (unranked Minnesota upset #25 Arkansas, 29–14)

The GMAC Bowl.

1. 2001   A. Only season in which the GMAC Bowl featured a team that scored less than 13 points in the game (Southern Mississippi defeated Ohio, 28–7)

2. 1999   B. Only GMAC Bowl to feature a ranked team (#14 Miami of Ohio defeated Louisville, 49–28)

3. 2003   C. The GMAC Bowl game considered to be one of the top 25 college games ever played (Marshall beat East Carolina, 64–61, in two overtimes)

4. 2006   D. Year LaDainian Tomlinson won the GMAC Bowl MVP Award, even though his TCU team lost to Southern Mississippi, 28–21

5. 2002   E. Only year the game was known as the Mobile Alabama Bowl (TCU defeated East Carolina, 28–14)

6. 2000   F. Year Byron Leftwich won his second consecutive GMAC Bowl MVP Award (Marshall defeated Louisville, 38–15)

7. 2004   G. Year Omar Jacobs tossed five TD passes as he led his Bowling Green team to a 52–35 win over Memphis

Miscellaneous newer bowl games.

1. Houston Bowl

    A. First played in 2003 as the PlainsCapital Bowl(#18 Boise State defeated #19 TCU, 34–31)

2. New Orleans Bowl

    B. Trick question; this bowl game doesn't really exist

3. Hawaii Bowl

    C. First played in 2002 as the Diamond Walnut San Francisco Bowl (#21 Virginia Tech defeated unranked Air Force, 20–13)

4. Meineke Car Care Bowl

    D. First played in 2002 as the Continental Tire Bowl (unranked Virginia defeated #15 West Virginia, 48–22)

5. Emerald Bowl

    E. First played in 2002 as the ConAgra Foods Bowl (Tulane defeated Hawaii, 36–28)

6. Fort Worth Bowl

    F. First played in 2000 and was then known as the galleryfurniture.com Bowl (East Carolina defeated Texas Tech, 40–27)

7. Kellogg's Cereal Bowl

    G. First game played in 2001 (Colorado State defeated North Texas, 45–20) and in 2004 Wyndham was added to the game's name

CHAPTER 19

THE SUPER BOWL

All right, here's the chapter you've been waiting for. Easily the most widely watched program on television—worldwide—is the Super Bowl. With an audience of one billion people, including tens of millions in China—*China?*—the Super Bowl deserves a super chapter in *Super Football Challenge*, and that's exactly what you're getting. With nearly 800 trivia questions in 112 games—all about the Super Bowl—even the most voracious football trivia appetite will be sated. And with the knowledge you'll gain from this chapter, you'll win all the bar bets, get all the girls, and even impress your friends in China, 'cuz this book isn't being published in Chinese. At least not yet.

Match these unforgettable Super Bowls with their final scores.

1. Super Bowl I   A. 14–7
   (Packers-Chiefs)

2. Super Bowl VII   B. 20–19
   (Dolphins-Redskins)

3. Super Bowl XXV   C. 21–17
   (Giants-Bills)

4. Super Bowl X   D. 16–13
   (Steelers-Cowboys)

5. Super Bowl XXXIV   E. 16–7
   (Rams-Titans)

6. Super Bowl III   F. 35–10
   (Jets-Colts)

7. Super Bowl V   G. 23–16
   (Colts-Cowboys)

Now try these blowout scores with their Super Bowls.

1. Super Bowl XXVII   A. 38–9
   (Cowboys-Bills)

2. Super Bowl XXXV   B. 55–10
   (Ravens-Giants)

3. Super Bowl XIX   C. 49–26
   (49ers-Dolphins)

4. Super Bowl XVIII   D. 48–21
   (Raiders-Redskins)

5. Super Bowl XXXVII   E. 52–17
   (Buccaneers-Raiders)

6. Super Bowl XXIX   F. 38–16
   (49ers-Chargers)

7. Super Bowl XXIV   G. 34–7
   (49ers-Broncos)

More Super Bowl trivia.

1. Super Bowl XXIX   A. The lowest scoring Super Bowl—21
   (49ers-Chargers)   total points

2. Super Bowl XIV   B. The highest scoring Super Bowl—75
   (Steelers-Rams)   total points

3. Super Bowl XXXVI
   (Patriots-Rams)

C. Super Bowl with the smallest attendance—61,946

4. Super Bowl VII
   (Dolphins-Redskins)

D. Super Bowl with the largest attendance—103,985

5. Super Bowl I
   (Packers-Chiefs)

E. The first Super Bowl played in February

6. Super Bowl XLI
   (Colts-Bears)

F. By date (January 9), the earliest Super Bowl played

7. Super Bowl XI
   (Raiders-Vikings)

G. The first Super Bowl played in the rain

How well do you remember the halftime shows of the earlier Super Bowls?

1. Super Bowl XI
   (Vikings-Raiders)

A. Mardi Gras with Carol Channing

2. Super Bowl VI
   (Cowboys-Dolphins)

B. "Salute to Superstars of the Silver Screen"

3. Super Bowl XVI
   (49ers-Bengals)

C. Disney's "It's A Small World" with the Los Angeles Unified All-City Band

4. Super Bowl X
   (Cowboys-Steelers)

D. Carnival Salute to Caribbean with various Caribbean bands

5. Super Bowl XVIII
   (Redskins-Raiders)

E. Up With the People's "Salute to the 1960s and Motown"

6. Super Bowl IV
   (Vikings-Chiefs)

F. The first of the "Up With People" halftime shows, (a tribute to America's bicentennial)

7. Super Bowl XIII
   (Cowboys-Steelers)

G. Salute to Louis Armstrong with Ella Fitzgerald, Carol Channing, Al Hirt, and the US Marine Corps Drill Team

More memorable halftime shows.

1. Super Bowl XIX
   (49ers-Dolphins)

2. Super Bowl XXIII
   (Bengals-49ers)

3. Super Bowl XXVII
   (Bills-Cowboys)

4. Super Bowl XXII
   (Redskins-Broncos)

5. Super Bowl XXVIII
   (Cowboys-Bills)

6. Super Bowl XXV
   (Bills-Giants)

7. Super Bowl XXI
   (Broncos-Giants)

A. New Kids on the Block

B. Wynonna and Naomi Judd, Clint Black, Travis Tritt, and Tanya Tucker

C. Michael Jackson

D. Chubby Checker and The Rockettes

E. "Be Bop Bamboozled" and 3-D effects

F. "Salute to Hollywood's 100th Anniversary"

G. "World of Children's Dreams" with the US Air Force Tops in Blue

One final game of memorable halftime shows.

1. Super Bowl XXXIX
   (Patriots-Eagles)

2. Super Bowl XXXV
   (Ravens-Giants)

3. Super Bowl XXX
   (Cowboys-Steelers)

4. Super Bowl XXXVII
   (Raiders-Buccaneers)

A. Aerosmith, Britney Spears, NSYNC, Nelly, and Mary J. Blige

B. Shania Twain, No Doubt, and Sting

C. Paul McCartney

D. Diana Ross

5. Super Bowl XXXII   E. James Brown, ZZ Top, and the Blues
   (Packers-Broncos)   Brothers

6. Super Bowl XXXVIII   F. Janet Jackson, Justin Timberlake,
   (Panthers-Patriots)   P. Diddy, Kid Rock, and Nelly

7. Super Bowl XXXI   G. Boyz II Men, Smokey Robinson, The
   (Patriots-Packers)   Temptations, and The Four Tops

And what about those who sang the national anthem?

1. Super Bowl IV   A. Vikki Carr
   (Vikings-Chiefs)

2. Super Bowl VIII   B. Charley Pride
   (Vikings-Dolphins)

3. Super Bowl XIV   C. Andy Williams
   (Rams-Steelers)

4. Super Bowl XVI   D. Cheryl Ladd
   (49ers-Bengals)

5. Super Bowl XI   E. Anita Bryant
   (Vikings-Raiders)

6. Super Bowl VII   F. Diana Ross
   (Dolphins-Redskins)

7. Super Bowl III   G. Al Hirt
   (Jets-Colts)

More anthem singers.

1. Super Bowl XXI   A. Barry Manilow
   (Broncos-Giants)

2. Super Bowl XXV   B. Neil Diamond
(Bills-Giants)

3. Super Bowl XXIX   C. Herb Alpert
(Chargers-49ers)

4. Super Bowl XVIII   D. Whitney Houston
(Redskins-Raiders)

5. Super Bowl XXIII   E. Garth Brooks
(Bengals-49ers)

6. Super Bowl XXII   F. Kathie Lee Gifford
(Redskins-Broncos)

7. Super Bowl XXVII   G. Billy Joel
(Bills-Cowboys)

One final game of those who sang the national anthem.

1. Super Bowl XXXII   A. Jewel
(Packers-Broncos)

2. Super Bowl XXXIV   B. Cher
(Rams-Titans)

3. Super Bowl XXXVI   C. Backstreet Boys
(Rams-Patriots)

4. Super Bowl XXXVII   D. Celine Dion and the Dixie Chicks
(Raiders-Buccaneers)

5. Super Bowl XXXV   E. Mariah Carey
(Ravens-Giants)

6. Super Bowl XXXIII   F. Faith Hill
(Broncos-Falcons)

7. Super Bowl XXX   G. Vanessa Williams
(Cowboys-Steelers)

Now try your hand at some interesting Super Bowl tidbits.

1. Super Bowl VII
   (Dolphins-Redskins)

2. Super Bowl VIII
   (Vikings-Dolphins)

3. Super Bowl X
   (Cowboys-Steelers)

4. Super Bowl XII
   (Cowboys-Broncos)

5. Super Bowl XLI
   (Colts-Bears)

6. Super Bowl XV
   (Raiders-Eagles)

7. Super Bowl XVI
   (49ers-Bengals)

A. Still to this day, the Super Bowl with the highest Nielsen TV ratings ever

B. First Super Bowl between two teams who met in the regular season the same year they met later in the Super Bowl.

C. First Super Bowl in which an *official* wild card team won the game

D. Super Bowl featuring the longest time a team was held without scoring (scored with 2:07 left in the 4th quarter).

E. First Super Bowl to feature a wide receiver as the game's MVP

F. First Super Bowl held on a truly neutral site. All previous Super Bowls had been held on an NFL field.

G. Only Super Bowl whose winner had a losing record in December (2–3) of their Super Bowl year

As with all things Super Bowl, even the pregame coin toss has been made into a celebrity production. Test your memory on which celebrities oversaw these Super Bowl coin tosses.

1. Super Bowl XII
   (Cowboy-Broncos)

2. Super Bowl XIII
   (Steelers-Cowboys)

A. Marie Lombardi

B. Ronald Reagan (via satellite from the White House)

3. Super Bowl XV   C. Red Grange
   (Raiders-Eagles)

4. Super Bowl XVII   D. George Halas
   (Dolphins-Redskins)

5. Super Bowl XVIII   E. Bart Starr
   (Redskins-Raiders)

6. Super Bowl XIX   F. Bronko Nagurski
   (Dolphins-49ers)

7. Super Bowl XX   G. Elroy "Crazy Legs" Hirsch
   (Bears-Patriots)

One more game of celebrity coin-toss observers.

1. Super Bowl XXV   A. Tom Brady
   (Bills-Giants)

2. Super Bowl XXVII   B. Members of the 1972 Miami Dolphins
   (Bills-Cowboys)

3. Super Bowl XXVIII   C. George H. W. Bush and Roger
   (Cowboys-Bills)   Staubach

4. Super Bowl XXX   D. Joe Namath
   (Cowboys-Steelers)

5. Super Bowl XXXVI   E. O.J. Simpson
   (Rams-Patriots)

6. Super Bowl XXXVII   F. Pete Rozelle
   (Raiders-Buccaneers)

7. Super Bowl XL   G. Joe Montana
   (Seahawks-Steelers)

Miscellaneous early Super Bowl trivia.

1. Super Bowl I
   (Packers-Chiefs)

2. Super Bowl II
   (Packers-Raiders)

3. Super Bowl III
   (Jets-Colts)

4. Super Bowl IV
   (Vikings-Chiefs)

5. Super Bowl V
   (Colts-Cowboys)

6. Super Bowl VI
   (Cowboys-Dolphins)

7. Super Bowl VII
   (Redskins-Dolphins)

A. The first Super Bowl to feature a
   two-time winner of the Super Bowl
   MVP Award

B. The only Super Bowl ever to feature a
   team that didn't score a touchdown

C. The last Super Bowl played before the
   NFL and AFL merged

D. The first Super Bowl played after three
   NFL teams voluntarily moved to the
   AFC (Pittsburgh, Cleveland, and
   Baltimore)

E. The only Super Bowl telecast in the
   United States by two networks
   simultaneously (CBS and NBC)

F. Only Super Bowl ever to cap a perfect
   season by one of the participants

G. The first Super Bowl to officially go by
   that name rather than the AFL-NFL
   Championship Game

More miscellaneous early Super Bowl trivia.

1. Super Bowl VIII
   (Vikings-Dolphins)

2. Super Bowl IX
   (Steelers-Vikings)

A. Super Bowl which featured a
   game-saving, end zone
   interception as time expired

B. First Super Bowl to feature a team
   appearing for the third straight year

3. Super Bowl X
(Steelers-Cowboys)

C. First Super Bowl to feature a four-time winner of the big event

4. Super Bowl XI
(Vikings-Raiders)

D. First Super Bowl to feature a safety

5. Super Bowl XII
(Cowboys-Broncos)

E. First Super Bowl to feature co-MVPs

6. Super Bowl XIII
(Cowboys-Steelers)

F. First Super Bowl to feature a four-time loser of the big event

7. Super Bowl XIV
(Steelers-Rams)

G. First Super Bowl played after the NFL regular season was expanded to 16 games from 14

Still more miscellaneous early Super Bowl trivia.

1. Super Bowl XV
(Raiders-Eagles)

A. First time in history a Super Bowl team shut out both of its opponents in the playoffs before the Super Bowl

2. Super Bowl XVI
(49ers-Bengals)

B. First Super Bowl to feature $1 million per minute commercials

3. Super Bowl XVII
(Dolphins-Redskins)

C. Super Bowl known as "Black Sunday" because of the convincing beating inflicted by the underdog on the heavy favorite

4. Super Bowl XVIII
(Raiders-Redskins)

D. Super Bowl which featured a quarterback completing 88% of his passes (22-for-25), not only a Super Bowl record, but an all-time postseason record as well

5. Super Bowl XIX
(49ers-Dolphins)

E. Only Super Bowl played using a 16-team playoff system with 1–8 seeding in each conference rather than divisional winners and wild card teams

6. Super Bowl XX
   (Bears-Patriots)

F. The first Super Bowl played in a northern city (Pontiac, Michigan)

7. Super Bowl XXI
   (Giants-Broncos)

G. First Super Bowl won by a wild card team

Super Bowl trivia from the middle years.

1. Super Bowl XXII
   (Redskins-Broncos)

A. First Super Bowl to feature zero turnovers

2. Super Bowl XXIII
   (49ers-Bengals)

B. Only Super Bowl ever to feature a team that scored five touchdowns in one quarter

3. Super Bowl XXIV
   (49ers-Broncos)

C. The second of only three Super Bowls to be played in a northern city (Minneapolis)

4. Super Bowl XXV
   (Giants-Bills)

D. In January 2006, an on-line poll at NFL.com ranked this game as the #1 Super Bowl of all time

5. Super Bowl XXVI
   (Redskins-Bills)

E. Super Bowl which featured an alleged child molester providing the half-time entertainment and an alleged murderer presiding over the coin toss

6. Super Bowl XXVII
   (Cowboys-Bills)

F. The Super Bowl with the largest margin of victory, 45 points

7. Super Bowl XXVIII
   (Cowboys-Bills)

G. Super Bowl that featured fans holding signs which read, "Yes, we're in the Super Bowl again. Deal with it."

More recent miscellaneous Super Bowl trivia.

1. Super Bowl XXIX
   (49ers-Chargers)

2. Super Bowl XXX
   (Cowboys-Steelers)

3. Super Bowl XXXI
   (Patriots-Packers)

4. Super Bowl XXXII
   (Packers-Broncos)

5. Super Bowl XXXIII
   (Broncos-Falcons)

6. Super Bowl XXXIV
   (Rams-Titans)

7. Super Bowl XXXV
   (Giants-Ravens)

A. Super Bowl featuring the oldest player
   (38) ever to win the MVP Award

B. First Super Bowl since Super Bowl IX
   in which one team held the other
   team's offense scoreless, allowing only
   a special team touchdown

C. First Super Bowl hosted in Arizona
   after the state officially and belatedly
   recognized Martin Luther King Day, a
   stumbling block that had previously
   caused the NFL to cancel Super Bowl
   XXVII scheduled for Tempe, Arizona

D. First AFC win in the Super Bowl after
   13 straight wins by the NFC

E. Super Bowl that featured the game
   ending play which became known as
   "The Tackle"

F. First Super Bowl to feature commercials
   at more than $2 million per minute

G. Only Super Bowl ever to feature a
   special teams player as the game's MVP

More of the same.

1. Super Bowl XXXVI
   (Rams-Patriots)

2. Super Bowl XXXVII
   (Buccaneers-Raiders)

3. Super Bowl XXXVIII
   (Panthers-Patriots)

4. Super Bowl XXXIX
   (Patriots-Eagles)

5. Super Bowl I
   (Chiefs-Packers)

6. Super Bowl XL
   (Steelers-Seahawks)

7. Super Bowl II
   (Raiders-Packers)

A. Super Bowl which had to redo the second half kickoff because the network was late coming back from a commercial break

B. One of the biggest upsets in Super Bowl history, won by the 14-point underdogs with a field goal as time expired

C. Only the second of two Super Bowls in history to be tied at halftime (7–7)

D. The winning quarterback entered this Super Bowl with more interceptions (17) than touchdowns (9) in the regular season

E. Super Bowl that added the term "wardrobe malfunction" to the American lexicon

F. Super Bowl that was watched in more homes (45.9 million) than any program in U.S. history other than the final episode of M*A*S*H*

G. Super Bowl that featured a quarterback throwing five interceptions

Same game, more trivia.

1. Super Bowl I
   (Packers-Chiefs)

A. Los Angeles was awarded this Super Bowl only six weeks before it took place

2. Super Bowl II
   (Packers-Raiders)

   B. This Super Bowl featured a team whose defense entered the game having allowed only one touchdown in the previous 25 quarters, then didn't allow one in the Super Bowl, either

3. Super Bowl III
   (Colts-Jets)

   C. One of the teams in this Super Bowl had a 12-game regular-season winning streak, longest in the NFL in 35 years

4. Super Bowl IV
   (Vikings-Chiefs)

   D. First Super Bowl to be played in Miami's Orange Bowl

5. Super Bowl V
   (Colts-Cowboys)

   E. This Super Bowl featured three running backs who had reached the 1,000-yard mark during the regular season, two on the same team

6. Super Bowl VI
   (Cowboys-Dolphins)

   F. Super Bowl known as the "Blooper Bowl" because of all the turnovers, penalties, officiating mistakes, and generally poor play

7. Super Bowl VII
   (Dolphins-Redskins)

   G. Super Bowl with 2nd largest betting point spread—18 points

We're just getting warmed up with Super Bowl trivia.

1. Super Bowl VIII
   (Dolphins-Vikings)

   A. The Super Bowl known for the "Terrible Towels"

2. Super Bowl IX
   (Steelers-Vikings)

   B. Last Super Bowl in which the individual or group who performed the national anthem was the same one who performed the halftime show

3. Super Bowl X
   (Steelers-Cowboys)

   C. The first Super Bowl to feature crowd participation in the halftime show (fans waved colored placards on cue)

4. Super Bowl XI
   (Vikings-Raiders)

D. First Super Bowl to feature a team playing in its fifth Super Bowl

5. Super Bowl XII
   (Cowboys-Broncos)

E. First Super Bowl to feature a running back as MVP

6. Super Bowl XIII
   (Steelers-Cowboys)

F. First Super Bowl to feature a wide receiver as MVP

7. Super Bowl XIV
   (Steelers-Rams)

G. The Super Bowl which featured the losing quarterback completing only eight passes—four to his teammates and four interceptions to the opponents

You know the routine by now.

1. Super Bowl XV
   (Raiders-Eagles)

A. First Super Bowl in history in which the team that gained the most yardage lost (356 to 275)

2. Super Bowl XVI
   (49ers-Bengals)

B. Only Super Bowl to take place on the same day as a presidential inauguration (Ronald Reagan)

3. Super Bowl XVII
   (Dolphins-Redskins)

C. This Super Bowl's pregame festivities honored the end of the Iran hostage crisis

4. Super Bowl XVIII
   (Raiders-Redskins)

D. First Super Bowl played in a Florida city other than Miami

5. Super Bowl XIX
   (49ers-Dolphins)

E. Super Bowl featuring the "Big Blue Wrecking Crew"

6. Super Bowl XX
   (Bears-Patriots)

F. Super Bowl featuring the first running back in history to to have four 100-yard rushing games in one postseason

7. Super Bowl XXI
   (Giants-Broncos)

G. Super Bowl in which the losing team was sacked seven times and collected only seven rushing yards

1. Super Bowl XXII
   (Redskins-Broncos)

A. Super Bowl which featured a 92-yard, game-winning drive in the last three minutes

2. Super Bowl XXIII
   (49ers-Bengals)

B. First Super Bowl ever played in Atlanta

3. Super Bowl XXIV
   (49ers-Broncos)

C. The halftime show of this Super Bowl featured a salute to the 40th anniversary of the comic strip *Peanuts*

4. Super Bowl XXV
   (Bills-Giants)

D. Super Bowl that featured an offensive line that allowed only nine sacks all season, ten fewer than their closest competitor

5. Super Bowl XXVI
   (Redskins-Bills)

E. The only Super Bowl ever decided by just one point

6. Super Bowl XXVII
   (Bills-Cowboys)

F. Super Bowl that was relocated to the Rose Bowl from Sun Devil Stadium in Tempe, Arizona, as punishment from the NFL for Arizona voters not recognizing Martin Luther King Day like the rest of the country

7. Super Bowl XXVIII
   (Cowboys-Bills)

G. The second Super Bowl played in the same season as a players' strike

1. Super Bowl XXIX
(Chargers-49ers)

A. Super Bowl featuring a team whose 16 offensive possessions all ended in either a punt or interception except for the last, which ended as time mercifully expired

2. Super Bowl XXX
(Cowboys-Steelers)

B. Only Super Bowl ever to feature a running back who rushed for 2,000 yards in the regular season

3. Super Bowl XXXI
(Packers-Patriots)

C. The first Super Bowl to feature the "Minister of Defense"

4. Super Bowl XXXII
(Packers-Broncos)

D. Super Bowl featuring the quarterback with the highest regular season passing rating (112.8); and it was deserved, since he threw for six touchdowns that day.

5. Super Bowl XXXIII
(Broncos-Falcons)

E. Super Bowl featuring a quarterback who threw a record 45 passes without an interception

6. Super Bowl XXXIV
(Titans-Rams)

F. Super Bowl featuring the game's MVP who missed most of the second quarter with a migraine headache

7. Super Bowl XXXV
(Giants-Ravens)

G. First Super Bowl to feature a cornerback as MVP

1. Super Bowl XXXVI
(Rams-Patriots)

A. Super Bowl featuring a team that was 1–15 just two years earlier

2. Super Bowl XXXVII
(Buccaneers-Raiders)

B. Super Bowl sometimes called the "Gruden Bowl"

3. Super Bowl XXXVIII
(Patriots-Panthers)

C. Super Bowl with the halftime show considered to be the best in Super Bowl history (performed by U2)

4. Super Bowl XXXIX
(Eagles-Patriots)

D. Super Bowl featuring the "No Name Defense"

5. Super Bowl XL
(Seahawks-Steelers)

E. Super Bowl which allowed Miami to tie New Orleans as the city hosting the most Super Bowls—9

6. Super Bowl XLI
(Colts-Bears)

F. Last Super Bowl played in a domed stadium

7. Super Bowl VII
(Dolphins-Redskins)

G. Super Bowl that featured a team which had broken the all-time record for consecutive regular season wins—18

1. Super Bowl I
(Packers-Chiefs)

A. Super Bowl featuring a team whose defensive unit was nicknamed "The Doomsday Defense"

2. Super Bowl II
(Packers-Raiders)

B. Super Bowl featuring a team whose defensive unit was nicknamed "The Purple People Eaters"

3. Super Bowl III
(Jets-Colts)

C. Last Super Bowl to be blacked out in the host city

4. Super Bowl IV
(Chiefs-Vikings)

D. Super Bowl nicknamed "The Guarantee"

5. Super Bowl V
(Colts-Cowboys)

E. Super Bowl featuring a team whose defensive unit was nicknamed "The 11 Angry Men"

6. Super Bowl VI
(Dolphins-Cowboys)

F. Super Bowl whose most famous play was a fumble by a placekicker that was returned for a touchdown

7. Super Bowl VII
(Dolphins-Redskins)

G. First Super Bowl to feature the team nicknamed "Titletown, USA"

1. Super Bowl VIII
(Dolphins-Vikings)

A. First Super Bowl to feature the appearance of the defensive unit known as "The Steel Curtain"

2. Super Bowl IX
(Steelers-Vikings)

B. First Super Bowl played outside the Miami, Los Angeles, New Orleans markets

3. Super Bowl X
(Cowboys-Steelers)

C. Super Bowl that featured both teams wearing a patch bearing the Bicentennial logo

4. Super Bowl XI
(Raiders-Vikings)

D. First Super Bowl to feature a team whose regular-season record was a paltry 9–7

5. Super Bowl XII
(Cowboys-Broncos)

E. First Super Bowl to be played in prime time

6. Super Bowl XIII
(Steelers-Cowboys)

F. First Super Bowl ever to feature a rematch between two teams who played in a previous Super Bowl

7. Super Bowl XIV
(Rams-Steelers)

G. Last Super Bowl to utilize only six referees, as well the last outdoor Super Bowl to end before dusk

1. Super Bowl XV
   (Raiders-Eagles)

2. Super Bowl XVI
   (49ers-Bengals)

3. Super Bowl XVII
   (Redskins-Dolphins)

4. Super Bowl XVIII
   (Raiders-Redskins)

5. Super Bowl XIX
   (49ers-Dolphins)

6. Super Bowl XX
   (Patriots-Bears)

7. Super Bowl XXI
   (Giants-Broncos)

A. Super Bowl featuring the first placekicker ever to be named the NFL's MVP in the regular season

B. Super Bowl featuring two teams who were both 6–10 the previous season

C. First Super Bowl to feature a team that scored two non-offensive touchdowns in one Super Bowl

D. Super Bowl known for "The Drive," a 98-yard scoring drive that tied the game with 39 seconds left

E. First Super Bowl to feature a wild card team that won three playoff games before reaching the Super Bowl

F. First Super Bowl to feature a quarterback who had passed for over 5,000 yards in the regular season

G. Last Super Bowl to feature two franchises that had never been to the Super Bowl before

1. Super Bowl XXII
   (Redskins-Broncos)

2. Super Bowl XXIII
   (Bengals-49ers)

3. Super Bowl XXIV
   (49ers-Broncos)

A. Super Bowl most remembered for a 47-yard field goal attempt that sailed barely wide right with 4 seconds left

B. Super Bowl that featured the first team to lose three consecutive Super Bowls

C. Super Bowl that featured the fourth team to win three Super Bowls

4. Super Bowl XXV
   (Giants-Bills)

D. Super Bowl that featured a third-time Super Bowl MVP who completed a record 13 consecutive passes

5. Super Bowl XXVI
   (Redskins-Bills)

E. First Super Bowl to be tied at halftime (3–3)

6. Super Bowl XXVII
   (Cowboys-Bills)

F. First Super Bowl ever played in San Diego

7. Super Bowl XXVIII
   (Bills-Cowboys)

G. Only Super Bowl in history to feature the same two teams that played in the previous Super Bowl

1. Super Bowl XXIX
   (49ers-Chargers)

A. Super Bowl that featured one team whose head coach had major coronary bypass surgery after Week 14 of the season

2. Super Bowl XXX
   (Steelers-Cowboys)

B. Super Bowl that featured that year's regular-season MVP, a second-year quarterback who had previously played for the Iowa Barnstormers and Amsterdam Admirals

3. Super Bowl XXXI
   (Patriots-Packers)

C. First Super Bowl in which both teams wore a Super Bowl logo patch

4. Super Bowl XXXII
   (Broncos-Packers)

D. Super Bowl that featured a record 99-yard kickoff return

5. Super Bowl XXXIII
   (Broncos-Falcons)

E. Super Bowl that featured the first team in NFL history to hold their regular-season opponents to less than 1,000 yards rushing on the season (16-game schedule)

6. Super Bowl XXXIV
   (Titans-Rams)

F. Super Bowl that featured the second team to win five Super Bowls

7. Super Bowl XXXV
   (Ravens-Giants)

G. Super Bowl which featured a Miss
   America singing the national anthem
   for the hearing impaired

1. Super Bowl XXXVI
   (Patriots-Rams)

A. Super Bowl that featured "The Super
   Bowl Shuffle," a rap song performed
   by members of one of that year's
   Super Bowl teams, which reached #41
   on the charts, and received a Grammy
   nomination

2. Super Bowl XXXVII
   (Buccaneers-Raiders)

B. First Super Bowl to be played on a
   FieldTurf surface rather than AstroTurf
   or natural grass

3. Super Bowl XXXVIII
   (Panthers-Patriots)

C. Super Bowl that featured pregame
   ceremonies honoring the Space
   Shuttle Columbia disaster which had
   occurred exactly one year before

4. Super Bowl XXXIX
   (Eagles-Patriots)

D. First Super Bowl to be declared a
   National Special Security Event
   (NSSE) by the Department of
   Homeland Security

5. Super Bowl XL
   (Steelers-Seahawks)

E. Super Bowl sometimes called the
   "Pirate Bowl"

6. Super Bowl XXIX
   (Chargers-49ers)

F. Super Bowl which featured the first
   quarterback in NFL history to throw at
   least 30 touchdowns in the regular
   season and have less than 10
   interceptions (31 TDs, 8 Int.)

7. Super Bowl XX
   (Bears-Patriots)

G. Super Bowl with the largest point
   spread—18$^{1}/_{2}$ points

1. Super Bowl I
   (Packers-Chiefs)

2. Super Bowl II
   (Packers-Raiders)

3. Super Bowl III
   (Jets-Colts)

4. Super Bowl IV
   (Chiefs-Vikings)

5. Super Bowl V
   (Colts-Cowboys)

6. Super Bowl VI
   (Cowboys-Dolphins)

7. Super Bowl VII
   (Dolphins-Redskins)

A. Super Bowl that featured the winner of the longest game in NFL history, an 82 minute-40 second, first-round playoff game

B. Super Bowl that featured the "Over the Hill Gang"

C. First Super Bowl to be televised on only one network

D. Super Bowl that featured the loser of the infamous "Heidi Game" earlier in the season

E. Only Super Bowl in history that was not an attendance sellout

F. Only Super Bowl in history in which the MVP came from the losing team

G. First Super Bowl to feature a head coach wearing a hidden microphone during the game

1. Super Bowl VIII
   (Dolphins-Vikings)

2. Super Bowl IX
   (Vikings-Steelers)

A. First Super Bowl to feature a team taking the opening kickoff and marching down the field for a touchdown

B. Super Bowl that featured a team that failed to score in the first half for its fourth straight Super Bowl

3. Super Bowl X
   (Cowboys-Steelers)

C. Super Bowl in which Hollywood Henderson said of the opposing team's quarterback: "He's so dumb, he couldn't spell "cat" if you spotted him the "c" and the "a"

4. Super Bowl XI
   (Raiders-Vikings)

D. First Super Bowl to feature a running back who threw a touchdown pass

5. Super Bowl XII
   (Cowboys-Broncos)

E. Super Bowl with the most lead changes—7

6. Super Bowl XIII
   (Steelers-Cowboys)

F. Super Bowl with the lowest halftime score ever, 2–0

7. Super Bowl XIV
   (Rams-Steelers)

G. Super Bowl that featured a team whose defense sent eight of its 11 players to that year's Pro Bowl

1. Super Bowl XV
   (Raiders-Eagles)

A. First Super Bowl in which both starting quarterbacks threw for more than 300 yards

2. Super Bowl XVI
   (49ers-Bengals)

B. Only Super Bowl ever in which a quarterback rushed for two touchdowns

3. Super Bowl XVII
   (Redskins-Dolphins)

C. Super Bowl that featured the most second half points by one team—30

4. Super Bowl XVIII
   (Raiders-Redskins)

D. Super Bowl that featured the "Killer Bees"

5. Super Bowl XIX
   (49ers-Dolphins)

E. Only Super Bowl ever to feature a turnover on the opening kickoff

6. Super Bowl XX
   (Bears-Patriots)

F. First Super Bowl to feature offensive, defensive, and special teams touchdowns by one team in the same game

7. Super Bowl XXI
   (Giants-Broncos)

G. First Super Bowl to feature a man who was a member of a winning Super Bowl team both as a player and head coach

1. Super Bowl XXII
   (Redskins-Broncos)

A. Last Super Bowl to feature both placekickers wearing helmets with only one bar on their facemasks

2. Super Bowl XXIII
   (Bengals-49ers)

B. Super Bowl that featured one team that gained 356 yards—in one quarter!

3. Super Bowl XXIV
   (49ers-Broncos)

C. First Super Bowl since the AFL-NFL merger that the two participants won their conference championships on the road

4. Super Bowl XXV
   (Bills-Giants)

D. The last Super Bowl presided over by Pete Rozelle as NFL commissioner

5. Super Bowl XXVI
   (Bills-Redskins)

E. The last Super Bowl to feature the two No. 1 seeds

6. Super Bowl XXVII
   (Cowboys-Bills)

F. Only Super Bowl in which one team scored at least two touchdowns in each quarter

7. Super Bowl XXVIII
   (Cowboys-Bills)

G. First Super Bowl to have a touchdown overruled by instant replay

1. Super Bowl XXIX
   (49ers-Chargers)

A. Super Bowl in which the favored team—for the first time ever—was a wild card team

2. Super Bowl XXX
   (Steelers-Cowboys)

B. Super Bowl referred to as the dot-com Super Bowl because of the game's 17 Internet-based advertisers

3. Super Bowl XXXI
   (Patriots-Packers)

C. First Super Bowl to feature a kickoff return for a touchdown by the *winning* team (previous 3 were all by the losing teams)

4. Super Bowl XXXII
   (Broncos-Packers)

D. First Super Bowl in which one player had the most passing and rushing yards in the game

5. Super Bowl XXXIII
   (Broncos-Falcons)

E. First Super Bowl to feature four 1-yard touchdown runs by one team

6. Super Bowl XXXIV
   (Rams-Titans)

F. Super Bowl that featured the only quarterback ever to start five Super Bowls

7. Super Bowl XXXV
   (Giants-Ravens)

G. Super Bowl which featured one team's 8th appearance

1. Super Bowl XIX
   (49ers-Dolphins)

A. Super Bowl that featured all four military service academy choirs performing together for the first time in more than 30 years as they sang the national anthem

2. Super Bowl XXXVI
   (Patriots-Rams)

B. Super Bowl with the best combined record of its two participants—33–3 (17–1 and 16–2)

3. Super Bowl XXXVII
   (Buccaneers-Raiders)

C. Super Bowl that featured former
   players reading excerpts from the
   Declaration of Independence during
   pregame ceremonies and former
   presidents reading speeches of
   Abraham Lincoln

4. Super Bowl XXXVIII
   (Patriots-Panthers)

D. First Super Bowl ever played at Joe
   Robbie Stadium

5. Super Bowl XXXIX
   (Patriots-Eagles)

E. First Super Bowl ever to feature a
   wide receiver who threw a
   touchdown pass

6. Super Bowl XL
   (Steelers-Seahawks)

F. Super Bowl which featured the most
   4th quarter points in Super Bowl
   history—37

7. Super Bowl XXIII
   (49ers-Bengals)

G. First Super Bowl to feature one team
   scoring three defensive touchdowns

**Much of what makes up the Super Bowl is the pregame hype,
press coverage, and brash statements made by the players and
coaches. See if you can remember these Super Bowls and the
pregame hype that surrounded them.**

1. Super Bowl I
   (Chiefs-Packers)

A. On the media hype of how
   outmatched one team was going into
   the game, one player said, "We were
   scared to death. Guys in the tunnel
   were throwing up and wetting their
   pants."

2. Super Bowl II
   (Raiders-Packers)

B. On being linked to a federal gambling
   investigation just five days before the
   Super Bowl, one of the game's
   quarterbacks said, "It was, beyond a
   doubt, the toughest week of my life."

3. Super Bowl III
(Jets-Colts)

C. Will they or won't they complete their perfect season?

4. Super Bowl IV
(Chiefs-Vikings)

D. "We know we're going to win the game, let's make sure we play the last 30 minutes for the old man."

5. Super Bowl V
(Colts-Cowboys)

E. "We're gonna win the game. I guarantee it."

6. Super Bowl VI
(Cowboys-Dolphins)

F. Intense media coverage of how one of the teams in the Super Bowl just couldn't "win the big games."

7. Super Bowl VIII
(Dolphins-Redskins)

G. Continuing media coverage of how one of the teams involved "still couldn't win the big games."

526

More pregame hype.

1. Super Bowl VIII
(Dolphins-Vikings)

A. Intense media coverage of one team's safety's remarks about the other team's star receiver who was in the hospital with a concussion from the previous playoff game. "I'm not going to hurt anyone intentionally, but getting hit again must be in the back of his mind. I know it would be in mine."

2. Super Bowl IX
(Steelers-Vikings)

B. The predictions by one team's linebacker that his team would shut out the other team, just like he had predicted (correctly) before his team's conference title game

3. Super Bowl X
(Steelers-Cowboys)

C. Would they lose their fourth Super Bowl in four tries?

4. Super Bowl XI
(Vikings-Raiders)

D. Most media coverage was about the battle between the two teams' quarterbacks, both of whom had played for the same team a few years before

5. Super Bowl XII
(Broncos-Cowboys)

E. The game was considered so one-sided that sportswriters suggested the favored team's quarterback should throw left-handed and the underdog team should be allowed to play with 12 men on the field just to make it even

6. Super Bowl XIII
(Cowboys-Steelers)

F. The game was predicted to be the lowest-scoring Super Bowl ever because of the two outstanding defenses

7. Super Bowl XIV
(Steelers-Rams)

G. The Super Bowl was going to be a question of who could exploit the other team's terrific defense

Still more pregame hype.

1. Super Bowl XV
(Raiders-Eagles)

A. The outrageous antics of one team's quarterback, including the wearing of various sloganed headbands and mooning photographers to show off his injured buttocks

2. Super Bowl XVI
(49ers-Bengals)

B. Heavy speculation on whether or not Pete Rozelle would present the Lombardi Trophy after the game if one particular team won because of the friction between him and the team's owner over the team's lawsuit against the NFL

3. Super Bowl XVII   C. One team was supposedly overmatched
   (Redskins-Dolphins)   because 26 of their 45 players were
       free agents, 14 of whom had never
       been drafted by an NFL team

4. Super Bowl XVIII   D. Game was predicted to be a high
   (Raiders-Redskins)   scoring shootout because of the two
       teams' prolific quarterbacks

5. Super Bowl XIX   E. Most pregame coverage centered
   (49ers-Dolphins)   around one team's quarterback and
       whether or not he would be able to
       escape the clutches of the other
       team's star defender

6. Super Bowl XX   F. Most media coverage centered on
   (Bears-Patriots)   how evenly matched the game
       seemed to be

7. Super Bowl XXI   G. Media coverage centered on how one
   (Giants-Broncos)   team was a heavy favorite because of
       their high-powered offense and #1
       defense against the run

Again, you know the routine.

1. Super Bowl XXII   A. One team was the heavy favorite because
   (Redskins-Broncos)   of the proven winning record of their
       quarterback and the other team was in
       disarray after their running back was
       suspended from the game after being
       caught using drugs in his hotel room

2. Super Bowl XXIII   B. Most publicity surrounded the ongoing
   (49ers-Bengals)   battle between one team's owner and the
       head coach, two men with huge egos

3. Super Bowl XXIV
   (Broncos-49ers)

C. Much discussion of how one team's potent offense had been shut down in the conference championship game, and questions about whether or not it could be revived

4. Super Bowl XXV
   (Giants-Bills)

D. One team was once again the heavy favorite because of their proven winning track record, even though the other team's young star quarterback had proven himself, too

5. Super Bowl XXVI
   (Bills-Redskins)

E. One team was the heavy favorite because of their team's proven veteran quarterback while the other team featured a young, unproven quarterback

6. Super Bowl XXVII
   (Bills-Cowboys)

F. One team was facing questions of how they would feel if they became the first team ever to lose three consecutive Super Bowls

7. Super Bowl XXVIII
   (Cowboys-Bills)

G. One team considered the heavy favorite because of its "turbo-charged, no-huddle offense"; also, because of terrorist threats, FBI sharpshooters were placed around the upper levels of the stadium

1. Super Bowl XXIX
   (49ers-Chargers)

A. Speculation centered on whether or not the underdogs could pull off another miracle to win the Super Bowl

2. Super Bowl XXX
   (Steelers-Cowboys)

B. The game was going to be a snoozer because one conference had won 13 straight Super Bowls

3. Super Bowl XXXI
   (Packers-Patriots)

C. Two teams both vying for their fifth Super Bowl win, and relief among many that the NFL's two most popular teams were once again facing off in the big game

4. Super Bowl XXXII   D. Super Bowl referred to as "Festivus Maximus"
   (Broncos-Packers)   by one team's players after a Seinfeld
                            episode that banned mentioning Christmas;
                            the coach thought talk of the Super Bowl
                            was premature until they were in it

5. Super Bowl XXXIII   E. The distraction faced by one team after one
   (Falcons-Broncos)   of their players was arrested for solicitation
                            of a prostitute the night before the Super
                            Bowl after being awarded the Bart Starr
                            Award for his "high moral character" the
                            same day

6. Super Bowl XXXIV   F. The distraction for one team because of
   (Titans-Rams)   reports that were circulating days before the
                            Super Bowl that their head coach would be
                            leaving after the Super Bowl to coach
                            another NFL team

7. Super Bowl XXXV   G. Speculation was that this would be the
   (Ravens-Giants)   least-watched Super Bowl in history
                            because of the TV markets involved and the
                            apparent one-sidedness of the game

No football trivia book worth it's salt would be without some
questions around those great Super Bowl commercials. Do you
remember when these commercials made their Super Bowl
debuts?

1. Super Bowl XXXIII   A. Apple: "1984" introduces the Mac
   (Broncos-Falcons)   computer

2. Super Bowl XXXV   B. Budweiser: "Frogs" sing the Budweiser
   (Ravens-Giants)   name

3. Super Bowl XI   C. Pepsi: "Apt. 10-G" a sexy new neighbor
   (Raiders-Vikings)   wants to borrow a Diet Pepsi from
                            Michael J. Fox

4. Super Bowl XVIII
   (Raiders-Redskins)

    D. Xerox:"Monks" need a miracle to duplicate 500 copies of an old manuscript

5. Super Bowl XXIX
   (49ers-Chargers)

    E. McDonald's:"Showdown" is a game of H-O-R-S-E between Larry Bird and Michael Jordan

6. Super Bowl XXVII
   (Cowboys-Bills)

    F. Monster.com:"When I Grow Up" has kids expressing their surprising dreams

7. Super Bowl XXI
   (Giants-Broncos)

    G. Budweiser:"Cedric" has a hot date that ends prematurely

More commercials.

1. Super Bowl XIV
   (Steelers-Rams)

    A. Pepsi:"Diner" Things turn sour when two cola drivers exchange sodas

2. Super Bowl VIII
   (Dolphins-Vikings)

    B. Budweiser:"Dalmatians" Two Dalmatians are reunited after two years apart

3. Super Bowl XXXIII
   (Broncos-Falcons)

    C. Nike:"Hare Jordan" The animated icon and celebrity icon meet on the basketball court

4. Super Bowl XXXIV
   (Titans-Rams)

    D. Master Lock:"Marksman" A sharpshooter blasts a bullet into a lock and it still works

5. Super Bowl XXVI
   (Redskins-Bills)

    E. Coke:"Mean Joe Greene" gives his game-used jersey to a kid who gave him his Coke

6. Super Bowl XXX
   (Steelers-Cowboys)

    F. Budweiser:"Clydesdales Play Ball" A game of pick-up football in the snow between two teams of horses

7. Super Bowl XXIX
   (Chargers-49ers)

G. EDS:"Herding Cats"The trials and tribulations of herding 10,000 cats

Still more commercials.

1. Super Bowl XL
   (Steelers-Seahawks)

A. Pepsi:"Security Camera"A camera detects a Coke driver attempting to steal a can of Pepsi from a machine

2. Super Bowl XXXI
   (Packers-Patriots)

B. Pepsi:"Sucked In"A boy gets sucked into his bottle of Pepsi

3. Super Bowl XXIX
   (49ers-Chargers)

C. Pepsi:"Ozzy's Nightmare"The rock legend has a bad dream

4. Super Bowl XXXIV
   (Rams-Titans)

D. Pepsi:"Dancing Bears" Grizzlies dance to a version of the Village People's song YMCA

5. Super Bowl XXX
   (Steelers-Cowboys)

E. FedEx:"Caveman"A caveman who failed to use FedEx suffers the consequences

6. Super Bowl XXXV
   (Ravens-Giants)

F. EDS:"Running With Squirrels" seeks to help business owners straighten out their problems

7. Super Bowl XXXVI
   (Buccaneers-Raiders)

G. Budweiser:"Rex's Bad Day" Rex the dog has to produce the required yowl on cue

One last round of commercials, titles only, because that's all you should need to identify these classics.

1. Super Bowl XXXIV
   (Rams-Titans)

2. Super Bowl XXXV
   (Ravens-Giants)

3. Super Bowl XXXVI
   (Patriots-Rams)

4. Super Bowl XXXVII
   (Buccaneers-Raiders)

5. Super Bowl XXXVIII
   (Patriots-Panthers)

6. Super Bowl XXXI
   (Packers-Patriots)

7. Super Bowl XXIII
   (49ers-Bengals)

A. E*trade:"Monkey Dance"

B. Budweiser:"Horny Talking Monkey"

C. FedEx:"The Blow Up Doll"

D. Budweiser:"The Bud Bowl"

E. M & M's:"Complimentary Chocolate
   on Your Pillow"

F. Reebok:"Terry Tate the Linebacker"

G. Nissan Maxima:"Pigeons"

See if you can match these teams with their Super Bowl accomplishments.

1. Minnesota Vikings

2. Buffalo Bills

3. Denver Broncos

A. Team that has given up the most total
   points in Super Bowl history—206

B. Team that is 5–1 in Super Bowl play
   even though they have only outscored
   their opponents 141–110

C. Team which is 2–1 in Super Bowl play
   even though they've been outscored
   by their opponents, 66–73

4. Dallas Cowboys

D. Outscored 34–95 in their 0–4 Super Bowl career

5. Pittsburgh Steelers

E. Of all the undefeated Super Bowl teams, they're the best at 5–0

6. San Francisco 49ers

F. Only team to lose four Super Bowls in four years

7. New York Giants

G. Team that has played in the most Super Bowls—8

Now try your hand at some players who aren't exactly household names and their Super Bowl records.

1. Mike Nelms

A. Highest career kickoff return average—42.0

2. Mike Lodish

B. Most Super Bowls played in—6

3. Ken Bell

C. Most career kickoff returns—10

4. Tim Dwight

D. First of only two players ever to return eight kickoffs in one Super Bowl

5. Charles Haley

E. Most yards gained on fumble recoveries in one Super Bowl—64

6. Leon Lett

F. Most times played on the winning team—5

7. Andre Coleman

G. First of only two players to return six punts in one Super Bowl

Let's try one game of Super Bowl kicking records.

1. Steve Christie   A. First kicker to attempt five field goals in one Super Bowl

2. John Kasay   B. Only kicker with at least five field goal attempts to be perfect in his Super Bowl career (he was 5-for-5)

3. Don Chandler   C. First kicker to make 7 PATs in one Super Bowl

4. Adam Vinatieri   D. Most kicking points in one Super Bowl—15

5. Mike Cofer   E. Last kicker to make a field goal from at least 50 yards

6. Jim Turner   F. Longest field goal—54 yards

7. Ray Wersching   G. Most career field goals (7) and PATs—(13)

Do you know your Super Bowl running back records?

1. Timmy Smith   A. Longest run from scrimmage—75 yards

2. Franco Harris   B. Most career rushing touchdowns—5

3. Willie Parker   C. Highest average per rush in one game—10.5 (116 yards on 11 carries)

4. John Riggins   D. Most rushing yards gained in one Super Bowl—204

5. Emmitt Smith   E. Most rushing touchdowns in one Super Bowl—3

6. Terrell Davis   F. Most rushing attempts in one Super Bowl—38

7. Tom Matte   G. Most yards gained in a Super Bowl career—354

Now for the quarterbacks.

1. John Elway   A. Most pass attempts in one Super Bowl—58

2. Jim Kelly   B. Most pass completions in one Super Bowl—32

3. Joe Montana   C. Most career Super Bowl pass attempts—152

4. Tom Brady   D. Longest touchdown pass—85 yards

5. Jake Delhomme   E. Most career pass completions—83

6. Kurt Warner   F. Highest completion percentage in one Super Bowl—88.0% (22-for-25)

7. Phil Simms   G. Most passing yards in one Super Bowl—414

More quarterbacks.

1. Rich Gannon   A. Highest career completion percentage— 70.0 (56-for-80)

2. Jim Plunkett   B. Most consecutive completions in one Super Bowl—13

3. Terry Bradshaw   C. Most interceptions thrown in a Super Bowl career—8

4. Troy Aikman   D. Most touchdown passes in one Super Bowl—6

5. Joe Montana   E. Only quarterback with at least 40 career passing attempts in Super Bowl play never to have been intercepted

6. Steve Young   F. Highest average gain per passing attempt in a Super Bowl career—11.10 (932 yards on 84 attempts)

7. John Elway   G. Most passes had intercepted in one Super Bowl—5

Now for the Super Bowl records of receivers.

1. Dan Ross   A. First receiver to catch 11 passes in one Super Bowl

2. Jerry Rice   B. Most career receptions—33

3. Lynn Swann   C. Most career receiving yards after Jerry Rice—364 (Rice had 589 yards)

4. Ricky Sanders   D. Longest pass reception—85 yards

5. Muhsin Muhammad   E. Highest average gain per reception in a career—24.4

6. John Stallworth   F. Most recent receiver to catch 11 passes in one Super Bowl

7. Deion Branch   G. Most yards receiving in one game after Jerry Rice—193 (Rice had 215 yards)

A game of miscellaneous Super Bowl records.

1. Rod Martin   A. Most yards gained in one Super Bowl on interception returns—108

2. Kelly Herndon

B. Most interceptions returned for touchdowns in one Super Bowl—2

3. Darrien Gordon

C. Longest punt return in Super Bowl history—45 yards

4. Dwight Smith

D. Most interceptions in one Super Bowl—3

5. Fulton Walker

E. Most career punt returns—8

6. John Taylor

F. Most career yards gained on kickoff returns—283

7. Troy Brown

G. Longest interception return—76 yards

542

Now for Super Bowl punting records.

1. Lee Johnson

A. Only punter besides the two referred to in Clue D to collect 15 career Super Bowl punts

2. Mike Eischeid

B. Second longest punt in Super Bowl history—62 yards

3. Larry Seiple

C. Longest punt in Super Bowl history—63 yards

4. Jerrell Wilson

D. Most career punts—17 (3 games; tied with Mike Horan, but Horan accomplished his total in 4 games)

5. Tom Rouen

E. Highest punting average in one Super Bowl—50.2

6. Rich Camarillo

F. Highest career punting average—46.5 (511 yards on 11 punts)

7. Brad Maynard

G. Most punts in one Super Bowl—11

Now for some Super Bowl team records.

1. Buffalo Bills

2. Miami Dolphins

3. Green Bay Packers

4. Minnesota Vikings

5. Denver Broncos

6. San Francisco 49ers

7. Dallas Cowboys

A. Second team to lose back-to-back Super Bowls

B. Only team to play in four consecutive Super Bowls

C. Only team besides the answer to Clue B to play in three consecutive Super Bowls

D. Most points scored in a Super Bowl—55

E. First team to lose back-to-back Super Bowls

F. Only team besides the answer to Clue D to score over 50 points in a Super Bowl

G. First team to win back-to-back Super Bowls

More team records.

1. Miami Dolphins

2. Minnesota Vikings

3. San Francisco 49ers

4. Washington Redskins

5. Denver Broncos

6. New York Giants

7. Dallas Cowboys

A. Loser of lowest scoring Super Bowl

B. Loser of the biggest rout in Super Bowl history

C. Scored most second-half points in Super Bowl history—30

D. Scored most 4th quarter points in Super Bowl history—21

E. Winner of highest scoring Super Bowl

F. Second fewest points scored in a Super Bowl—6

G. Fewest points scored in a Super Bowl—3

1. Chicago Bears

2. Washington Redskins

3. New England Patriots

4. San Francisco 49ers

5. Miami Dolphins

6. San Diego Chargers

7. New York Jets

A. Only Super Bowl team that failed to score a touchdown

B. First team to attempt five field goals in one Super Bowl

C. Scored most 3rd quarter points in Super Bowl history—21

D. Most recent of five teams to score 14 1st quarter points

E. Only team to score two 2-point conversions in one Super Bowl

F. Only team to score 8 touchdowns in one Super Bowl

G. Scored most 2nd quarter points in Super Bowl history—35

546

1. Green Bay Packers

2. Pittsburgh Steelers

3. Buffalo Bills

4. Minnesota Vikings

5. New England Patriots

A. First team to make four field goals in one Super Bowl

B. Last team to make a safety in the Super Bowl

C. Only team to make 19 first downs by passing in one Super Bowl

D. Only team in history to achieve just one first down by passing in a Super Bowl

E. Only team in Super Bowl history with more than one safety

6. San Francisco 49ers   F. One of only two teams (Miami is the other) to make just 9 first downs in a Super Bowl

7. Denver Broncos   G. Last team to make four field goals in one Super Bowl

1. Washington Redskins   A. 2nd fewest yards gained in a Super Bowl—123

2. San Francisco 49ers   B. 2nd most yards gained in a Super Bowl—537

3. Minnesota Vikings   C. First of only two teams (Washington is the other) to average 7.0 yards per carry in a Super Bowl

4. New England Patriots   D. Most rushing attempts in a Super Bowl—57

5. Pittsburgh Steelers   E. Fewest yards gained in a Super Bowl—119

6. Miami Dolphins   F. Most yards gained in a Super Bowl—602

7. Los Angeles Raiders   G. Fewest rushing attempts in a Super Bowl—9

1. New England Patriots   A. Fewest yards gained passing in a Super Bowl—35

2. Washington Redskins   B. Most yards gained rushing in a Super Bowl—280

3. Minnesota Vikings   C. Most passes attempted in a Super Bowl—59

4. Buffalo Bills   D. Most yards gained passing in a Super Bowl—407

5. Miami Dolphins   E. Fewest yards gained rushing in a Super Bowl—7

6. St. Louis Rams

    F. 2nd fewest yards gained rushing in a Super Bowl—17

7. Denver Broncos

    G. Fewest passes attempted in a Super Bowl—7

549

Now for some combined team Super Bowl records.

1. Super Bowl XXII
   (Redskins-Broncos)

    A. Most recent Super Bowl of only three to see just one field goal attempt by both teams

2. Super Bowl XXXVII
   (Buccaneers-Raiders)

    B. Most first half points, both teams—45

3. Super Bowl XXIX
   (49ers-Chargers)

    C. Only Super Bowl to see ten combined touchdowns

4. Super Bowl III
   (Jets-Colts)

    D. Of only two Super Bowls to feature 50 first downs, this was the most recent

5. Super Bowl XXXIX
   (Eagles-Patriots)

    E. Of only two Super Bowls not to have a field goal, this was the most recent

6. Super Bowl IX
   (Steelers-Vikings)

    F. Most second half points, both teams—46

7. Super Bowl XXXIV
   (Titans-Rams)

    G. Only Super Bowl to see just two combined touchdowns

550

More combined team Super Bowl records.

1. Super Bowl XXII
   (Redskins-Broncos)

    A. Fewest rushing attempts by both teams in a Super Bowl—45

2. Super Bowl XXXV
   (Ravens-Giants)

    B. Most pass attempts by both teams in a Super Bowl—93

3. Super Bowl XVII
(Redskins-Dolphins)

C. Fewest pass attempts by both teams in a Super Bowl—35

4. Super Bowl XXXIX
(Eagles-Patriots)

D. Most yards gained by both teams in a Super Bowl—929

5. Super Bowl XXIX
(Chargers-49ers)

E. Fewest yards gained by both teams in a Super Bowl—396

6. Super Bowl VIII
(Dolphins-Vikings)

F. Most rushing attempts by both teams in a Super Bowl—81

7. Super Bowl XXXVIII
(Patriots-Panthers)

G. Most passing yards by both teams in a Super Bowl—649

More team Super Bowl records.

1. New England Patriots

A. Only team to have six touchdown passes in one Super Bowl

2. Denver Broncos

B. Most passes completed in one Super Bowl—32

3. New York Giants

C. Lowest completion percentage in one Super Bowl with at least 20 attempts—32.0 (8-for-25)

4. Miami Dolphins

D. Highest completion percentage in one Super Bowl with at least 20 attempts—88.0 (22-for-25)

5. Buffalo Bills

E. Fewest passes completed in one Super Bowl—4

6. Dallas Cowboys

F. Second most passes completed in one Super Bowl—31

7. San Francisco 49ers

G. First of only two teams to suffer seven sacks in one Super Bowl

1. Tampa Bay Bucs

2. New York Giants

3. Washington Redskins

4. Green Bay Packers

5. San Francisco 49ers

6. Oakland Raiders

7. New York Jets

A. Highest average punt return yardage in one Super Bowl (with at least three returns)—18.7

B. Most total punt return yards in one Super Bowl—90

C. First of only two teams to return 6 punts in one Super Bowl

D. Only team to punt 11 times in one Super Bowl

E. Only team to intercept five passes in one Super Bowl

F. Most recent of only two teams to return 9 kickoffs in one Super Bowl (Denver is the other)

G. First of only three teams to return just one kickoff in a Super Bowl

1. San Diego Chargers

2. Atlanta Falcons

3. Washington Redskins

4. Los Angeles Raiders

5. Cincinnati Bengals

A. First Super Bowl team to return a kickoff for a touchdown

B. Second fewest kickoff return yards in one Super Bowl—17

C. Most kickoff return yards in one Super Bowl—244

D. Most recent of only two teams to suffer 12 penalties in one Super Bowl (Dallas was the other)

E. Fewest kickoff return yards in one Super Bowl—16

6. Miami Dolphins

F. Highest average kickoff return in one Super Bowl (with at least three returns)—44.0

7. Carolina Panthers

G. Second most kickoff return yards in one Super Bowl—227

More team records.

(Note: Two teams are the answers to two clues each.)

1. Miami Dolphins

A. First of only four teams not to suffer a penalty in the Super Bowl

2. Atlanta Falcons

B. Only team to commit nine turnovers in one Super Bowl

3. Dallas Cowboys

C. Most recent team to be penalty free in a Super Bowl

4. Pittsburgh Steelers

D. Only team to recover eight fumbles in one Super Bowl

5. Buffalo Bills

E. Suffered the most penalty yards in a Super Bowl—133

F. Only team to commit eight fumbles in one Super Bowl

G. Suffered the 2nd most penalty yards in a Super Bowl—122

More combined team records.

(Note: one Super Bowl is the answer to two clues.)

1. Super Bowl V
   (Colts-Cowboys)

2. Super Bowl XXV
   (Bills-Giants)

3. Super Bowl XXVII
   (Cowboys-Bills)

4. Super Bowl XL
   (Steelers-Seahawks)

5. Super Bowl XIV
   (Steelers-Rams)

6. Super Bowl VI
   (Cowboys-Dolphins)

A. First of only three Super Bowls that didn't have a fumble

B. Super Bowl with the most total penalty yards—164

C. Super Bowl that featured the most lost fumbles—7

D. Most recent of only three Super Bowls with no fumbles

E. Super Bowl with the fewest total penalty yards—15

F. First of only two Super Bowls to feature 11 turnovers

G. First of only two Super Bowls to feature zero turnovers

More combined team records.

1. Super Bowl X
   (Steelers-Cowboys)

2. Super Bowl XXXV
   (Ravens-Giants)

3. Super Bowl VII
   (Dolphins-Redskins)

4. Super Bowl XXXVII
   (Raiders-Buccaneers)

A. Most recent of only two Super Bowls to feature 20 penalties

B. Super Bowl with the most total kickoff return yards—292

C. Only Super Bowl to feature 13 kickoff returns

D. Super Bowl with the fewest penalties—2

5. Super Bowl XXXI
   (Packers-Patriots)

E. Only Super Bowl to feature ten punt
   returns

6. Super Bowl XXXVIII
   (Panthers-Patriots)

F. Super Bowl with the fewest total
   kickoff return yards—78

7. Super Bowl XXIX
   (Chargers-49ers)

G. Only Super Bowl to feature kickoff
   returns for touchdowns by both teams

The next 41 games deal with the individual Super Bowls from I–XLI. See how well you remember what happened in each Super Bowl.

557

Super Bowl I (Green Bay Packers-Kansas City Chiefs).

1. Max McGee

A. Won the game's Most Valuable Player Award

2. Elijah Pitts

B. Kicked the only field goal of the game

3. Curtis McClinton

C. Opened the scoring with a 37-yard
   touchdown catch

4. Willie Wood

D. Made a key 50-yard interception return

5. Bart Starr

E. Scored the only touchdown for the losing
   team

6. Mike Mercer

F. Closed out the scoring with a 1-yard
   touchdown run

7. Boyd Dowler

G. Star who got hurt, allowing Max McGee to
   play

Super Bowl II (Green Bay Packers-Oakland Raiders).

1. Don Chandler   A. Kicked four field goals in the game

2. Bart Starr   B. Passed for two touchdowns

3. Boyd Dowler   C. Fumbled a fair catch that led to the other team scoring a field goal with just 23 seconds left in the first half

4. Bill Miller   D. Won the game's Most Valuable Player Award

5. Daryle Lamonica   E. Returned an interception 60 yards for a touchdown

6. Rodger Bird   F. Scored twice on 23-yard pass receptions

7. Herb Adderly   G. Scored the game's first touchdown on a 62-yard pass

Super Bowl III (New York Jets-Baltimore Colts).

1. Earl Morrall   A. Led the Colts to their only score

2. Johnny Unitas   B. Closed out the scoring with a 1-yard plunge

3. Joe Namath   C. The game's leading scorer

4. Tom Matte   D. Opened the scoring with a 4-yard touchdown run

5. Matt Snell   E. Starting quarterback for the Colts

6. Jim Turner   F. Made a critical fumble on the 2nd half's opening play

7. Jerry Hill   G. Won the game's Most Valuable Player Award

Super Bowl IV (Minnesota Vikings-Kansas City Chiefs).

1. Otis Taylor   A. Won the game's Most Valuable Player Award

2. Jan Stenerud   B. Opened the scoring with a 48-yard field goal

3. Dave Osborn   C. Accused of sucker-punching Len Dawson

4. Alan Page   D. His fumble was considered the key play of the game

5. Len Dawson   E. Closed out the scoring with a 46-yard touchdown catch

6. Mike Garrett   F. Scored Minnesota's only touchdown

7. Charlie West   G. Scored Kansas City's only rushing touchdown

Super Bowl V (Dallas Cowboys-Baltimore Colts).

1. Chuck Howley   A. Rookie kicker whose field goal won the game with 5 seconds left in the game

2. John Mackey.   B. Made the key interception late in the game and returned it to the other team's 3-yard line, leading to an easy score

3. Jim O'Brien   C. Top passer of the game with 147 yards

4. Rick Volk   D. Scored the game's first touchdown on a 75-yard pass reception from Johnny Unitas

5. Tom Nowatzke   E. Threw three interceptions

6. Craig Morton   F. Won the game's Most Valuable Player Award

7. Earl Morrall   G. Scored the game's only rushing touchdown

Super Bowl VI (Dallas Cowboys-Miami Dolphins).

1. Duane Thomas	A. The game's leading passer with 134 yards
2. Mike Ditka	B. Scored the game's only rushing touchdown
3. Mike Clark	C. Won the game's Most Valuable Player Award
4. Roger Staubach	D. Scored the game's first touchdown
5. Garo Yepremian	E. Closed out the scoring with a 7-yard pass reception
6. Lance Alworth	F. Accounted for the Dolphins' only scoring
7. Bob Griese	G. Opened the game's scoring with a 9-yard field goal, tied for the shortest field goal in Super Bowl history

Super Bowl VII (Washington Redskins-Miami Dolphins).

1. Howard Twilley	A. Entered the game as the NFL's regular season leader in touchdown passes
2. Jim Kiick	B. Scored the game's only rushing touchdown
3. Billy Kilmer	C. Made a key interception with 2 minutes left in the half
4. Bob Griese	D. Won the game's Most Valuable Player Award
5. Nick Buoniconti	E. The game's leading rusher with 112 yards
6. Jake Scott	F. Opened the game's scoring with a 28-yard touchdown catch
7. Larry Csonka	G. Threw the game's only touchdown pass

Super Bowl VIII (Minnesota Vikings-Miami Dolphins).

1. Larry Csonka

A. Won the game's Most Valuable Player Award

2. John Gilliam

B. Lost a fumble at the opposing team's 5-yard line with less than a minute left in the first half

3. Fran Tarkenton

C. Was just 6-for-7 passing for 73 yards

4. Bob Griese

D. Returned the second half kickoff 65 yards, but it was nullified by a penalty

5. Oscar Reed

E. Recovered the critical fumble in Clue B

6. Jake Scott

F. The game's top receiver with 46 yards

7. Stu Voight

G. The game's leading passer with 182 yards

Super Bowl IX (Pittsburgh Steelers-Minnesota Vikings).

1. Dwight White

A. Blocked the Steelers punt that led to a touchdown

2. Larry Brown

B. Won the game's Most Valuable Player Award

3. Fran Tarkenton

C. Player responsible for scoring the first Super Bowl safety

4. Terry Brown

D. Forced and recovered a fumble at the Steelers 5-yard line by Chuck Foreman to squelch a late Viking threat

5. Matt Blair

E. Player who was downed in the end zone for the safety

6. Joe Greene   F. Scored Minnesota's only touchdown

7. Franco Harris   G. Scored the game's final touchdown

Super Bowl X (Pittsburgh Steelers-Dallas Cowboys).

1. Hollywood
   Henderson

A. Sacked the opposing team's quarterback on the game's first play from scrimmage, forcing a fumble

2. Lynn Swann

B. Blocked a punt in the end zone for a safety

3. L.C. Greenwood

C. Scored the game's opening touchdown on a 29-yard pass reception

4. Drew Pearson

D. The game's top rusher with 82 yards

5. Percy Howard

E. Won the game's Most Valuable Player Award

6. Reggie Harrison

F. Took a handoff on the opening kickoff and returned it 48 yards

7. Franco Harris

G. Closed out the game's scoring with a 34-yard pass reception with 1:48 left in the game

Super Bowl XI (Minnesota Vikings-Oakland Raiders).

1. Fran Tarkenton

A. The game's top passer with 205 yards

2. Willie Brown

B. Won the game's Most Valuable Player Award

3. Fred Biletnikoff

C. The game's leading rusher with 137 yards

4. Stu Voight

D. Closed out the game's scoring with a 13-yard touchdown reception

5. Dave Casper   E. Scored the game's first touchdown on a 1-yard pass reception

6. Brent McClanahan   F. Returned an interception 75 yards for a touchdown

7. Clarence Davis   G. Fumbled away early in the game at the opponents' 3-yard line, setting the tone for the game

Super Bowl XII (Dallas Cowboys-Denver Broncos).

1. Tony Dorsett   A. Made a spectacular diving catch in the end zone for a 45-yard touchdown reception

2. Butch Johnson   B. Scored Denver's only touchdown

3. Robert Newhouse C. The game's leading rusher with 66 yards

4. Golden Richards   D. Running back who tossed a 29-yard touchdown pass

5. Rob Lytle   E. Scored the game's final touchdown on a trick play pass reception

6. Rick Upchurch   F. Won the game's Most Valuable Player Award along with Harvey Martin, the only Super Bowl to feature co-MVPs

7. Randy White   G. Returned a kickoff 67 yards, a record at the time

Super Bowl XIII (Pittsburgh Steelers-Dallas Cowboys).

1. Roger Staubach

A. Won the game's Most Valuable Player Award

2. John Stallworth

B. The game's top rusher with 96 yards

3. Terry Bradshaw

C. Threw two touchdowns in the game's final 2:23

4. Franco Harris

D. Scored the game's final touchdown with 22 seconds left on a 4-yard pass

5. Butch Johnson

E. Opened the game's scoring with a 28-yard touchdown pass reception

6. Mike Hegman

F. Scored on a 37-yard fumble recovery return

7. Tony Dorsett

G. Scored the only rushing touchdown of the game's nine total touchdowns

Super Bowl XIV (Pittsburgh Steelers-Los Angeles Rams).

1. Terry Bradshaw

A. Threw the only touchdown pass of the game for the Rams

2. Wendell Tyler

B. Scored the game's first touchdown on a 1-yard run

3. Franco Harris

C. Scored on a 73-yard pass reception

4. Cullen Bryant

D. Closed out the game's scoring with a 1-yard touchdown run

5. Lawrence McCutcheon

E. Scored on a 47-yard pass reception

6. John Stallworth

F. The game's leading rusher with 60 yards

7. Lynn Swann

G. Won the game's Most Valuable Player Award

Super Bowl XV (Philadelphia Eagles-Oakland Raiders).

1. Cliff Branch   A. Scored the only touchdown of the game for the Eagles

2. Kenny King   B. Intercepted three passes, a Super Bowl record

3. Wilbert Montgomery   C. The game's leading rusher with 75 yards

4. Mark van Eeghen   D. Won the game's Most Valuable Player Award

5. Rod Martin   E. Scored on an 80-yard touchdown pass, the longest play in Super Bowl history up to then

6. Keith Krepfle   F. Scored two touchdowns in the game

7. Jim Plunkett   G. The game's leading receiver with 91 yards

Super Bowl XVI (Cincinnati Bengals-San Francisco 49ers).

1. Ken Anderson   A. Scored on an 11-yard pass reception to climax a Super Bowl record 92-yard scoring drive

2. Dan Ross   B. Fumbled away a kickoff return with just 15 seconds left in the half on his own 4-yard line, leading to a score by the other team

3. Earl Cooper   C. Scored two touchdowns in the 4th quarter

4. Ray Wersching   D. Won the game's Most Valuable Player Award

5. Archie Griffin   E. Intercepted a pass at the 5-yard line to thwart the other team's opening drive just minutes into the game

6. Joe Montana

F. Kicked four field goals to tie the Super Bowl record

7. Dwight Hicks

G. The game's top passer with 300 yards

Super Bowl XVII (Washington Redskins-Miami Dolphins).

1. Jimmy Cefalo

A. Made a spectacular one-handed interception at the 5-yard line as he was falling to the ground

2. John Riggins

B. Quarterback who finished the game 4-for-14 for 97 yards

3. Fulton Walker

C. Opened the game's scoring with a 76-yard touchdown pass reception

4. Charlie Brown

D. Closed out the game's scoring with a 6-yard touchdown pass reception

5. Joe Theismann

E. The game's leading passer with 143 yards

6. David Woodley

F. Won the game's Most Valuable Player Award

7. Mark Murphy

G. Scored on a 98-yard kickoff return

Super Bowl XVIII (Washington Redskins-Los Angeles Raiders).

1. Derrick Jensen

A. Placed 5 of his 7 punts inside the opponent's 20-yard line

2. Marcus Allen

B. Won the game's Most Valuable Player Award

3. John Riggins

C. The game's top passer with 243 yards

4. Jack Squirek   D. Scored the game's first offensive touchdown on a 12-yard pass reception

5. Cliff Branch   E. Scored a touchdown on a 5-yard interception return with only 7 seconds left in the first half

6. Joe Theismann   F. Scored Washington's only touchdown on a 1-yard run

7. Ray Guy   G. Opened the game's scoring by blocking a punt in the end zone for a touchdown

Super Bowl XIX (San Francisco 49ers-Miami Dolphins).

1. Roger Craig   A. Won the game's Most Valuable Player Award

2. Carl Monroe   B. Scored three touchdowns on pass receptions

3. Joe Montana   C. The game's top receiver with 92 yards

4. Mark Clayton   D. Finished with 29 completions in 50 attempts for 318 yards

5. Dan Marino   E. Kicked three field goals

6. Wendell Tyler   F. Scored the game's opening touchdown on a 33-yard pass reception

7. Uwe von Schamann   G. The game's leading rusher with 65 yards

Super Bowl XX (New England Patriots-Chicago Bears).

1. Matt Suhey   A. Scored the game's first touchdown on an 11-yard run

2. Tony Franklin

B. Scored the game's last touchdown on an 8-yard pass reception

3. Irving Fryar

C. Won the game's Most Valuable Player Award

4. Reggie Phillips

D. Made the game's first score after just 1:19 of the first quarter, the fastest score in Super Bowl history

5. Henry Waechter

E. Scored a touchdown on a 28-yard interception return

6. Richard Dent

F. Closed out the game's scoring by sacking the opposing team's quarterback in the end zone

7. Jim McMahon

G. Only player in the game to score two touchdowns, one on a 1-yard run, the other on a 2-yard run

Super Bowl XXI (New York Giants-Denver Broncos).

1. Joe Morris

A. Scored the game's first touchdown on a 6-yard pass reception

2. Vance Johnson

B. Kicked a Super Bowl record-tying field goal of 48 yards

3. John Elway

C. Closed out the game's scoring with a 47-yard pass reception

4. Phil Simms

D. Was tackled in the end zone for a safety

5. Ottis Anderson

E. The game's leading rusher with 67 yards

6. Zeke Mowatt

F. Won the game's Most Valuable Player Award

7. Rich Karlis

G. Scored the final touchdown for the Giants on a 2-yard run

Super Bowl XXII (Denver Broncos-Washington Redskins).

1. Ricky Nattiel   A. Had two interceptions in the game

2. Barry Wilburn   B. Scored on a 56-yard pass reception on the team's first play from scrimmage

3. Doug Williams   C. Scored on a 27-yard pass reception, giving his team the lead for good

4. Timmy Smith   D. Scored his team's fifth touchdown of the second quarter on an 8-yard pass reception

5. Ricky Sanders   E. The game's leading rusher with 204 yards

6. Clint Didier   F. The game's leading receiver with 193 yards

7. Gary Clark   G. Won the game's Most Valuable Player Award

Super Bowl XXIII (San Francisco 49ers-Cincinnati Bengals).

1. Mike Cofer   A. Won the game's Most Valuable Player Award

2. Jerry Rice   B. Made a Super Bowl record 63-yard punt

3. Stanford Jennings   C. Returned a kickoff 93 yards for a touchdown

4. Ickey Woods   D. Missed a 19-yard field goal, the shortest miss in Super Bowl history

5. Lee Johnson   E. The game's leading scorer with 10 points

6. John Taylor   F. Set a Super Bowl record with 56 punt return yards

7. Jim Breech   G. The game's top rusher with 79 yards

Super Bowl XXIV (San Francisco 49ers-Denver Broncos).

1. Jerry Rice

2. Joe Montana

3. John Elway

4. Roger Craig

5. Tom Rathman

6. Bobby Humphrey

7. Brent Jones

A. The leading rusher *and* receiver for his team

B. Scored three touchdowns in the game

C. Won the game's Most Valuable Player Award

D. Scored on a 7-yard touchdown pass with just 3 seconds left in the first quarter

E. Scored the losing team's only touchdown on a 3-yard run

F. The game's leading rusher with 69 yards

G. Scored two rushing touchdowns in the game

Super Bowl XXV (New York Giants-Buffalo Bills).

1. Stephen Baker

2. Matt Bahr

3. James Lofton

4. Ottis Anderson

5. Thurman Thomas

6. Don Smith

7. Bruce Smith

A. Had the game's only pass-receiving touchdown, a 14-yarder

B. Both opened and closed the game's scoring with field goals

C. Won the game's Most Valuable Player Award

D. Caught a 61-yard tipped pass reception to set up his team's first score

E. Scored the game's final touchdown on a 31-yard run

F. Sacked the opposing team's quarterback in the end zone for a safety

G. Scored the game's first touchdown on a 1-yard run

Super Bowl XXVI (Buffalo Bills-Washington Redskins).

1. Mark Rypien

2. Earnest Byner

3. Gerald Riggs

4. Don Beebe

5. Art Monk

6. Gary Clark

7. Ricky Ervins

A. Lost a touchdown on an instant replay ruling

B. The game's leading rusher with 79 yards

C. Scored the game's first touchdown on a 10-yard pass reception

D. Closed out the game's scoring with a 4-yard touchdown pass reception

E. The game's leading receiver with 114 yards

F. Won the game's Most Valuable Player Award

G. Scored two touchdowns on runs of 1 and 2 yards

Super Bowl XXVII (Dallas Cowboys-Buffalo Bills).

1. Andre Reed

2. Steve Tasker

3. Thurman Thomas

4. Michael Irvin

A. Won the game's Most Valuable Player Award

B. Opened the game's scoring with a 2-yard touchdown run

C. Lost a 64-yard touchdown when the ball was knocked out of his hands just before he crossed the goal line after he began showboating early in anticipation of his touchdown

D. Blocked a punt, knocking the ball out at the 16-yard line

5. Ken Norton Jr.   E. Scored the third of three touchdowns for Dallas in a span of 2:33 of the fourth quarter to close out the game's scoring

6. Leon Lett   F. The game's leading receiver with 152 yards

7. Troy Aikman   G. Scored two touchdowns in 18 seconds just before the end of the first half

Super Bowl XXVIII (Buffalo Bills-Dallas Cowboys).

1. Emmitt Smith   A. Kicked a Super Bowl record 54-yard field goal

2. Thurman Thomas   B. Returned a fumble 46 yards for a game-tying touchdown

3. James Washington   C. Won the game's Most Valuable Player Award

4. Eddie Murray   D. The game's top passer with 260 yards

5. Steve Christie   E. Both opened and closed the game's scoring with field goals

6. Jim Kelly   F. Scored the game's first touchdown on a 4-yard run

7. Kevin Williams   G. Returned the opening kickoff 50 yards

Super Bowl XXIX (San Diego Chargers-San Francisco 49ers).

1. Andre Coleman   A. Opened the game's scoring with a 44-yard touchdown pass reception

2. Stan Humphries   B. Scored the first of his three touchdowns on a 51-yard pass reception

3. Ricky Watters   C. Threw for two 2-point conversions in the game

4. Jerry Rice   D. Scored the record-setting game's final touchdown on a 30-yard pass reception

5. Steve Young   E. Scored San Diego's only rushing touchdown on a 1-yard run

6. Natrone Means   F. Won the game's Most Valuable Player Award

7. Tony Martin   G. Returned a kickoff 98 yards for a touchdown

Super Bowl XXX (Pittsburgh Steelers-Dallas Cowboys).

1. Larry Brown   A. Closed out the game's scoring with a 4-yard touchdown run

2. Troy Aikman   B. Got the game's first touchdown on the board with a 3-yard touchdown pass

3. Yancey Thigpen   C. The game's leading rusher with 73 yards

4. Neil O'Donnell   D. Scored on a 6-yard pass reception just 13 seconds before the end of the first half

5. Emmitt Smith   E. The game's leading receiver with 98 yards

6. Bam Morris   F. The game's leading passer with 239 yards

7. Andre Hastings   G. Won the game's Most Valuable Player Award

Super Bowl XXXI (Green Bay Packers-New England Patriots).

1. Andre Rison   A. Set a Super Bowl record with 3 sacks

2. Antonio Freeman   B. The game's leading rusher with 61 yards

3. Desmond Howard   C. Opened the game's scoring with a 54-yard touchdown pass reception on his team's second play from scrimmage

4. Reggie White   D. Won the game's Most Valuable Player Award

5. Drew Bledsoe   E. The game's leading passer with 253 yards

6. Dorsey Levens   F. Ran for one touchdown and passed for two more

7. Brett Favre   G. Scored on a Super Bowl record 81-yard touchdown pass

Super Bowl XXXII (Denver Broncos-Green Bay Packers).

1. Mark Chmura   A. Had three touchdown passes in the game

2. Terrell Davis   B. Won the game's Most Valuable Player Award

3. Jason Elam   C. Opened the game's scoring with a 22-yard touchdown pass reception

4. Brett Favre   D. Became the first player ever to be a member of six Super Bowl teams, though he didn't play in all six games

5. Don Beebe   E. Was hit so hard on one 8-yard run that his body spun in the air sideways; this play was later dubbed "The Helicopter"

6. John Elway   F. Kicked a 51-yard field goal, second longest in Super Bowl history

7. Antonio Freeman   G. Scored on a 6-yard pass reception with 12 seconds left in the first half

Super Bowl XXXIII (Atlanta Falcons-Denver Broncos).

1. Howard Griffith

2. Terance Mathis

3. Tim Dwight

4. Rod Smith

5. Darrien Gordon

6. Shannon Sharpe

7. John Elway

A. Scored the game's first touchdown on a 1-yard run

B. Injured on his team's first drive and didn't return to the game

C. Scored on an 80-yard touchdown pass reception

D. Closed out the game's scoring with a touchdown on a 3-yard pass reception

E. Won the game's Most Valuable Player Award

F. Returned 2 interceptions for a Super Bowl record 108 yards

G. Returned a kickoff 94 yards for a touchdown

Super Bowl XXXIV (St. Louis Rams-Tennessee Titans).

1. Eddie George

2. Jeff Wilkins

3. Kurt Warner

4. Torry Holt

A. Won the game's Most Valuable Player Award

B. Scored the game's first touchdown on a 9-yard pass reception

C. Opened the game's scoring by kicking three field goals

D. Tied the game with a 43-yard field goal with just 2:12 left in the fourth quarter, but earlier missed a field goal and had another one blocked

5. Al Del Greco	E. Scored two touchdowns on runs of 1 and 2 yards
6. Isaac Bruce	F. Closed out the game's scoring with a 73-yard touchdown pass reception
7. Steve McNair	G. Set a Super Bowl record for rushing yards by a quarterback with 64

Super Bowl XXXV (New York Giants-Baltimore Ravens).

1. Ray Lewis	A. Returned an interception 49 yards for a touchdown
2. Brandon Stokley	B. Returned a kickoff 84 yards for a touchdown
3. Ron Dixon	C. The game's leading passer with 153 yards
4. Duane Starks	D. Opened the game's scoring with a 38-yard touchdown pass reception
5. Jermaine Lewis	E. Scored the game's final touchdown on a 3-yard run
6. Jamal Lewis	F. Won the game's Most Valuable Player Award
7. Trent Dilfer	G. Returned a kickoff 97 yards for a touchdown

Super Bowl XXXVI (New England Patriots-St. Louis Rams).

1. Jeff Wilkins	A. Scored on an 8-yard pass reception with 31 seconds left in the first half
2. Ty Law	B. The game's leading passer with 365 yards

3. David Patten

C. Won the game's Most Valuable Player Award

4. Ricky Proehl

D. Won the game with a 48-yard field goal as time expired

5. Adam Vinatieri

E. Returned an interception 47 yards for a touchdown

6. Tom Brady

F. Scored the game's last touchdown on a 26-yard pass reception with 1:30 left in the game

7. Kurt Warner

G. Opened the game's scoring with a 50-yard field goal

Super Bowl XXXVII (Tampa Bay Buccaneers-Oakland Raiders).

1. Dwight Smith

A. The game's leading rusher with 124 yards

2. Derrick Brooks

B. Won the game's Most Valuable Player Award

3. Dexter Jackson

C. Returned two interceptions for touchdowns

4. Jerry Rice

D. Returned an interception 44 yards for a touchdown

5. Mike Alstott

E. Scored the last offensive touchdown of the game on a 48-yard pass reception

6. Rich Gannon

F. Scored the game's first touchdown on a 2-yard run

7. Michael Pittman

G. The game's leading passer with 272 yards

594

Super Bowl XXXVIII (Carolina Panthers-New England Patriots).

1. John Kasay	A. Won the game's Most Valuable Player Award
2. Muhsin Muhammad	B. Opened the game's scoring on a 5-yard touchdown pass reception
3. Deion Branch	C. Passed for 323 yards and three touchdowns
4. Jake Delhomme	D. Kicked a 41-yard field goal with 4 seconds left to win the game
5. Tom Brady	E. The game's leading rusher with 83 yards
6. Adam Vinatieri	F. Scored on an 85-yard touchdown pass reception
7. Antowain Smith	G. Kicked a 50-yard field goal as time expired in the first half

595

Super Bowl XXXIX (New England Patriots-Philadelphia Eagles).

1. Corey Dillon	A. The game's leading passer with 357 yards
2. Donovan McNabb	B. The game's leading rusher with 75 yards
3. Tom Brady	C. Opened the game's scoring on a 6-yard touchdown pass reception
4. Greg Lewis	D. The game's leading receiver with 122 yards
5. Terrell Owens	E. Scored the game's final touchdown on a 30-yard pass reception
6. Deion Branch	F. Threw two touchdown passes of 2 and 4 yards
7. L.J. Smith	G. Won the game's Most Valuable Player Award

Super Bowl XL (Pittsburgh Steelers-Seattle Seahawks).

1. Antwaan Randle El
2. Hines Ward
3. Shaun Alexander
4. Ben Roethlisberger
5. Willie Parker
6. Matt Hasselbeck
7. Darrell Jackson

A. The game's leading rusher with 95 yards

B. Scored the game's first touchdown on a 1-yard run

C. Threw a 43-yard scoring pass for the game's final score

D. Won the game's Most Valuable Player Award

E. The game's leading passer with 273 yards

F. Had a 16-yard touchdown catch nullified by pass interference

G. Set a Super Bowl record with a 75-yard touchdown run

Super Bowl XLI (Indianapolis Colts-Chicago Bears).

1. Tank Johnson
2. Peyton Manning
3. Devin Hester
4. Joseph Addai
5. Kelvin Hayden
6. Dominic Rhodes

A. The game's top rusher with 113 yards

B. Scored the game's final touchdown on a 56-yard interception return

C. Due to legal difficulties, he had to secure permission from a judge to leave his state to play in the Super Bowl

D. Scored the game's first *offensive* touchdown on a 53-yard pass reception

E. Won the game's Most Valuable Player Award

F. Caught 10 passes, a Super Bowl record for running backs

7. Reggie Wayne   G. Returned the opening kickoff 92 yards for a touchdown

See if you can match the following Super Bowl won-lost records with the franchise that owns that record. (Through Super Bowl XLI. Franchise records include Super Bowls played for all cities that franchise has played in.)

1. 5–0   A. Green Bay Packers

2. 3–1   B. Chicago Bears

3. 3–2   C. New York Giants

4. 5–3   D. Dallas Cowboys

5. 2–1   E. San Francisco 49ers

6. 1–1   F. Pittsburgh Steelers

7. 5–1   G. Oakland Raiders

Another game of all-time Super Bowl records.

1. 2–4   A. Minnesota Vikings

2. 3–2   B. Miami Dolphins

3. 2–3   C. Denver Broncos

4. 1–2   D. Kansas City Chiefs

5. 0–4   E. Cincinnati Bengals

6. 1–1   F. New England Patriots

7. 0–2   G. St. Louis Rams

One last game of all-time Super Bowl records.

(Note: one W–L record is the answer for two teams. And don't forget, the record listed is for the franchise's all-time record for all cities they have ever played in.)

1. 3–2
2. 0–4
3. 2–1
4. 0–2
5. 1–0
6. 0–1

A. Indianapolis Colts

B. Philadelphia Eagles

C. Tampa Bay Buccaneers

D. Atlanta Falcons

E. Buffalo Bills

F. San Diego Chargers

G. Washington Redskins

ANSWERS

The answers are arranged by tens, starting with numbers ending in one and ending with numbers ending in zero.

#1: 1-A, 2-E, 3-B, 4-F, 5-C, 6-G, 7-D

#11: 1-A, 2-E, 3-F, 4-B, 5-C, 6-G, 7-D

#21: 1-F, 2-A, 3-G, 4-C, 5-E, 6-D, 7-B

#31: 1-C, 2-B, 3-A, 4-G, 5-E, 6-F, 7-D

#41: 1-A, 2-E, 3-G, 4-B, 5-C, 6-D, 7-F

#51: Art Rooney

#61: Lynn Swann

#71: 1-C, 2-D, 3-F, 4-E, 5-G, 6-A, 7-B

#81: 1-C, 2-F, 3-B, 4-E, 5-A, 6-D, 7-G

#91: 1-C, 2-D, 3-F, 4-G, 5-E, 6-A, 7-B

#101: 1-G, 2-B, 3-D, 4-F, 5-A, 6-C, 7-E

#111: 1-G, 2-B, 3-D, 4-F, 5-E, 6-C, 7-A

#121: 1-C, 2-A, 3-F, 4-D, 5-B, 6-G, 7-E

#131: 1-C, 2-G, 3-A, 4-F, 5-D, 6-E, 7-B

#141: 1-D, 2-A, 3-G, 4-F, 5-B, 6-E, 7-C

#151: 1-B, 2-E, 3-F, 4-C, 5-A, 6-G, 7-D

#161: 1-C, 2-A, 3-F, 4-D, 5-B, 6-G, 7-E

#171: 1-E, 2-A, 3-D, 4-G, 5-C, 6-F, 7-B

#181: 1-E, 2-A, 3-D, 4-G, 5-C, 6-F, 7-B

#191: 1-E, 2-A, 3-B, 4-G, 5-F, 6-C, 7-D

#201: 1-E, 2-A, 3-D, 4-G, 5-C, 6-B, 7-F

#211: 1-E, 2-A, 3-D, 4-G, 5-C, 6-F, 7-B

#221: 1965

#231: 1934

#241: 1-G, 2-B, 3-D, 4-F, 5-A, 6-C, 7-E

#251: 1-B, 2-D, 3-F, 4-G, 5-E, 6-C, 7-A

#261: 1-C, 2-F, 3-B, 4-E, 5-A, 6-G, 7-D

#271: 1-D, 2-E, 3-F, 4-B, 5-G, 6-C, 7-A

#281: 1-H, 2-B, 3-E, 4-G, 5-C, 6-A, 7-F, 8-D

#291: 1-E, 2-B, 3-H, 4-G, 5-D, 6-A, 7-C, 8-F

#301: 1-F, 2-C, 3-D, 4-A, 5-G, 6-E, 7-B, 8-H

#311: 1-B, 2-F, 3-A, 4-E, 5-G, 6-D, 7-C

#321: 1-B, 2-C, 3-F, 4-D, 5-G, 6-E, 7-A

#331: 1-A, 2-F, 3-C, 4-E, 5-G, 6-D, 7-B

#341: 1-F, 2-D, 3-E, 4-A, 5-G, 6-B, 7-C

#351: 1-B, 2-F, 3-A, 4-C, 5-G, 6-E, 7-D

#361: 1-F, 2-A, 3-D, 4-G, 5-B, 6-C, 7-E

#371: 1-B, 2-F, 3-C, 4-G, 5-D, 6-A, 7-E

#381: 1-B, 2-F, 3-E, 4-A, 5-C, 6-D

#391: 1-I, 2-B, 3-H, 4-A, 5-E, 6-G, 7-F, 8-D, 9-C

#401: 1-D, 2-C, 3-A, 4-G, 5-B, 6-E, 7-F

#411: 1-G, 2-A, 3-E, 4-B, 5-D, 6-F, 7-C

#421: 1-B, 2-A, 3-F, 4-C, 5-E, 6-D, 7-G

#431: 1-C, 2-F, 3-B, 4-E, 5-G, 6-D, 7-A

#441: 1-A, 2-E, 3-B, 4-F, 5-C, 6-G, 7-D

#451: 1-C, 2-F, 3-E, 4-B, 5-A, 6-D, 7-G

#461: 1-B, 2-C, 3-F, 4-A, 5-E, 6-D, 7-G

#471: 1-A, 2-F, 3-C, 4-B, 5-D, 6-G, 7-E

#481: 1-A, 2-G, 3-C, 4-F, 5-E, 6-B, 7-D

#491: 1-B, 2-D, 3-E, 4-A, 5-C, 6-G, 7-F

#501: 1-E, 2-A, 3-G, 4-C, 5-D, 6-B, 7-F

#511: 1-D, 2-G, 3-C, 4-F, 5-B, 6-E, 7-A

#521: 1-G, 2-E, 3-D, 4-F, 5-A, 6-B, 7-C

#531: 1-E, 2-D, 3-B, 4-G, 5-C, 6-F, 7-A

#541: 1-D, 2-G, 3-A, 4-B, 5-F, 6-C, 7-E

#551: 1-B, 2-C, 3-D, 4-E, 5-F, 6-G, 7-A

#561: 1-F, 2-D, 3-A, 4-B, 5-G, 6-E, 7-C

#571: 1-F, 2-E, 3-G, 4-C, 5-B, 6-A, 7-D

#581: 1-A, 2-B, 3-D, 4-C, 5-E, 6-G, 7-F

#591: 1-F, 2-D, 3-G, 4-A, 5-B, 6-E, 7-C

#2: 1-B, 2-D, 3-F, 4-A, 5-C, 6-E, 7-G

#12: 1-B, 2-C, 3-E, 4-F, 5-D, 6-G, 7-A

#22: 1-D, 2-F, 3-C, 4-G, 5-A, 6-B, 7-E

#32: 1-C, 2-E, 3-A, 4-G, 5-B, 6-D, 7-F

#42: 1-B, 2-D, 3-A, 4-E, 5-F, 6-C, 7-G

#52: Paul Hornung

#62: Dan Fouts

#72: 1-C, 2-F, 3-B, 4-E, 5-A, 6-D, 7-G

#82: 1-D, 2-G, 3-C, 4-F, 5-B, 6-E, 7-A

#92: 1-E, 2-G, 3-A, 4-D, 5-B, 6-C, 7-F

#102: 1-A, 2-F, 3-D, 4-B, 5-G, 6-E, 7-C

#112: 1-A, 2-F, 3-B, 4-E, 5-G, 6-D, 7-C

#122: 1-E, 2-G, 3-B, 4-D, 5-F, 6-A, 7-C

#132: 1-A, 2-E, 3-C, 4-B, 5-G, 6-D, 7-F

#142: 1-A, 2-C, 3-E, 4-B, 5-G, 6-F, 7-D

#152: 1-E, 2-A, 3-D, 4-F, 5-B, 6-G, 7-C

#162: 1-B, 2-G, 3-E, 4-C, 5-A, 6-F, 7-D

#172: 1-F, 2-B, 3-E, 4-A, 5-D, 6-G, 7-C

#182: 1-F, 2-B, 3-E, 4-A, 5-D, 6-G, 7-C

#192: 1-F, 2-B, 3-A, 4-E, 5-C, 6-D, 7-G

#202: 1-F, 2-B, 3-E, 4-A, 5-D, 6-G, 7-C

#212: 1-F, 2-B, 3-A, 4-E, 5-D, 6-G, 7-C

#222: 1971

#232: 1943

#242: 1-A, 2-B, 3-G, 4-D, 5-F, 6-E, 7-C

#252: 1-A, 2-F, 3-D, 4-B, 5-G, 6-E, 7-C

#262: 1-D, 2-G, 3-E, 4-C, 5-F, 6-B, 7-A

#272: 1-B, 2-F, 3-G, 4-A, 5-C, 6-E, 7-D

#282: 1-D, 2-F, 3-E, 4-A, 5-H, 6-C, 7-G, 8-B

#292: 1-H, 2-G, 3-E, 4-F- 5A, 6-C, 7-D,
8-B

#302: 1-D, 2-H, 3-E, 4-F, 5-B, 6-G, 7-C, 8-A

#312: 1-D, 2-G, 3-E, 4-F-5-C, 6-B, 7-A

#322: 1-C, 2-G, 3-E, 4-H, 5-F, 6-D, 7-B, 8-A

#332: 1-G, 2-E, 3-A, 4-F, 5-B, 6-D, 7-C

#342: 1-B, 2-E, 3-F, 4-C, 5-A, 6-G, 7-D

#352: 1-B, 2-E, 3-G, 4-A, 5-C, 6-F, 7-D

#362: 1-F, 2-H, 3-B, 4-A, 5-D, 6-E, 7-C, 8-G

#372: 1-D, 2-A, 3-E, 4-F, 5-B, 6-G, 7-C

#382: 1-D, 2-E, 3-B, 4-C, 5-A, 6-F

#392: 1-A, 2-F, 3-H, 4-C, 5-G, 6-B, 7-E, 8-D

#402: 1-A, 2-E, 3-B, 4-F, 5-C, 6-G, 7-D

#412: 1-A, 2-G, 3-E, 4-D, 5-H, 6-f, 7-C, 8-B

#422: 1-E, 2-G, 3-A, 4-F, 5-D, 6-C 7-B

#432: 1-D, 2-G, 3-C, 4-F, 5-B, 6-A, 7-E

#442: 1-B, 2-D, 3-F, 4-A, 5-C, 6-E, 7-G

#452: 1-F, 2-E, 3-A, 4-B, 5-G, 6-D, 7-C

#462: 1-A, 2-D, 3-G, 4-C, 5-F, 6-B, 7-E

#472: 1-B, 2-E, 3-F, 4-C, 5-A, 6-G, 7-D

#482: 1-B, 2-D, 3-E, 4-A, 5-G, 6-C, 7-F

#492: 1-C, 2-G, 3-E, 4-F, 5-B, 6-A, 7-D

#502: 1-B, 2-D, 3-A, 4-F, 5-E, 6-G, 7-C

#512: 1-C, 2-B, 3-A, 4-G, 5-F, 6-E, 7-D

#522: 1-B, 2-D, 3-F, 4-A, 5-G, 6-C, 7-E

#532: 1-E, 2-D, 3-B, 4-G, 5-A, 6-F, 7-C

#542: 1-C, 2-D, 3-A, 4-F, 5-E, 6-B, 7-G

#552: 1-E, 2-D, 3-C, 4-B, 5-A, 6-F, 7-G

#562: 1-B, 2-E, 3-G, 4-C, 5-F, 6-D, 7-A

#572: 1-G, 2-C, 3-A, 4-F, 5-B, 6-D, 7-E

#582: 1-F, 2-C, 3-G, 4-D, 5-A, 6-E, 7-B

#592: 1-G, 2-E, 3-A, 4-F, 5-D, 6-C, 7-B

#3: 1-C, 2-F, 3-B, 4-E, 5-A, 6-G, 7-D

#13: 1-A & D, 2-G, 3-B, 4-C, 5-F, 6-E

#23: 1-E, 2-F, 3-G, 4-C, 5-D, 6-A, 7-B

#33: 1-F, 2-D, 3-G, 4-A, 5-C, 6-E, 7-B

#43: 1-G, 2-D, 3-B, 4-F, 5-E, 6-A, 7-C

#53: Jim Brown

#63: O.J. Simpson

#73: 1-D, 2-G, 3-C, 4-F, 5-B, 6-E, 7-A

#83: 1-E, 2-C, 3-A, 4-F, 5-D, 6-G, 7-B

#93: 1-A, 2-B, 3-F, 4-D, 5-G, 6-E, 7-C

#103: 1-B, 2-F, 3-C, 4-G, 5-D, 6-A, 7-E

#113: 1-B, 2-E, 3-F, 4-A, 5-C, 6-D, 7-G

#123: 1-F, 2-C, 3-G, 4-D, 5-A, 6-E, 7-B

#133: 1-G, 2-E, 3-D, 4-C, 5-F, 6-B, 7-A

#143: 1-G, 2-D, 3-F, 4-E, 5-C, 6-B, 7-A

#153: 1-B, 2-D, 3-G, 4-C, 5-A, 6-E, 7-F

#163: 1-A, 2-C, 3-E, 4-G, 5-B, 6-D, 7-F

#173: 1-F, 2-E, 3-C, 4-A, 5-A, 6-D, 7-B

#183: 1-F, 2-C, 3-D, 4-B, 5-E, 6-D, 7-A

#193: 1-G, 2-C, 3-F, 4-B, 5-E, 6-D, 7-A

#203: 1-G, 2-C, 3-F, 4-B, 5-E, 6-A, 7-D

#213: 1-G, 2-C, 3-F, 4-B, 5-E, 6-A, 7-D

#223: 1989

#233: 1995

#243: 1-B, 2-F, 3-C, 4-D, 5-A, 6-E, 7-G

#253: 1-B, 2-F, 3-C, 4-G, 5-D, 6-A, 7-E

#263: 1-E, 2-G, 3-B, 4-F, 5-D, 6-A, 7-C

#273: 1-G, 2-B, 3-E, 4-A, 5-D, 6-F, 7-C

#283: 1-G, 2-F, 3-E, 4-H, 5-A, 6-D, 7-C, 8-B

#293: 1-B, 2-E, 3-F, 4-G, 5-D, 6-C, 7-A, 8-H

#303: 1-B, 2-G, 3-D, 4-A, 5-F, 6-C, 7-E

#313: 1-B, 2-F, 3-A, 4-G, 5-D, 6-C, 7-E

#323: 1-D, 2-G, 3-E, 4-C, 5-B, 6-A, 7-F

#333: 1-F, 2-A, 3-G, 4-C, 5-D, 6-B, 7-E

#343: 1-G, 2-A, 3-F, 4-D, 5-C, 6-B, 7-E

#353: 1-F, 2-B, 3-D, 4-E, 5-C, 6-G, 7-A

#363: 1-A, 2-B, 3-G, 4-C, 5-E, 6-H, 7-F, 8-D

#373: 1-A, 2-C, 3-E, 4-F, 5-B, 6-D

#383: 1-C, 2-A, 3-F, 4-B, 5-E, 6-D

#393: 1-C, 2-D, 3-A, 4-F, 5-H, 6-B, 7-G, 8-E

#403: 1-F, 2-A, 3-B, 4-C, 5-E, 6-D, 7-G

#413: 1-D, 2-E, 3-C, 4-F, 5-B, 6-G, 7-A

#423: 1-E, 2-G, 3-F, 4-D, 5-A, 6-B, 7-C

#433: 1-E, 2-C, 3-A, 4-F, 5-D, 6-B, 7-G

#443: 1-C, 2-F, 3-B, 4-E, 5-A, 6-D, 7-G

#453: 1-A, 2-B, 3-F, 4-C, 5-D, 6-G, 7-E

#463: 1-B, 2-G, 3-C, 4-D, 5-A, 6-F, 7-E

#473: 1-D, 2-C, 3-G, 4-E, 5-F, 6-B, 7-A

#483: 1-C, 2-F, 3-A, 4-E, 5-G, 6-B, 7-D

#493: 1-G, 2-E, 3-C, 4-D, 5-B, 6-A, 7-F

#503: 1-G, 2-F, 3-E, 4-C, 5-B, 6-A, 7-D

#513: 1-G, 2-E, 3-D, 4-B, 5-A, 6-C, 7-F

#523: 1-D, 2-G, 3-C, 4-E, 5-F, 6-B, 7-A

#533: 1-A, 2-C, 3-E, 4-F, 5-B, 6-G, 7-D

#543: 1-B, 2-C, 3-G, 4-E, 5-A, 6-D, 7-F

#553: 1-C, 2-G, 3-E, 4-B, 5-F, 6-A, 7-D

#563: 1-F, 2-B, 3-A, 4-G, 5-C, 6-D, 7-E

#573: 1-C, 2-F, 3-G, 4-D, 5-E, 6-B, 7-A

#583: 1-F, 2-D, 3-B, 4-G, 5-E, 6-C, 7-A

#593: 1-C, 2-D, 3-B, 4-E, 5-F, 6-G, 7-A

#4: 1-A & D, 2-G, 3-C, 4-F, 5-B, 6-E

#14: 1-F, 2-E, 3-B, 4-D, 5-C, 6-G, 7-A

#24: 1-D, 2-F, 3-A, 4-B, 5-G, 6-C, 7-E

#34: 1-G, 2-C, 3-E, 4-D, 5-B, 6-F, 7-A

#44: 1-F, 2-D, 3-E, 4-G, 5-A, 6-B, 7-C

#54: George Blanda

#64: Walter Payton

#74: 1-E, 2-C, 3-A, 4-F, 5-D, 6-B, 7-G

#84: Bill Peterson

#94: 1-B, 2-E, 3-G, 4-C, 5-F, 6-D, 7-A

#104: 1-C, 2-G, 3-A, 4-D, 5-B, 6-E, 7-F

#114: 1-C, 2-E, 3-G, 4-A, 5-B, 6-F, 7-D

#124: 1-G, 2-D, 3-A, 4-E, 5-B, 6-F, 7-C

#134: 1-B, 2-A, 3-G, 4-F, 5-C, 6-E, 7-D

#144: 1-C, 2-G, 3-E, 4-F, 5-B, 6-A, 7-D

#154: 1-G, 2-B, 3-A, 4-F, 5-D, 6-C, 7-E

#164: 1-C, 2-G, 3-D, 4-A, 5-F, 6-B, 7-E

#174: 1-D, 2-B, 3-G, 4-E, 5-C, 6-A, 7-F

#184: 1-D, 2-B, 3-G, 4-E, 5-C, 6-A, 7-F

#194: 1-D, 2-B, 3-G, 4-E, 5-C, 6-A, 7-F

#204: 1-D, 2-B, 3-A, 4-F, 5-E, 6-G, 7-C

#214: 1-D, 2-B, 3-G, 4-E, 5-C, 6-A, 7-F

#224: 1946

#234: 1973

#244: 1-F, 2-C, 3-B, 4-A, 5-G, 6-E, 7-D

#254: 1-C, 2-G, 3-D, 4-A, 5-F, 6-E, 7-B

#264: 1-F, 2-E, 3-G, 4-B, 5-A, 6-C, 7-D

#274: 1-C, 2-D, 3-A, 4-G, 5B, 6-E, 7-F

#284: 1-D, 2-E, 3-G, 4-F, 5-H, 6-A, 7-C, 8-B

#294: 1-B, 2-F, 3-H, 4-G, 5-D, 6-C, 7-E, 8-A

#304: 1-E, 2-F, 3-C, 4-G, 5-D, 6-A, 7-B

#314: 1-A, 2-E, 3-B, 4-F, 5-C, 6-G, 7-D

#324: 1-F, 2-A, 3-B, 4-C, 5-G, 6-E, 7-D

#334: 1-C, 2-D, 3-E, 4-B, 5-G, 6-A, 7-F

#344: 1-B, 2-E, 3-F, 4-C, 5-D, 6-G, 7-A

#354: 1-F, 2-E, 3-A, 4-D, 5-G, 6-B, 7-C

#364: 1-H, 2-D, 3-G, 4-C, 5-F, 6-B, 7-E, 8-A

#374: 1-B, 2-D, 3-F, 4-A, 5-C, 6-E

#384: 1-A, 2-E, 3-D, 4-F, 5-C, 6-B

#394: 1-H, 2-A, 3-E, 4-G, 5-F, 6-D, 7-B, 8-C

#404: 1-F, 2-E, 3-G, 4-D, 5-A, 6-C, 7-B

#414: 1-G, 2-E, 3-D, 4-F, 5-C, 6-B, 7-A

#424: 1-C, 2-D, 3-F, 4-A, 5-B, 6-G, 7-E

#434: 1-F, 2-C, 3-D, 4-G, 5-B, 6-A, 7-E

#444: 1-D, 2-G, 3-C, 4-F, 5-A, 6-E, 7-B

#454: 1-A, 2-D, 3-E, 4-G, 5-F, 6-B, 7-C

#464: 1-D, 2-F, 3-G, 4-E, 5-C, 6-B, 7-A

#474: 1-C, 2-G, 3-A, 4-B, 5-F, 6-D, 7-E

#484: 1-B, 2-A, 3-D, 4-C, 5-F, 6-G, 7-E

#494: 1-C, 2-A, 3-D, 4-B, 5-G, 6-F, 7-E

#504: 1-B, 2-D, 3-F, 4-A, 5-C, 6-E, 7-G

#514: 1-B, 2-A, 3-C, 4-G, 5-E, 6-F, 7-D

#524: 1-B, 2-C, 3-G, 4-F, 5-A, 6-E, 7-D

#534: 1-D, 2-F, 3-A, 4-G, 5-B, 6-E, 7-C

#544: 1-G, 2-F, 3-E, 4-A, 5-B, 6-C, 7-D

#554: 1-A, 2-C, 3-D & E, 4-G, 5-B & F

#564: 1-A, 2-D, 3-G, 4-C, 5-B, 6-E, 7-F

#574: 1-G, 2-B, 3-F, 4-E, 5-D, 6-C, 7-A

#584: 1-C, 2-F, 3-B, 4-E, 5-A, 6-D, 7-G

#594: 1-G, 2-F, 3-B, 4-C, 5-A, 6-D, 7-E

#5: 1-B & E, 2-C, 3-A, 4-F, 5-D, 6-G

#15: 1-E, 2-D, 3-A, 4-B, 5-F, 6-G, 7-C

#25: 1-B, 2-G, 3-F, 4-E, 5-A, 6-C, 7-D

#35: 1-G, 2-A, 3-C, 4-E, 5-B, 6-D, 7-F

#45: Troy Aikman

#55: Earl Campbell

#65: Dick Butkus

#75: 1-F, 2-C, 3-G, 4-D, 5-A, 6-E, 7-B

#85: 1-F, 2-A, 3-D, 4-G, 5-B, 6-E, 7-C

#95: 1-E, 2-C, 3-F, 4-B, 5-A, 6-G, 7-D

#105: 1-A, 2-C, 3-E, 4-G, 5-B, 6-D, 7-F

#115: 1-A, 2-C, 3-D, 4-E, 5-F, 6-B, 7-G

#125: 1-D, 2-G, 3-C, 4-F, 5-B, 6-E, 7-A

#135: 1-A, 2-B, 3-C, 4-D, 5-E, 6-F, 7-G

#145: 1-D, 2-C, 3-G, 4-A, 5-F, 6-B, 7-E

#155: 1-A, 2-G, 3-C, 4-D, 5-F, 6-B, 7-E

#165: 1-A, 2-E, 3-B, 4-F, 5-D, 6-G, 7-C

#175: 1-C, 2-A, 3-F, 4-D, 5-B, 6-G, 7-E

#185: 1-C, 2-A, 3-F, 4-D, 5-B, 6-G, 7-E

#195: 1-C, 2-F, 3-A, 4-D, 5-B, 6-G, 7-E

#205: 1-C, 2-A, 3-F, 4-D, 5-B, 6-E, 7-G

#215: 1976

#225: 1978

#235: 1-D, 2-A, 3-E, 4-B, 5-F, 6-C, 7-G

#245: 1-G, 2-F, 3-E, 4-D, 5-C, 6-A, 7-B

#255: 1-A, 2-C, 3-E, 4-G, 5-B, 6-D, 7-F

#265: 1-D, 2-B, 3-F, 4-A, 5-G, 6-E, 7-C

#275: 1-C, 2-F, 3-E, 4-A, 5-G, 6-B, 7-D

#285: 1-C, 2-E, 3-G, 4-H, 5-D, 6-B, 7-A, 8-F

#295: 1-E, 2-B, 3-H, 4-G, 5-D, 6-A, 7-I, 8-C, 9-F

#305: 1-E, 2-B, 3-F, 4-C, 5-D, 6-G, 7A

#315: 1-D, 2-A, 3-E, 4-C, 5-B, 6-G, 7-F

#325: 1-C, 2-D, 3-B, 4-E, 5-A, 6-F, 7-G

#335: 1-E, 2-F, 3-C, 4-A, 5-B, 6-D, 7-G

#345: 1-C, 2-D, 3-A, 4-E, 5-F, 6-B, 7-G

#355: 1-A, 2-D, 3-C, 4-G, 5-F, 6-E, 7-B

#365: 1-A, 2-F, 3-D, 4-B, 5-E, 6-G, 7-C

#375: 1-E, 2-A, 3-F, 4-D, 5-B, 6-C, 7-G

#385: 1-B, 2-A, 3-E, 4-C, 5-D

#395: 1-E, 2-D, 3-A, 4-B, 5-F, 6-G, 7-C

#405: 1-C, 2-A, 3-F, 4-B, 5-E, 6-G, 7-D

#415: 1-E, 2-C, 3-A, 4-G, 5-D, 6-B, 7-F

#425: 1-D, 2-A, 3-B, 4-G, 5-F, 6-C, 7-E

#435: 1-G, 2-C, 3-F, 4-E, 5-A, 6-D, 7-B

#445: 1-A, 2-B, 3-C, 4-G, 5-D, 6-F, 7-E

#455: 1-C, 2-F, 3-B, 4-A, 5-G, 6-D, 7-E

#465: 1-B, 2-G, 3-F, 4-E, 5-A, 6-D, 7-C

#475: 1-B, 2-G, 3-A, 4-F, 5-D, 6-E, 7-C

#485: 1-E, 2-C, 3-B, 4-F, 5-A, 6-D, 7-G

#495: 1-G, 2-B, 3-D, 4-F, 5-A, 6-C, 7-E

#505: 1-F, 2-C, 3-G, 4-D, 5-A, 6-E, 7-B

#515: 1-E, 2-B, 3-A, 4-C, 5-F, 6-G, 7-D

#525: 1-A, 2-D, 3-E, 4-B, 5-F, 6-G, 7-C

#535: 1-G, 2-B, 3-C, 4-A, 5-F, 6-E, 7-D

#545: 1-C, 2-G, 3-D, 4-F, 5-A, 6-E, 7-B

#555: 1-B & F, 2-G, 3-C, 4-D, 5-A, 6-E

#565: 1-C, 2-G, 3-E, 4-F, 5-A, 6-D, 7-B

#575: 1-B, 2-F, 3-A, 4-C, 5-D, 6-G, 7-E

#585: 1-G, 2-C, 3-B, 4-A, 5-F, 6-E, 7-D

#595: 1-B, 2-A, 3-F, 4-E, 5-D, 6-G, 7-C

#6: 1-F, 2-C, 3-G, 4-D, 5-A, 6-E, 7-B

#16: 1-C, 2-B, 3-F, 4-A, 5-E, 6-G, 7-D

#26: 1-C, 2-G, 3-B, 4-A, 5-F, 6-D, 7-E

#36: 1-B, 2-F, 3-D, 4-G, 5-A, 6-C, 7-E

#46: Joe Montana

#56: Merlin Olsen

#66: Terry Bradshaw

#76: 1-G, 2-B, 3-D, 4-F, 5-A, 6-C, 7-E

#86: 1-D, 2-C, 3-A, 4-B, 5-G, 6-F, 7-E

#96: 1-D, 2-A, 3-E, 4-B, 5-F, 6-C, 7-G

#106: 1-B, 2-D, 3-F, 4-A, 5-C, 6-E, 7-G

#116: 1-B, 2-D, 3-C, 4-F, 5-A, 6-G, 7-E

#126: 1-A, 2-F, 3-D, 4-B, 5-G, 6-C, 7-E

#136: 1-D, 2-E, 3-G, 4-F, 5-C, 6-B, 7-A

#146: 1-A, 2-B, 3-F, 4-E, 5-G, 6-D, 7-C

#156: 1-B, 2-F, 3-E & C, 4-G, 5-D, 6-A

#166: 1-A, 2-E, 3-B, 4-F, 5-C, 6-G, 7-D

#176: 1-B, 2-C, 3-B, 4-E, 5-A, 6-C, 7-D

#186: 1-B, 2-F, 3-C, 4-G, 5-D, 6-A, 7-E

#196: 1-B, 2-F, 3-C, 4-G, 5-D, 6-A, 7-E

#206: 1-B, 2-F, 3-C, 4-G, 5-D, 6-A, 7-E

#216: 1961

#226: 1997

#236: 1-F, 2-B, 3-G, 4-D, 5-E, 7-A

#246: 1-B, 2-D, 3-F, 4-A, 5-E, 6-C, 7-G

#256: 1-B, 2-C, 3-D, 4-E, 5-A, 6-G, 7-F

#266: 1-C, 2-G, 3-B, 4-E, 5-F, 6-A, 7-D

#276: 1-A, 2-E, 3-B, 4-F, 5-G, 6-C, 7-D

#286: 1-E, 2-D, 3-H, 4-G, 5-F, 6-C, 7-A, 8-B

#296: 1-B, 2-E, 3-G, 4-C, 5-F, 6-H, 7-D, 8-A

#306: 1-B, 2-A, 3-G, 4-C, 5-F, 6-D, 7-E

#316: 1-C, 2-G, 3-F, 4-A, 5-D, 6-B, 7-E

#326: 1-F, 2-B, 3-D, 4-A, 5-C, 6-G, 7-E

#336: 1-A, 2-D, 3-E, 4-F, 5-B, 6-G, 7-C

#346: 1-E, 2-F, 3-C, 4-B, 5-A, 6-G, 7-D

#356: 1-C, 2-E, 3-A, 4-B, 5-G, 6-D, 7-F

#366: 1-F, 2-C, 3-G, 4-D, 5-A, 6-E, 7-B

#376: 1-B, 2-G, 3-A, 4-E, 5-D, 6-H, 7-F, 8-C

#386: 1-E, 2-G, 3-A, 4-C, 5-F, 6-H, 7-B, 8-D

#396: 1-B, 2-F, 3-G, 4-C, 5-E, 6-D, 7-A

#406: 1-D, 2-E, 3-A, 4-G, 5-C, 6-F, 7-B

#416: 1-D, 2-E, 3-C, 4-F, 5-B, 6-G, 7-A

#426: 1-C, 2-G, 3-F, 4-B, 5-E, 6-D, 7-A

#436: 1-F, 2-C, 3-G, 4-D, 5-A, 6-B, 7-E

#446: 1-F, 2-C, 3-G, 4-A, 5-B, 6-D, 7-E

#456: 1-B, 2-D, 3-F, 4-A, 5-E, 6-C, 7-G

#466: 1-F, 2-G, 3-B, 4-A, 5-C, 6-D, 7-E

#476: 1-C, 2-D, 3-G, 4-A, 5-F, 6-E, 7-B

#486: 1-G, 2-A, 3-F, 4-E, 5-C, 6-B, 7-D

#496: 1-B, 2-D, 3-F, 4-A, 5-G, 6-C, 7-E

#506: 1-B, 2-G, 3-E, 4-C, 5-A, 6-F, 7-D

#516: 1-F, 2-E, 3-D, 4-A, 5-C, 6-B, 7-G

#526: 1-G, 2-F, 3-A, 4-C, 5-D, 6-B, 7-E

#536: 1-F, 2-E, 3-D, 4-G, 5-C, 6-A, 7-B

#546: 1-A, 2-E, 3-B, 4-F, 5-C, 6-G, 7-D

#556: 1-D, 2-G, 3-F, 4-C, 5-E, 6-A, 7-B

#566: 1-F, 2-E, 3-A, 4-C, 5-G, 6-B, 7-D

#576: 1-A, 2-D, 3-B, 4-E, 5-F, 6-C, 7-G

#586: 1-G, 2-B, 3-D, 4-F, 5-A, 6-C, 7-E

#596: 1-C, 2-D, 3-A, 4-B, 5-G, 6-E, 7-F

#7: 1-G, 2-B, 3-E, 4-D, 5-F, 6-A, 7-C

#17: 1-D, 2-F, 3-A, 4-G, 5-C, 6-E, 7-B

#27: 1-A, 2-D, 3-G, 4-E, 5-B, 6-C, 7-F

#37: 1-C, 2-A, 3-D, 4-F, 5-G, 6-E, 7-B

#47: Jim Thorpe

#57: Johnny Unitas

#67: Barry Sanders

#77: 1-C, 2-F, 3-D, 4-B, 5-G, 6-E, 7-A

#87: 1-B, 2-F, 3-G, 4-A, 5-E, 6-D, 7-C

#97: 1-B, 2-D, 3-F, 4-G, 5-E, 6-C, 7-A

#107: 1-C, 2-F, 3-B, 4-E, 5-A, 6-D, 7-G

#117: 1-A, 2-F, 3-E, 4-G, 5-D, 6-C, 7-B

#127: 1-B, 2-F, 3-C, 4-G, 5-D, 6-A, 7-E

#137: 1-E, 2-A, 3-D, 4-G, 5-C, 6-B, 7-H, 8-F

#147: 1-E, 2-C, 3-G, 4-B, 5-F, 6-A, 7-D

#157: 1-G, 2-C, 3-F, 4-B, 5-E, 6-A, 7-D

#167: 1-D, 2-G, 3-C, 4-F, 5-B, 6-E, 7-A

#177: 1-A, 2-C, 3-E, 4-B, 5-C, 6-D, 7-F

#187: 1-A, 2-C, 3-E, 4-G, 5-F, 6-D, 7-B

#197: 1-A, 2-G, 3-C, 4-E, 5-F, 6-D, 7-B

#207: 1-A, 2-C, 3-E, 4-C, 5-F, 6-D, 7-B

#217: 1984

#227: 1963

#237: 1-C, 2-F, 3-B, 4-E, 5-A, 6-D, 7-G

#247: 1-C, 2-G, 3-F, 4-E, 5-A, 6-B, 7-D

#257: 1-G, 2-E, 3-A, 4-B, 5-C, 6-F, 7-D

#267: 1-B, 2-A, 3-G, 4-E, 5-F, 6-C, 7-D

#277: 1-D, 2-B, 3-A, 4-G, 5-F, 6-E, 7-C

#287: 1-C, 2-F, 3-G, 4-H, 5-A, 6-D, 7-B, 8-E

#297: 1-H, 2-E, 3-B, 4-G, 5-A, 6-F, 7-D, 8-C

#307: 1-D, 2-G, 3-A, 4-E, 5-F, 6-C, 7-B

#317: 1-G, 2-D, 3-E, 4-A, 5-B, 6-C, 7-F

#327: 1-B, 2-C, 3-G, 4-F, 5-D, 6-E, 7-A

#337: 1-G, 2-B, 3-F, 4-C, 5-A, 6-E, 7-C

#347: 1-F, 2-E, 3-G, 4-D, 5-C, 6-B, 7-A

#357: 1-D, 2-G, 3-F, 4-C, 5-E, 6-A, 7-B

#367: 1-E, 2-G, 3-B, 4-D, 5-F, 6-A, 7-C	**#128:** 1-C, 2-E, 3-G, 4-B, 5-D, 6-A, 7-F
#377: 1-A, 2-D, 3-G, 4-F, 5-B, 6-E, 7-C	**#138:** 1-H, 2-F, 3-A, 4-G, 5-E, 6-D, 7-B, 8-C
#387: 1-C, 2-B, 3-E, 4-F, 5-D, 6-A, 7-G	**#148:** 1-A, 2-E, 3-B, 4-F, 5-G, 6-D, 7-C
#397: 1-G, 2-C, 3-B, 4-A, 5-E, 6-D, 7-F	**#158:** 1-C, 2-F, 3-A, 4-B, 5-E, 6-D
#407: 1-G, 2-A, 3-E, 4-B, 5-F, 6-D, 7-C	**#168:** 1-C, 2-G, 3-D, 4-A, 5-E, 6-B, 7-F
#417: 1-D, 2-B, 3-A, 4-G, 5-E, 6-F, 7-C	**#178:** 1-C, 2-G, 3-D, 4-A, 5-E, 6-B, 7-F
#427: 1-B, 2-F, 3-A, 4-G, 5-C, 6-E, 7-D	**#188:** 1-C, 2-G, 3-D, 4-A, 5-E, 6-B, 7-F
#437: 1-G, 2-B, 3-D, 4-F, 5-A, 6-C, 7-E	**#198:** 1-C, 2-G, 3-D, 4-A, 5-E, 6-B, 7-F
#447: 1-G, 2-B, 3-A, 4-F, 5-E, 6-D, 7-C	**#208:** 1-C, 2-G, 3-D, 4-A, 5-E, 6-B, 7-F
#457: 1-E, 2-G, 3-A, 4-B, 5-F, 6-C, 7-D	**#218:** 1990
#467: 1-A, 2-D, 3-B, 4-F, 5-C, 6-G, 7-E	**#228:** 1956
#477: 1-G, 2-A, 3-C, 4-B, 5-F, 6-E, 7-D	**#238:** 1-E, 2-F, 3-G, 4-A, 5-C, 6-B, 7-D
#487: 1-C, 2-E, 3-B, 4-A, 5-F, 6-D, 7-G	**#248:** 1-D, 2-G, 3-C, 4-F, 5-B, 6-E, 7-A
#497: 1-A, 2-F, 3-E, 4-D, 5-C, 6-B, 7-G	**#258:** 1-D, 2-G, 3-C, 4-F, 5-B, 6-E, 7-A
#507: 1-A, 2-D, 3-G, 4-C, 5-F, 6-B, 7-E	**#268:** 1-E, 2-B, 3-G, 4-F, 5-C, 6-D, 7-A
#517: 1-G, 2-F, 3-D, 4-C, 5-A, 6-B, 7-E	**#278:** 1-D, 2-E, 3-F, 4-H, 5-C, 6-G, 7-B, 8-A
#527: 1-B, 2-F, 3-C, 4-G, 5-D, 6-A, 7-E	**#288:** 1-G, 2-E, 3-B, 4-A, 5-F, 6-D, 7-B, 8-C
#537: 1-D, 2-G, 3-A, 4-F, 5-B, 6-E, 7-C	**#298:** 1-F, 2-C, 3-D, 4-H, 5-G, 6-A, 7-B, 8-E
#547: 1-F, 2-B, 3-E, 4-A, 5-D, 6-G, 7-C	**#308:** 1-B, 2-C, 3-E, 4-F, 5-G, 6-A, 7-D
#557: 1-C, 2-F, 3-E, 4-D, 5-A, 6-B, 7-G	**#318:** 1-G, 2-C, 3-F, 4-B, 5-E, 6-A, 7-D
#567: 1-A, 2-F, 3-B, 4-D, 5-E, 6-G, 7-C	**#328:** 1-G, 2-D, 3-A, 4-E, 5-B, 6-C, 7-F
#577: 1-E, 2-C, 3-D, 4-F, 5-G, 6-A, 7-B	**#338:** 1-E, 2-D, 3-A, 4-F, 5-C, 6-G, 7-B
#587: 1-C, 2-G, 3-D, 4-A, 5-E, 6-B, 7-F	**#348:** 1-A, 2-C, 3-D, 4-G, 5-B, 6-E, 7-F
#597: 1-C, 2-E, 3-G, 4-F, 5-B, 6-A, 7-D	**#358:** 1-C, 2-E, 3-B, 4-G, 5-H, 6-F, 7-A, 8-D
#8: 1-A, 2-C, 3-G, 4-B, 5-F, 6-E, 7-D	**#368:** 1-G, 2-D, 3-A, 4-E, 5-B, 6-C, 7-F
#18: 1-E, 2-B, 3-G, 4-C, 5-F, 6-D, 7-A	**#378:** 1-C, 2-F, 3-D, 4-H, 5-G, 6-A, 7-E, 8-B
#28: 1-B, 2-G, 3-E, 4-D, 5-C, 6-F, 7-A	**#388:** 1-E, 2-D, 3-G, 4-A, 5-F, 6-C, 7-B
#38: 1-G, 2-A, 3-D, 4-B, 5-F, 6-E, 7-C	**#398:** 1-E, 2-A, 3-H, 4-C, 5-F, 6-D, 7-G, 8-B
#48: Harold "Red" Grange	**#408:** 1-C, 2-E, 3-F, 4-A, 5-G, 6-D, 7-B
#58: Vince Lombardi	**#418:** 1-E, 2-D, 3-B, 4-C, 5-G, 6-A, 7-F
#68: Fran Tarkenton	**#428:** 1-G, 2-F, 3-E, 4-A, 5-B, 6-C, 7-D
#78: 1-B, 2-F, 3-C, 4-G, 5-D, 6-A, 7-E	**#438:** 1-A, 2-F, 3-D, 4-B, 5-G, 6-E, 7-C
#88: 1-C, 2-D, 3-G, 4-E, 5-F, 6-B, 7-A	**#448:** 1-C, 2-G, 3-D, 4-A, 5-F, 6-E, 7-B
#98: 1-E, 2-A, 3-G, 4-B, 5-F, 6-D, 7-C	**#458:** 1-C, 2-A, 3-E, 4-D, 5-G, 6-F, 7-B
#108: 1-G, 2-D, 3-C, 4-F, 5-B, 6-A, 7-E	**#468:** 1-B, 2-E, 3-A, 4-G, 5-F, 6-D, 7-C
#118: 1-A, 2-C, 3-E, 4-G, 5-B, 6-D, 7-F	**#478:** 1-F, 2-G, 3-A, 4-C, 5-B, 6-E, 7-D

#488: 1-F, 2-G, 3-E, 4-D, 5-C, 6-A, 7-B

#498: 1-D, 2-F, 3-E, 4-B, 5-G, 6-C, 7-A

#508: 1-E, 2-B, 3-F, 4-C, 5-G, 6-D, 7-A

#518: 1-D, 2-E, 3-C, 4-F, 5-B, 6-G, 7-A

#528: 1-E, 2-A, 3-D, 4-G, 5-C, 6-F, 7-B

#538: 1-C, 2-A, 3-E, 4-B, 5-D, 6-G, 7-F

#548: 1-E, 2-B, 3-F, 4-C, 5-G, 6-D, 7-A

#558: 1-A, 2-D, 3-G, 4-F, 5-B, 6-C, 7-E

#568: 1-C, 2-A, 3-D, 4-E, 5-B, 6-G, 7-F

#578: 1-B, 2-A, 3-G, 4-E, 5-F, 6-D, 7-C

#588: 1-G, 2-B, 3-F, 4-A, 5-D, 6-E, 7-C

#598: 1-E, 2-A, 3-G, 4-D, 5-C, 6-B, 7-F

#9: 1-B, 2-F, 3-C, 4-G, 5-E, 6-D, 7-A

#19: 1-D, 2-G, 3-B, 4-F, 5-C, 6-A, 7-E

#29: 1-E, 2-G, 3-A, 4-D, 5-C, 6-F, 7-B

#39: 1-F, 2-C, 3-A, 4-B, 5-E, 6-G, 7-D

#49: Gale Sayers

#59: Paul Warfield

#69: Jim Kelly

#79: 1-C, 2-G, 3-D, 4-A, 5-E, 6-B, 7-F

#89: 1-B, 2-E, 3-F, 4-G, 5-C, 6-A, 7-D

#99: 1-C, 2-D, 3-G, 4-F, 5-B, 6-A, 7-E

#109: 1-E, 2-C, 3-A, 4-F, 5-G, 6-B, 7-D

#119: 1-D, 2-A, 3-E, 4-B, 5-F, 6-C, 7-G

#129: 1-F, 2-A, 3-C, 4-E, 5-G, 6-B, 7-D

#139: 1-G, 2-E, 3-C, 4-A, 5-B, 6-D, 7-F, 8-H

#149: 1-B, 2-D, 3-F, 4-C, 5-G, 6-A, 7-E

#159: 1-G, 2-C, 3-F, 4-B, 5-E, 6-A, 7-D

#169: 1-A, 2-E, 3-A, 4-E, 5-C, 6-B, 7-D

#179: 1-A, 2-E, 3-B, 4-F, 5-C, 6-G, 7-D

#189: 1-A, 2-E, 3-B, 4-F, 5-C, 6-G, 7-D

#199: 1-A, 2-B, 3-E, 4-F, 5-C, 6-G, 7-D

#209: 1-A, 2-B, 3-E, 4-F, 5-C, 6-G, 7-D

#219: 2001

#229: 2002

#239: 1-A, 2-B, 3-F, 4-C, 5-D, 6-E, 7-G

#249: 1-E, 2-C, 3-A, 4-F, 5-G, 6-D, 7-B

#259: 1-A, 2-D, 3-E, 4-B, 5-G, 6-F, 7-C

#269: 1-D, 2-E, 3-A, 4-C, 5-F, 6-G, 7-B

#279: 1-E, 2-D, 3-H, 4-C, 5-G, 6-B, 7-A, 8-F

#289: 1-A, 2-D, 3-B, 4-A, 5-F, 6-E, 7-C, 8-G

#299: 1-G, 2-A, 3-E, 4-F, 5-B, 6-H, 7-C, 8-D

#309: 1-C, 2-D, 3-F, 4-A, 5-B, 6-G, 7-E

#319: 1-F, 2-G, 3-E, 4-D, 5-A, 6-B, 7-C

#329: 1-A, 2-G, 3-D, 4-F, 5-C, 6-E, 7-B

#339: 1-D, 2-G, 3-C, 4-F, 5-E, 6-A, 7-B

#349: 1-F, 2-A, 3-C, 4-E, 5-B, 6-G, 7-D

#359: 1-E, 2-D, 3-B, 4-H, 5-G, 6-C, 7-F, 8-A

#369: 1-D, 2-G, 3-C, 4-F, 5-B, 6-E, 7-A

#379: 1-G, 2-E, 3-A, 4-B, 5-F, 6-H, 7-D, 8-C

#389: 1-F, 2-A, 3-C, 4-B, 5-D, 6-G, 7-E

#399: 1-B, 2-E, 3-C, 4-G, 5-A, 6-H, 7-F, 8-D

#409: 1-C, 2-B, 3-D, 4-E, 5-A, 6-G, 7-F, 8-H

#419: 1-D, 2-G, 3-B, 4-F, 5-A, 6-E, 7-C

#429: 1-B, 2-D, 3-F, 4-E, 5-G, 6-A, 7-C

#439: 1-B, 2-F, 3-C, 4-G, 5-D, 6-A, 7-E

#449: 1-A, 2-E, 3-B, 4-F, 5-C, 6-D, 7-G

#459: 1-G, 2-F, 3-B, 4-A, 5-C, 6-E, 7-D

#469: 1-B, 2-G, 3-C, 4-E, 5-D, 6-A, 7-F

#479: 1-D, 2-B, 3-E, 4-C, 5-G, 6-A, 7-F

#489: 1-F, 2-A, 3-B, 4-C, 5-G, 6-E, 7-D

#499: 1-C, 2-D, 3-A, 4-G, 5-F, 6-B, 7-E

#509: 1-C, 2-A, 3-F, 4-D, 5-B, 6-G, 7-E

#519: 1-E, 2-C, 3-D, 4-G, 5-F, 6-A, 7-B

#529: 1-G, 2-C, 3-F, 4-B, 5-E, 6-A, 7-D

#539: 1-G, 2-E, 3-F, 4-A, 5-B, 6-D, 7-C

#549: 1-B, 2-F, 3-C, 4-G, 5-A, 6-E, 7-D

#559: 1-E, 2-A, 3-G, 4-F, 5-D, 6-C, 7-B

#569: 1-C, 2-E, 3-A, 4-G, 5-D, 6-F, 7-B

#579: 1-D, 2-A, 3-C, 4-G, 5-B, 6-F, 7-E

#589: 1-A, 2-D, 3-G, 4-C, 5-F, 6-B, 7-E

#599: 1-C, 2-F, 3-B, 4-G, 5-A, 6-D, 7-E

#10: 1-C, 2-G, 3-D, 4-A, 5-F, 6-E, 7-B

#20: 1-A, 2-G, 3-D, 4-E, 5-B, 6-C, 7-F

#30: 1-F, 2-A, 3-E, 4-B, 5-G, 6-C, 7-D

#40: 1-C, 2-F, 3-E, 4-A, 5-G, 6-B, 7-D

#50: Bronko Nagurski

#60: Thurman Thomas

#70: 1-E, 2-C, 3-F, 4-G, 5-D, 6-B, 7-A

#80: 1-A, 2-E, 3-B, 4-F, 5-C, 6-G, 7-D

#90: 1-D, 2-C, 3-G, 4-A, 5-B, 6-F, 7-E

#100: 1-A, 2-B, 3-F, 4-G, 5-E, 6-D, 7-C

#110: 1-F, 2-C, 3-G, 4-D, 5-B, 6-E, 7-A

#120: 1-B, 2-E, 3-A, 4-D, 5-G, 6-C, 7-F

#130: 1-D, 2-A, 3-E, 4-B, 5-F, 6-G, 7-C

#140: 1-B, 2-D, 3-F, 4-H, 5-G, 6-E, 7-C, 8-A

#150: 1-F, 2-G, 3-A, 4-D, 5-E, 6-C, 7-B

#160: 1-D, 2-B, 3-G, 4-E, 5-C, 6-A, 7-F

#170: 1-B, 2-D, 3-F, 4-A, 5-C, 6-E, 7-G

#180: 1-B, 2-D, 3-F, 4-A, 5-C, 6-E, 7-G

#190: 1-B, 2-D, 3-F, 4-C, 5-A, 6-E, 7-G

#200: 1-B, 2-D, 3-F, 4-A, 5-C, 6-E, 7-G

#210: 1-B, 2-D, 3-F, 4-A, 5-C, 6-E, 7-G

#220: 1959

#230: 1987

#240: 1-F, 2-C, 3-G, 4-D, 5-A, 6-E, 7-B

#250: 1-C, 2-G, 3-F, 4-A, 5-B, 6-D, 7-E

#260: 1-B, 2-D, 3-F, 4-A, 5-C, 6-E, 7-G

#270: 1-G, 2-A, 3-D, 4-E, 5-B, 6-F, 7-C

#280: 1-H, 2-A, 3-B, 4-F, 5-G, 6-C, 7-D, 8-E

#290: 1-D, 2-F, 3-A, 4-B, 5-G, 6-H, 7-C, 8-E

#300: 1-B, 2-A, 3-G, 4-E, 5-D, 6-C, 7-H, 8-F

#310: 1-E, 2-C, 3-G, 4-D, 5-F, 6-B, 7-A

#320: 1-C, 2-A, 3-F, 4-D, 5-G, 6-E, 7-B

#330: 1-C, 2-B, 3-G, 4-D, 5-F, 6-E, 7-A

#340: 1-B, 2-C, 3-G, 4-F, 5-D, 6-E, 7-A

#350: 1-C, 2-D, 3-G, 4-F, 5-B, 6-A, 7-E

#360: 1-C, 2-E, 3-A, 4-D, 5-G, 6-B, 7-F

#370: 1-A, 2-F, 3-D, 4-B, 5-G, 6-C, 7-E

#380: 1-A, 2-F, 3-D, 4-B, 5-C, 6-E, 7-G

#390: 1-A, 2-G, 3-B, 4-F, 5-E, 6-C, 7-D

#400: 1-C, 2-E, 3-F, 4-A, 5-G, 6-D, 7-B

#410: 1-E, 2-H, 3-F, 4-G, 5-D, 6-C, 7-B, 8-A

#420: 1-A, 2-E, 3-G, 4-B, 5-C, 6-F, 7-D

#430: 1-F, 2-C, 3-E, 4-D, 5-A, 6-B, 7-G

#440: 1-C, 2-G, 3-D, 4-A, 5-E, 6-B, 7-F

#450: 1-B, 2-C, 3-D, 4-E, 5-F, 6-G, 7-A

#460: 1-A, 2-C, 3-E, 4-F, 5-G, 6-D, 7-B

#470: 1-D, 2-F, 3-B, 4-C, 5-A, 6-G, 7-E

#480: 1-E, 2-D, 3-G, 4-B, 5-F, 6-C, 7-A

#490: 1-E, 2-G, 3-F, 4-A, 5-D, 6-C, 7-B

#500: 1-F, 2-E, 3-D, 4-G, 5-C, 6-B, 7-A

#510: 1-G, 2-A, 3-C, 4-E, 5-D, 6-F, 7-B

#520: 1-A, 2-F, 3-G, 4-B, 5-D, 6-C, 7-E

#530: 1-F, 2-G, 3-D, 4-A, 5-B, 6-E, 7-C

#540: 1-A, 2-B, 3-C, 4-G, 5-D, 6-E, 7-F

#550: 1-D, 2-E, 3-F, 4-A, 5-B, 6-C, 7-G

#560: 1-E, 2-B, 3-F, 4-C, 5-A, 6-G, 7-D

#570: 1-G, 2-F, 3-D, 4-B, 5-A, 6-C, 7-E

#580: 1-B, 2-C, 3-E, 4-F, 5-G, 6-A, 7-D

#590: 1-E, 2-C, 3-A, 4-B, 5-D, 6-F, 7-G

#600: 1-G, 2-E, 3-A, 4-B, 5-C, 6-D & F

ABOUT THE AUTHOR

Dennis Purdy is the author of seven books, two screenplays, and 160 magazine articles. A former teacher of baseball history on the college level, Purdy is the former editor and publisher of *The Vintage & Classic Baseball Collector* magazine and creator of the syndicated newspaper feature *Baseball Trivia Game*. His unique Traveling Baseball Card Museum and Baseball History exhibits have been displayed at memorabilia shows and shopping malls around the country. His 20,000-page web site, TheBaseballScribe.com, is a free site devoted to the preservation of baseball's history and its artifacts.

A former professional gambler who has appeared in his own poker advice segment on the Fox Sports Television Network, he has authored two books on poker and one on blackjack. Mr. Purdy, who lives in University Place, Washington with his wife Kathy and their four children, is currently at work on several more books.